A Critical Introduction
to Translation Studies

Also available from Continuum

A Critical Introduction to Phonology, Daniel Silverman
A Critical Introduction to Phonetics, Ken Lodge
A Critical Introduction to Syntax, Jim Miller
An Introduction to Syntax, Edith A. Moravcsik
An Introduction to Syntactic Theory, Edith A. Moravcsik

A Critical Introduction to Translation Studies

Jean Boase-Beier

Continuum Critical Introductions to Linguistics

continuum

Continuum International Publishing Group

The Tower Building   80 Maiden Lane
11 York Road   Suite 704
London, SE1 7NX   New York, NY 10038

www.continuumbooks.com

British Library Cataloguing-in-Publication Data
A catalogue record for this book is available from the British Library.

ISBN: 978-1-4411-8912-7 (hardcover)
        978-0-8264-3525-5 (paperback)

Library of Congress Cataloging-in-Publication Data
A catalog record for this book is available from the Library of Congress.

Typeset by Newgen Imaging Systems Pvt Ltd, Chennai, India
Printed and bound in India

Contents

Preface

This book is aimed mainly at postgraduate students of translation studies, their teachers and the general researcher. It is intended as background reading; as the series title suggests, it provides an introduction to the subject of translation which is rather different from existing ones. This introduction to translation studies engages with the concepts and ideas that can be found in more traditional introductions, but the perspective is that of cognitive poetics.

It will therefore also be of interest to students, teachers and researchers working in the areas of cognitive poetics, cognitive stylistics, cognitive linguistics and cognitive literary theory more generally. Advanced undergraduate students should find it provides them with interesting perspectives on old questions or, indeed, a critical introduction to new questions.

I hope very much that practising translators will also find things to interest them in this book. I am a literary translator myself and much of my research involves questions of burning interest to the translator: What is creativity? How creative can the translator be? Why do we feel we know what a text is saying? I hope the book will help give literary translators the confidence to try out new ways of seeing and doing their work.

Acknowledgements

The writing of this book has owed much to the help of others. Many of my students and colleagues have (often unconsciously) provided examples and ideas. In particular, for help with examples from languages outside my competence, I wish to thank B.J. Epstein, Hiroko Furukawa, Rosalind Harvey and Clara Stern Rodríguez. I should also like to thank current and past students of the MA in Literary Translation at UEA for their enthusiasm, support and suggestions, and in particular my present and former PhD students who do so much to help my research into literary translation. I am also extremely grateful to the School of Literature and Creative Writing for providing the funds to employ poet, translator and current PhD student Philip Wilson as my Research Assistant during a crucial phase of the writing of this book. I am especially indebted to Philip for his tireless work in providing references and examples, including a number of creative translations. These are attributed individually where possible. Finally, I should like, as always, to thank my husband Dieter Beier for his invaluable help in preparing the various drafts of the manuscript. It goes without saying that these helpers are not responsible for any of the errors I might have made.

I am grateful to the copyright-holders of the following material for permission to reprint extracts. Full details of all works used can be found in the Bibliography:

Bloodaxe Books, for 'Agnus Dei', by R.S. Thomas, reproduced from *Collected Later Poems 1988–2000*; copyright © 2004

Everyman, an imprint of the Orion Publishing Group, London, for 'The Gap' and 'Absence', by R.S. Thomas, reproduced from *Collected Poems 1945–1990*; copyright © 1993, and for 'In Memoriam (Easter 1915)', by Edward Thomas, reproduced from *Edward Thomas*; copyright © 1997

Suhrkamp Verlag, for 'Wann Herr . . .' and 'Beten will ich', by Thomas Bernhard, translated by James Reidel, reproduced from *In Hora Mortis; Under the Iron of the Moon*; copyright © 1991

Anvil Press Poetry, for 'Winter Solstice', by Michael Hamburger, reproduced from *Intersections*; copyright © 2000

Verlag Klaus Wagenbach GmbH, for 'Beim Lesen der Zeitung' and 'Aufruf', by Volker von Törne, reproduced from *Im Lande Vogelfrei: Gesammelte Gedichte*; copyright © 1981

Arc Publications, for 'The sun sets a trap . . .', by Anise Koltz, translated by Anne-Marie Glasheen, reproduced from *At the Edge of Night*; copyright © 2009

Literarisher Verlag Braun, for 'Weidenwort' and 'Wandlung', by Rose Ausländer, reproduced from *Gesammelte Gedichte*; copyright © 1977

Part I

Translation, Text, Mind and Context

What does Translation Involve?

1.1 The difficulty of definition

Most of us are aware that translation plays an important role in our daily lives. For example, we sense that translation must have been involved if we read a Swedish crime novel in English. Sometimes we pay little attention to the fact that it is translated, but occasionally something stands out: perhaps characters in a Swedish city speak English, and this incompatibility makes us aware that what we are reading has been written by someone who is not the author given on the book cover.

Dictionary definitions typically give a very narrow sense of translation: to translate is to express the sense of (words or texts) in another language (*Concise Oxford English Dictionary* 2008:1532). But it is also possible to think of other instances which, although they do not involve different languages, still seem to have something in common with rendering a Swedish crime novel into English. A new audience needs to know what someone has said, but there is a barrier of code, register or style. Consider the following example:

> (1.1) The woman in the station Enquiries Office said: 'There's been a big . . . '.
> She gave an apologetic shrug and a half-smile.

Is there any translation involved here?

The woman in the office uses gestures and facial expression to say something she is thinking, but cannot or does not want to put into words. Is she, then, translating thought into gesture? If we were to call this translation, then any speaking or writing would have to be considered a translation of thought into words. And this is indeed the view of some translation scholars (see e.g. Barnstone 1993:20). We might dismiss this as broadening the definition of translation so much as to render it meaningless. But suppose we say the woman's gestures are a translation, not of thoughts, but of unspoken words: to be precise, of the noun or noun phrase that syntactically would have to follow the word 'big' in (1.1); perhaps 'accident' or 'derailment at Stowmarket' or even 'cock-up'. Would this then be more of a translation than just putting vague thoughts into gestures?

If we are sure that it is not, because we feel that translation has to involve two languages, and not just thought and language, then what about a poem written on a painting, such as 'Marine Still Life', James Kirkup's poem 'after a painting by Edward Wadsworth' (Kirkup 2002:27). Is this a translation? Or an illustration that shows the 'Things' in *Where the Wild Things Are* (Sendak 1963)? In both these cases, there seems to be a transference of content between a non-linguistic and a linguistic representation. In 1958 Jakobson (2004:139) stated that such cases were 'intersemiotic translations' if the original was formulated in language. Turning the English translation of the Swedish crime novel into a film would thus be an intersemiotic translation, as would the illustration of Sendak's 'things', but writing a poem about a painting would not. For Jakobson, whose view of language was that it encoded meaning (2008:144), there must first be a process of decoding and this is only possible with an original which is a linguistic representation. Jakobson gives three types of translation; the other two are 'intralingual translation' (2004:139), which is the translation of, say, a poem in Yorkshire dialect into Standard English, and 'interlingual translation', which is what Jakobson, and almost everyone, regards as 'translation proper' (ibid.). This is the sort of translation exemplified by the first instance above: a Swedish crime novel in English.

Though Jakobson's categories – intersemiotic, intralingual and interlingual – may seem quite separate, none of them have exact defining characteristics. It is fairly clear, for example, that he would not regard the woman's action in (1.1) as intersemiotic translation, because 'semiotic' means to do with signs, and the woman's thoughts are not only not linguistically encoded, but they are also not signs at all, so 'translation' of thought to gesture only involves one semiotic system – gesture – and is by this definition not translation. What is less clear is whether a translation of the original Swedish crime novel into an English film would be intersemiotic translation, for the definition of the latter, according to Jakobson (2004:139), does not involve crossing a language boundary. Perhaps we could say that the English film involves two types of translation: interlingual (Swedish to English novel) and intersemiotic (novel to film). In fact one could argue that the translation of the English version into an English film also involves two acts of translation, for the English version itself was already a 'proper' or interlingual translation, and so traces of its having been originally Swedish (such as Swedish personal and place names) will be part of the English text.

Before this discussion becomes any more complicated, it is probably worth just picking up the main points, which are as follows:

(i) Some cases of translation would probably be deemed by everyone to be translations (the English translation of a Swedish crime novel).

(ii) There are cases such as putting thoughts into words which some scholars would consider to be translations, but many people would not.

(iii) Intersemiotic translations, such as novels made into films or poems captured in paintings, could reasonably be called translations.

(iv) A translation might involve a change of both language and medium (such as an English film of a Swedish novel).

(v) If a text that has already been translated is translated again (such as an English film of the English version of a Swedish novel), we might assume that the first act of translation plays a role in the second.

What the above discussion shows, then, is that it is not really clear what translation involves, a point made by many writers on translation (e.g. Munday 2009:5–9; Bassnett 1998).

Where one draws the boundaries between what is translation and what is not will depend upon one's views of language, thought and representation, and these will in turn be influenced by historical and personal context. But it might also depend upon issues of how we define such concepts as 'language' or 'dialect' or 'register'. For example, do the following qualify as translations?

(1.2) The label on the iron says 'The clothes with protrude fal-lals: avoid the fal-lals. This must mean that you shouldn't iron over the beading.'

(1.3) Once the reaction is triggered – the switch is flipped – the serotonin is then free to go back and float around in the space between the neurons.

(Oakley 2007:72)

(1.4) 'B – b – la' said the baby. 'He's saying "butterfly" ', said his mother, smiling confidently.

In the sentences in (1.2), the second sentence translates into Standard English a sentence which is not Standard English. We can tell this because 'protrude' is not an adjective in English and 'fal-lal' would not be recognized by most speakers of English today as a word at all, though it was used by Hardy in *Jude the Obscure* (1974:114) in 1895 and is included in the 1976 *Concise Oxford Dictionary*, though not in the 2008. But what do we call the language of the label itself? Is it a sort of dialect? If so, is it a language, since one could argue that, linguistically speaking, a dialect is a language (see Crystal 2003:25)? Or is it an idiolect, the way the person (or machine) writing the label speaks English? Is a translation from an idiolect to a standard form of the language still a translation? And is the label itself perhaps a translation from a Chinese speaker's (imaginary or real) original Chinese instructions? In that case, perhaps it is less of a translation if there is no written original than if there is; this is again the question of whether thoughts 'count' for translation or not.

In example (1.3) further questions arise. Do we count the expression between dashes as a colloquial translation of 'the reaction is triggered'? But it is only marginally more colloquial than the first expression. Perhaps, then, it is a translation of a literal expression into a metaphorical one? But 'triggered' also seems metaphorical. An explanation which says that registers, which are different varieties of a language used in different contexts, count as languages for the purpose of translation will not really help here, because the register differences seem minimal. Many scholars have pointed out that metaphor (which means 'carrying over' in its original Greek, just as does originally the word 'translation', from Latin) is a type of translation (see Barnstone 1993:16). But if we are simply translating one metaphor to another (a trigger to a switch) then it seems that to say (1.3) involves translation would be to say that any rephrasing in different words is a translation.

In the case of (1.4), we have someone who understands the original language (the baby's babbling) translating to Standard English for the benefit of those who do not speak the baby's language. Whether we would call it translation or not might depend on whether we wish to regard the different stages in a child's acquisition of language as languages in their own right.

So it seems that not only is it unclear whether translation has to involve different languages, or whether thought counts as language, but that we must also now add the following to our list of points two pages back:

(vi) We might consider different varieties of a language, such as idiolects, registers, personal styles or even different stages of acquisition as different 'languages' for the purposes of translation.

These are not purely theoretical questions. For example, whether dialects are counted as languages for the purposes of translation has possible repercussions for questions of power and authority. A dialect might be perceived as carrying less authority than the standard form of the language. Questions such as this, and their relation to description and prescription, are considered within sociolinguistics (see, for example, Milroy and Milroy 1991).

Questions about varieties of language and the power invested in them are also of great importance to such areas of literary criticism as postcolonial theory, and to areas of translation such as postcolonial translation (see, for example, Bassnett and Trivedi 1999, Tymoczko 2007). In the study of translation, such considerations are always tied up with questions about the ethics of translation, an issue to which we shall return in Chapter 5.

One way to deal with points (i) to (vi), all of which make it clear that translation is difficult to define, is to define it as a process rather than trying to define its source and end products. That is, we might say that any process of transferring one section of language into another, which says the same thing in different words, is a process of translation. This would leave open the possibility that any reformulation is a translation. And in fact this does accord with what many people feel, as the following section of conversation (adapted from a real example) shows:

(1.5) A: I don't quite, well, maybe, you know . . .
　　　 B: Let me translate: no.

B might speak in an amused or ironical tone, suggesting that 'translate' is not being used in its core or most obvious sense. Nevertheless, the fact that the meaning of 'translate' can easily be extended to include such cases suggests that such a process of reformulating feels like an act of translation to many people. It appears, then, that we can describe translation as a process which has a source text (the Swedish novel, the baby's babble, the speaker's stumbling words) and a target text (the English film, the mother's interpretation, the other person's clarification). If the source and target texts are clearly in different languages, it is obviously translation. If we are not so sure whether they are in different languages or the same language, it is less obviously translation, but in a broad sense it is. If they are not languages but different sorts of representation (such as painting to poem), it is even less obviously translation.

But even if we accept that translation is best seen as a class of processes of the type that involves a transfer from a source to a target text, there is still another question we have to ask: What is it that is transferred in translation? Another way of putting the question (- a translation of the question -) is: What part of the language of the source text do we preserve?

In all the examples so far, we might say that it is content, or meaning, that is preserved. Intuitively, this seems correct. But consider the following example:

(1.6) 'Il pleure' means 'he is crying'

'He is crying' is not really the meaning of the French, but is an English translation. We often use 'means' to say 'is a foreign rendering of' because we intuitively consider English (or whatever our native language is) to somehow express the meaning directly. We think the English words *are* the meaning. Even if we leave aside this issue, though, it is not clear that 'He is crying' is an English translation of '*Il pleure*'. Suppose that the context of the expression '*il pleure*' was as follows:

(1.7) Il pleure dans mon cœur / Comme il pleut sur la ville (Verlaine 2001:25)

If '*il pleure*' means, or translates as 'he is crying', then we might translate (1.7) as:

(1.8) He is crying in my heart / just as it is raining in the town

But '*il pleure*' also suggests rain, because of the presence of what looks like an impersonal '*il*' ('it') with no antecedent, so perhaps:

(1.9) It is raining in my heart / as it is raining in the town

And yet, if (1.6) is in any sense correct, then the original French lines also mention crying. So a closer translation of the lines would be:

(1.10) There is crying in my heart, as the rain falls on the town

But this is not a good translation. It ignores the near-repetition of '*il pleure*' and '*il pleut*' by translating these phrases with two different verbs. It ignores the repetition of the impersonal '*il* V *dans*' and '*il* V *sur*' (V stands for verb), which suggests that one's heart, by analogy with the town, is a place in which things just happen and are outside of one's control, a problem avoided by translations such as Sorrell's 'Falling tears in my heart, / Falling rain on the town' (Sorrell 1999:69). And, crucially, (1.10) ignores the fact that the third person of the present tense of '*pleurer*' (to cry) and '*pleuvoir*' (to rain) are close in sound, even though not etymologically connected, so that crying and raining could be said to be linked in a French speaker's mind more closely than in an English speaker's. This latter point is connected to the notion of Linguistic Relativity, which we will come to shortly.

These are all aspects of the style, or the way that something is said, as opposed to what is said. What the above discussion shows is that style is as important as content – perhaps more so – in translation. This is an issue that will be revisited many times in the course of this book.

But does it make sense to say 'he is crying 'is somehow the meaning or content of '*il pleure*', as (1.6) suggested, whereas the style is something much more complex? To some extent, this does make sense, and leads us to one possible definition of style:

(1.11) Style is a set of weak implicatures

This is a definition based on Sperber and Wilson (1995:193–202) and it provides a useful way of understanding style and of understanding translation. In Relevance Theory, Sperber and Wilson's theory of communication, relevance is defined as the property of communicated utterances such that they do not involve more processing on the part of the hearer or reader than is appropriate to the amount of cognitive benefit derived. Such cognitive benefit, or cognitive effect, might be increased knowledge or changed ways of thinking. In this theory, explicatures are the parts of meaning directly encoded in utterances (1995:182) and implicatures are implications intended by the speaker (1995:182), but not made explicit. Weak implicatures are thus all those aspects of the meaning of a text which are left fairly open by the speaker. They are suggested to a greater or lesser degree. Literary texts typically contain a very large number of very weak implicatures, as has been frequently noted (e.g. Pilkington 2000:75–83). So part of what is implicated in (1.7) is the suggestion that '*il pleure*' represents an uncontrollable, natural phenomenon. That link is still there in (1.10), but it is much weaker than in (1.7). Interestingly, if style in literary texts typically consists of many weak implicatures, one might want to argue that (1.10), having even weaker implicatures, is even more literary than (1.7). The reader has to work harder, this argument would go, and therefore would obtain more cognitive effects. This is the argument behind the idea that literary texts should not be too obvious, or browbeat the reader, and views of style differ historically in this respect. In spite of this possibility, if we consider translation as a process that captures the style of the original, then a translation such as that in (1.10), which ignores the links of sound present in the word '*pleut*' itself, as well as those suggested by the repetition of '*il* V PP' (where PP is a prepositional phrase), is therefore translating only a fairly small proportion of what (1.7) says.

The importance of the style, in which the similarity of the French words '*pleure*' and '*pleut*' (which might be regarded as a play on words, sometimes called paronomasia; see e.g. Wales 2001:287) is underlined by the repetition in the sentence, will not be unexpected to the reader of the text in which (1.7) occurs, because the text has other characteristics, such as being written in lines, that mark it out as a literary text. In a text such as the following, on the other hand, the fact that there are two words beginning with 's' and two beginning with 'p' would probably be considered irrelevant:

> (1.12) You will need a strong sense of responsibility and proven project manage-
> ment skills.

A translation of (1.12) into another language would be unlikely to try and preserve the alliteration of 'strong sense' and 'proven project'. In fact, if alliteration – the repetition of sound (usually consonants or consonant clusters) at the beginning of words – is assumed to be a phenomenon of literary texts, it is doubtful that these examples would be considered alliteration at all. However, alliteration is not in fact merely a literary phenomenon, and the translator of a phrase such as

> (1.13) 'Why money messes with your mind' (*New Scientist* March 21st, 2009)

would probably want to echo the alliteration in some way.

Are we therefore saying that literary translation transfers both content and style, whereas non-literary translation is only concerned with content? And, if we are, are we saying that the *New Scientist* title in (1.13) is literary, whereas the advertisement in (1.12) is not?

The possible answers to these and other questions will form an important thread running throughout this book. But we can consider preliminary answers now, with the caveat that there is much more to say. One possible answer to the first question would be to say that yes, style is in general important in literary translation and not in non-literary translation because the main difference between literary and non-literary texts is a difference in the role of style. This is the difference expressed by Ross when he said: 'literary texts are not just about something; they do that thing' (1982:687; see also Iser 2006:58). This could be taken to mean that literary texts express meaning through iconicity, the stylistic phenomenon in which the language used physically resembles what it represents, rather than doing so in a purely arbitrary way. If arbitrariness is the basis of the form – meaning relation in language generally, a view that goes back to Saussure (1966:67–70) but is generally accepted in linguistics (see e.g. Pinker 1999:2–4), then one could argue that iconicity undermines or overturns this relation (see e.g. Lee 2001:77). Here are examples of iconicity:

(1.14) twitter, bark, ring

(1.15) flash, flutter, fling

(1.16) We must not use no double negatives

(1.17) Out of the corpse-warm antechamber of the heavens steps the sun

The examples in (1.14) are words which sound like the sounds they represent; this is referred to as onomatopoeia. Those in (1.15) illustrate a weaker type of iconicity, generally known as phonaesthesia: the consonant cluster 'fl' seems to suggest quick movement, but it is not a direct representation of movement, or speed. However, because 'fl' does not mean anything on its own, so the sequence is not simply a result of morphology – the structure of words in terms of meaningful elements – or etymology (their origins), many writers (e.g. Anderson 1998) would argue that the words in (1.15) illustrate iconicity. The example in (1.16) demonstrates syntactic iconicity: the syntactic structure of the sentence – the way its words are organized and the relationship between them – mimics what it says. And the example in (1.17) is also an instance of syntactic iconicity in which the line length, the difficulty of pronouncing 'heavens steps' and the position of the noun at the end of the line all echo the movement of the sun.

(1.17) is my translation of a line in a poem by Ingeborg Bachmann (in Boland 2004:94; for further discussion see Boase-Beier 2010a). If, as Ross says, poems do what they say, then (1.17) is an example of this; it is in fact translated in this way because Bachmann's original German also mirrors the sun's movement in a similar way. But Ross's statement could also be taken to mean that poems do things to their readers. In fact, the idea that language does things is a common one, and informs Speech Act Theory (e.g. Austin 1962); this includes the notion that, for example, by saying 'I baptize you Christopher' you actually do so. This example, just like those in (1.13), (1.14), (1.15) and (1.16), suggests that the difference between literary and non-literary texts is not clear-cut, because all these examples are, or could be, from non-literary language, yet the notion that texts do things to their readers is the basis of literary theories such as Reader-Response Theory (e.g. Iser 1979) and more general discussions of what defines literature (e.g. Attridge 2004; see Chapter 6). Iser (1979) argues that literary texts leave gaps that the reader has to fill. So if, for instance, the text in example (1.1) appeared at the start of a novel, the reader would be bound to imagine not only what noun goes in the space, but what might have happened in the story, and what its consequences might be. Iser (1979), in speaking of gaps and the reader's involvement, anticipated work such as that of Pilkington (2000), mentioned above, in which readers work through possible weak implicatures.

What this brief discussion of style has suggested is that the style of a literary text goes beyond its content to allow the text to do something besides just saying something, whereby what it does might be to echo a particular meaning in its form, or to make the reader supply a meaning (or indeed to do other things that this book will explore). If the translation of such texts does not go beyond content, the translated texts will only say something but will not 'do' anything and therefore could be considered not to be literary texts at all. But to return to our second question – is (1.13) in some sense more literary than (1.12) – we might recall that the notion of a text 'doing something' to the reader, just like the more general notion of style, is not confined to literary texts. Nevertheless, there are texts, such as that in example (1.12), whose style seems unimportant and where the translation could focus merely on content. Such texts will almost always be non-literary. Thus we can say that style always matters in literary translation, but conversely cannot always be ignored in non-literary translation. To the extent that style is an essential element in a text we might even want to say that it forms part of content or meaning, and that therefore a distinction between content and style (or what is said and how it is said) is at best an idealization, especially in literary texts.

The discussion above has made the implicit assumption that, when we say 'literary translation', we mean the translation of literary texts, assuming the definition of a literary text discussed in the last few pages. This is generally the sense in which I will speak of literary translation in this book. However, it is possible to use 'literary translation' as a term meaning the literary translation of non-literary texts, that is, a translation that takes into account the ways in which the text has literary elements, or characteristics, or effects. I will return to this point in the next chapter.

It seems common sense that, if the original text is a literary text such as a novel, the translation will be a novel, too. Or if the original is an advertisement, the translation will also be an advertisement. That this is not always the case is suggested by earlier examples, such as the making of an English film from a Swedish novel or the writing of a poem about a picture, where the original is not a text at all. Considerations such as these might lead us to ask what a text is. A picture would not usually be considered a text, but a film might possibly. A simple definition of text might be 'a stretch of writing or speech, not necessarily complete, which is the object of observation or analysis' (Wales 2001:391). This is in general the sense in which I will use 'text' in this book. It might include headlines or stretches of conversation, and also poems, advertisements, books, newspaper articles and so on. It will not in general include films or photographs.

Taking this simple definition of text as a starting point, then, it is reasonable to say that translation is a process that preserves meaning, style and text-type. We have already seen some exceptions: meaning was not kept in example (1.9) nor register in (1.13). And another exception, even based on the fairly narrow definition of text just given, might be a book like Burnshaw's *The Poem Itself* (1960), which includes prose translations of poems, and could be said to involve a change of text-type.

The question of text-type, and whether it is preserved, is clearly important for translation. The theory of text-types developed in parallel with text linguistics especially in Germany and the Netherlands, and overlaps with such areas of linguistics as text grammar and discourse analysis. Text grammar (e.g. van Dijk 1972) was originally an attempt to move away from the focus on the sentence common in the work of linguists such as Chomsky (e.g.1965) and discourse analysis is the analysis of language in use (e.g. van Dijk 1977). A brief discussion of these links can be found in Wales (2001:392). It seems clear that such ideas will be interesting for translators, because translation, especially of literary texts, has always been assumed to operate at a higher level than that of a sentence (see Qvale 2003:7–17).

It was the theory of texts that formed the basis for an important study of translation by Reiß and Vermeer in 1984. They argue that a text is an action, with a producer and recipient, and has a particular aim to fulfil (1984:18). The situation in which the original and translated texts are produced and received is subject to a vast array of linguistic, social and cultural influences. From this complex, detailed and loosely organized work the term *skopos*, or translation aim (1984:29) was taken over to become part of the vocabulary of translation theory, not just in the original German (see e.g. Agnorni 2002). Reiß and Vermeer point out that the *skopos* of a translation will include preserving or changing the text-type of the source text. Frequently the text-type will stay the same, as part of the necessary coherence between source and target texts (1984:171–216), though, as Reiß had pointed out in a much earlier work, especially in the case of literary translations the function of the target text might differ from that of the source text (Reiß 1971:104f.) as in the examples we saw above (see also Nord 1997:9–10 for discussion). Most of these 'functionalist' approaches, as Nord (1997) calls them, are not specifically concerned with literary translation, though Nord herself (1997:80–103) does discuss the particular 'poetic effect' that a literary text has on its readers as one of the functions of literature. In this sense, and in keeping with other German theories of text-types, which usually see the literary text as one of a number of such types (- others are journalistic texts, instructions and so on -) it can be seen that knowing the characteristics of a particular text-type is an essential prerequisite for the translator. Such knowledge might, for example, determine or affect the degree of freedom the translator has to deviate from the source text. This freedom will be linked both to the need for a translator to interpret the original (Nord 1997:85), as well as to the extent to which a text describes a state of affairs in the real world. Thus Kleist's *Der zerbrochne Krug* (1973), a German play originally set in 1770 on the German-Dutch border, can be translated into an English play set on the Yorkshire-Lancashire border, as happens in Blake Morrison's translation *The Cracked Pot* (Morrison 1996). Because the events the original play describes are assumed to be fictional, they can be set in England for an English audience. But it would not be considered acceptable to translate a report on an experiment performed on the German-Dutch border, and which had appeared in a scientific journal, in such a way that its English translation said the experiment had been conducted on the Yorkshire-Lancashire border. We might argue, then, that the fictionality of a literary text confers the freedom to change its content. But 'fiction' is not a clear-cut category in literary texts. What about literary biography, or novels based on historical events, or poems about the Holocaust? These will be semi-fictionalized accounts of the events, but it is not clear how much licence would generally be accorded to their translations. It might seem that the greater the degree of fictionality in the text the more important the style will be, and the more the translation will need to focus on style. However, it will not always be the case that the degree of fictionality and the importance of style are in direct proportion. A poem, for example, might have a high level of stylistic patterning, and yet the translator might feel constrained by the content or situation that gave rise to the poem. Thus Michael Hamburger, writing about translating Paul Celan's poetry, feels strongly that he should not make 'a merely aesthetic game of the existential struggle' (Hamburger 2007:421) which was the subject of much of Celan's poetry. Celan wrote many poems about the Holocaust, in which both his parents died, and eventually himself committed suicide. It is easy to see why a translator of these poems would feel more constrained by a notion of content than in, say, a translation of a nursery rhyme. Literariness might be assumed to depend to a great extent upon fictionality, but there are degrees of fictionality.

Another way to describe literary texts is to characterize them, as Nord (1997:82) did, as having poetic effects. Poetic effects are defined by Pilkington (2000:26) as the cognitive effects that a text has on its reader and that arise during the processing of the text, including searching for contexts in which it can be understood (2000:77,189), working out implicatures, or interpreting attitude. These effects may be general cognitive effects such as rearranged structures of knowledge or enhanced beliefs, and also, according to Pilkington, the emotional and affective states of mind (2000:190,191) particularly triggered by poetic texts.

Similarly for Attridge, literary texts evoke creative reading, that is, a type of reading which involves the reader in 'a suspension of habits, a willingness to rethink old positions' (2004:80), and this type of reading is signalled by the form of the text (2004:111).

In both these views, then, poetic effects result from the work done by the reader as such work is directed by the text (Pilkington 2000:190), and thus these views are partly a further development of the work of Ross (1982:682), who said poetic texts do things to readers, and of Iser (1971; 1979), who described how texts leave gaps for the reader to become involved with (e.g. 1979:19). These gaps may be places where there are actual gaps (see Boase-Beier 2004 for an example) or ambiguities that enable the reader to consider several possibilities at once. Such processing of possible cognitive contexts can happen in any text. But, whereas a scientific report of an experiment may involve processing and understanding on the part of the reader, it is unlikely to involve interpreting the writer's attitude or experiencing feelings of fear or joy or empathy. A work of popular science, on the other hand, will employ elements of literary style in order to involve the reader more. The popular science book *Evil Genes* (Oakley 2007), from which the example in (1.3) is taken, describes psychopaths both in terms of genetic variation, in a way unlikely to evoke emotion, and also in the following terms:

> (1.18) Psychopaths are so scary that roughly a quarter of psychology professionals who meet one wind up experiencing . . . hair standing up on the back of the neck, crawling skin, the 'creeps' . . . (Oakley 2007:52)

This is written in a colloquial style as the phrases 'wind up', 'crawling skin' show and the most colloquial expression, the 'creeps', is given as though it is a quotation from one of the psychologists in question. The effect of this is to make the reader think of people she knows who cause similar effects, to think about the physical symptoms, because they are listed, or to imagine the various associations of the 'creeps': creepy music, darkened houses, unexplainable phenomena and so on.

What this description does, then, is to cause cognitive effects of various types in the reader which seem similar to, but less complex and open-ended than the sort of poetic effects a literary text could be assumed to give rise to. A translation that merely conveyed the more scientific information about genetic variation and translated (1.18) as though it had said:

> (1.19) . . . psychology professionals who meet one experience a number of typical physical symptoms of fear

would risk not having any poetic effects on the reader but only the non-poetic cognitive effects of increased knowledge.

As we move on beyond the first five chapters that form Part I of this book, we shall consider what it means to see the style of texts not merely as a formal textual entity, nor just as a representation of a cognitive entity, but as itself a cognitive entity, and the effects of this view on translation. In other words, style is not just ways of saying but has as its counterpart ways of thinking, and their effects on the reader are, as Attridge (2004:80) quoted above, suggests, not just the appreciation of style or the experiencing of emotion but also more radical types of rethinking. This is the view behind cognitive poetics or cognitive stylistics, as it is sometimes called, a discipline situated at the cross over of linguistics and literary studies. Cognitive poetics is described by Stockwell

(2002:1–11) as a way of talking about the reading of literature which explains how particular readings are arrived at (2002:1–11), taking into account the ways the mind works, and not just the way language in a literary text works. Following Jakobson's 1958 statement (see Jakobson 2008), Stockwell uses the term 'poetics' to refer to all types of literary text, as I shall frequently do in this book. One of the particularly interesting consequences of cognitive poetics for translation is that it suggests a translation is not merely concerned with transferring the surface features of a source text into a target text, but that, because a text embodies a cognitive state, and has effects on the cognitive state of its reader, so also does its translation.

Another important aspect of cognitive poetics is that it sees the literary mind not as something that only comes into play when a literary text is to be read, but as the mind itself. In other words, not only are elements of style such as metaphor or ambiguity ways of thinking, but they are ways of thinking that are central to our cognitive functioning (Turner 1996:4–5). We can examine such aspects of style especially well by examining literature because it is here that many aspects of the mind such as the blending of concepts, the creating of analogies, the forming of narratives and so on, can be seen particularly clearly. If the literary mind is simply the mind, and the ways of thinking that literature requires are simply good examples of the way we think, this suggests that a literary text is simply a good example of a text. What this means is that translation of non-literary, as well as of literary texts will need to be concerned with stylistic figures and devices, with the cognitive counterparts of textual stylistic elements and with poetic effects. All texts will contain metaphor, because metaphor is central to the way we think, and by the same token texts of different types will all contain what we tend to think of as literary figures such as ambiguity or iconicity, as in examples (1.14), (1.15), (1.16) and (1.17). If there is a difference between literary and non-literary texts, and thus between literary and non-literary translation, it cannot be a purely linguistic one. To find out about translation, then, it makes sense to concentrate on those texts where these elements have the greatest role to play. Literary translation is a particularly good example of translation. The distinction between literary and non-literary translation is one to which we shall return in Chapter 2.

Up to now our discussion has been mainly about what elements of a text are preserved in translation. Some elements that we have considered are meaning, style and the type of text with its functions and characteristics. A further question we have to ask of translation, aside from what it transfers, is what it *can* transfer. If we recall the discussion of example (1.7) above, one of the issues was that the French words '*pleure*' and '*pleut*' were similar in sound. Thus there is a mismatch between what the source language can do and what the target language can do.

There has been much controversy, within both translation theory and linguistics, about the extent to which such mismatches suggest different ways of thinking. It is possible to hold different views about this question. One view would say that French and English people habitually think differently in some ways, and the languages encode these differences. This is a fairly uncontroversial view, known as Weak Linguistic Relativity (see Gumperz and Levinson 1996 for discussion). A stronger view is that, because the languages do different things, it is impossible for an English thinker to ever make the same link between crying and raining. This is Strong Linguistic Relativity, and is not accepted by most linguists or translation specialists today. It seems clear that an English speaker can understand the link between 'cry' and 'rain', once it has been explained, and possibly, in this case, even before it has been explained, because of the similarities of crying and raining, and their consequent association in images and metaphors, even as far back as Hildegard of Bingen in the twelfth century (Biedermann 1992:277). Generative linguists, in arguing against Strong Linguistic Relativity, have a tendency to ignore the consequences of Weak Linguistic Relativity. Pinker, for example, argues that Relativity is either untrue (in its strong form) or uninteresting (in its weak form; see Pinker 2007:124–151). In fact, Linguistic Relativity in its weaker forms is extremely interesting for translation. If a particular meaning in one language is not habitually expressed in another, then there are no easy ways to translate this meaning from the first to the second language, especially in texts in which style plays a major role, and where involved explanations are thus inappropriate. An example is the use of '*wenn*' in German, which means something close to 'if, and if so, when' in English. There is no conjunction in English with this meaning. This does not, of course, mean that the meaning of the German conjunction cannot be expressed, nor the concept conceived of, in English. I have just expressed in English what it means. But if it is used in a German poem, its translation risks losing compression or ambiguity (see Boase-Beier 2006:119–120; 2010). We will return to the question of Linguistic Relativity and how it affects translation in Chapter 2.

The simple definition of translation as the transfer of content between languages can, then, be seen to hide a number of questions about what counts as a language and what is actually meant by 'content', and whether this includes style, as well as questions about the extent to which the function of a particular text-type is preserved, and about the extent to which languages allow such transfer. But there are many other questions about the nature of translation, and the next section considers one of the most fundamental.

1.2 Source and target

A further set of issues, perhaps less obvious than those we have just considered, concerns the place of the translated text in relation to the source and the target contexts. This is a set of issues with various different emphases. If we were to take 'context' to mean linguistic context, and assume that a translation is always situated at some point on a scale between source and target languages, we might represent this as follows:

(1.20) source ── X ── X── X── target
        language   language
        context   context

The translation may be at any of the Xs on the line between source and target, or at any other point along the line. A translation may be closer to the language of the source text or of the target text. Here are some examples; the source text is a German idiom and appears in (1.21); possible translations follow in (1.22), (1.23) and (1.24):

(1.21) Es ist gehüpft wie gesprungen
      it is jumped like   sprung

(1.22) It's the same whether you jump or leap

(1.23) It's as broad as long

(1.24) It's all the same

It seems intuitively clear that (1.22) would be to the left of the scale in (1.20) and (1.24) to the right. Of course, (1.22) would not be at the far left as it still sounds more like an English idiom than does the gloss in (1.21). (1.23) keeps the idea of a comparison expressed metaphorically, so would be in the middle of the scale. (1.24) does none of these things.

The discussion in Section 1.1 about meaning and style has shown that, if one tries to separate the two – 'the what' from 'the how' – then it could be maintained that the meaning or content is kept in all the above translations, but the style is only kept in (1.22) and (1.23). So, one could argue that in terms of linguistic closeness to source, attention to style is more important than meaning. Alternatively, and as the discussion in 1.1 suggested, one could argue that style is part of the meaning. In Relevance Theory, as we have seen, it is possible to explain this by saying that the style embodies a set of weak implicatures which are additional to the explicatures in a text. Implicatures of (1.21) are that there is a balance of two similar actions, that the outcome in each case is likely to be the same, that the reader must visualize two actions which have different words to represent them but only seem different in execution in a very minor way: the sort of thing where one would have to weigh up the differences. Indeed, weighing up and finding little difference seems to be the main point of the idiom in (1.21). In this sense, (1.23) might be said to capture its essence rather well.

But the sort of degrees of closeness that (1.20) illustrates might not just be a question of linguistic equivalence. In fact it has been one of the main criticisms (see e.g. Venuti 1998:21) of the type of linguistically orientated studies of translation carried out in the 1960s (e.g. Catford 1965; Nida 1964) that they focused too much on the linguistic detail of the text and ignored such things as cultural background, the expectations of the audience, the allegiance of the translator, or the cognitive context of the various participants in the translation process. Though it is not true that they ignored such issues (see also Tymoczko 2007:31), they reflected the concerns of linguistics at that time. And developments in linguistics, including views of communication, of context and of mind, which go beyond the obvious linguistic structures of text, have had a strong influence on the way views of translation have developed.

One of these developments is the increasing concern with pragmatics. Pragmatics, or the study of language use rather than structure (see e.g. Verschueren 1999:1–11), dates back to the early 1970s, according to Mey (2001:4) and was developed because a focus on context-free syntactic phenomena in the generative grammar of that time left too many language phenomena unexplained. In stylistics, these developments were often expressed in terms of a growing concern with context (see, for example, Verdonk 1993:1–6). Equally important has been the recent growth of cognitive linguistics and cognitive poetics. All these developments have had profound influences on the way we view translation (see Boase-Beier 2006:15–21). Both 'contextualized stylistics' (Verdonk 1993:2) and 'cognitive stylistics' (Boase-Beier 2006:19), also, as we have seen, called 'cognitive poetics' (Stockwell 2002), are concerned with what is behind the text in the mind of author, reader, translator or critic, influenced by individual knowledge, belief and experience and shared knowledge of beliefs, which we can refer to as 'culture' (see, for example, Sperber 1996). Cultural objects, events, beliefs and knowledge always form part of the background against which a translator must work. This background also includes such things as historical and current political situation. Especially in views of translation that have been influenced by literary theory which focuses on this type of context (rather than just on the text itself), such background elements will be of great importance, as in, for example, the study of the translation of postcolonial texts. Bassnett and Trivedi (1999:2) point out that, when considering the cultural as well as the linguistic boundaries translation crosses, in fact translation 'rarely, if ever, involves a relationship of equality between texts, authors or systems'. We have already noted in passing that the power relationships between languages, cultures and texts will play a role in even such a fundamental issue as what constitutes a language. In translation, notions of language and power are central to the status of the translator, the translated text and the ethics of translation. The latter question involves the importance of not mentally adapting everything to our own narrow way of seeing. For the moment, and to keep things simple, we merely note that another way of measuring closeness to or distance from source or target along the lines of (1.20) would be to consider cultural, rather than linguistic closeness. An example such as (1.25), taken from a German advertisement for a car, illustrates this

```
(1.25) Katzensprung  zur   Kiesgrube
         cat-jump      to-the gravel-pit
```

The phrase can be taken to suggest (in conjunction with a picture showing a family getting into a car with sunshade, ball, etc.) that it is no problem, if one buys the car in question, to take a quick trip with the children out to the nearby man-made lake for a swim in hot weather. Possible translations of (1.25) might be:

(1.26) A stone's throw to the lake

(1.27) Be at the beach in the blink of an eye

(1.28) Have a picnic!

(1.26) preserves some cultural elements of the source text, in that the idiom 'Katzensprung' in German is replaced by an equivalent in English ('stone's throw'), and the notion of a family trip out would, at least given the illustration, be as clear as in the original. However, (1.26) would be strange and even slightly far-fetched in the English context. (1.27) tries to echo the alliteration of the original, which is more noticeable than the assonance in the expression 'stone's throw', and (1.28) uses a completely different strategy, playing on the double meaning of picnic as an open-air meal or something done easily.

The difference between German and English habits is great enough for (1.25) to pose real problems in translation: in England we do not have a typical mental representation (called a 'schema'; see Cook 1994:11) for getting out of town for a couple of hours to a water-filled gravel pit to swim and sunbathe. If we were translating into Inuit or Hausa or any language generally used in countries with no gravel extraction, the cultural difficulties would be much greater.

But closeness and distance might not only be measured in terms of the linguistic or cultural elements in the text. In a cognitive view of language and style, the likely thoughts and feelings embodied in a text, the likely effects on a reader, the work that a reader has to do, are of central importance. As we saw in Section 1.1, the reader will typically have to work harder to understand a text if it contains gaps, uncertainties, very weak implicatures and ambiguities. Consider the following three lines from a poem by R.S. Thomas:

> (1.29) The wrinkles will come upon her
>   calm though her brow be
>   under time's blowing.
>   (Thomas 2004:282)

A first reading suggests an enjambed (or run-on) structure: 'the wrinkles will come upon her calm' as in 'waves will disturb the calm' when speaking of the sea. Even though the rest of the sentence does not make this reading syntactically impossible, as one could understand 'though her brow be under time's blowing' to mean 'though her brow is affected by the passage of time', by the end of the sentence it seems semantically unlikely. 'Though' should introduce a contrast: 'she will get wrinkles even though subject to time passing' does not make sense. Therefore the reader assumes the correct interpretation is that 'her' is the object rather than 'her calm': 'the wrinkles will come upon her' even though she now appears calm.

This process of leading the reader in one direction only to change direction suddenly is known as 'garden-pathing' (see e.g. Ferreira et al 2000; Pinker 1994:212–217) and is also behind the sense of mild shock one feels in instances of zeugma such as:

(1.30) On the first evening she found a bed and breakfast and total happiness.

Here the shock (and pleasure) is not so much, as in (1.29), a feeling of having followed a path to a dead end but of having found the garden path leads to, say, a peacock's cage, rather than the expected back door of a house. It only works because 'a bed and breakfast' suggests one sense of the verb 'to find', but then 'happiness' suggests another.

One might therefore decide that this effect is the most important thing about (1.29); so a translation should not lose it, as in the following example:

(1.31) Die Falten werden über sie kommen
   the wrinkles will upon her come
      (Perryman 1998:18)

Here the object of 'come upon' is clearly 'her' (*sie*) and not 'her calm'; the garden-pathing effect has not been judged important.

Though the above discussion about (1.29) and its translation reflects the recent concern in cognitive stylistics with poetic effect, the discussion of effects on the reader in translation goes back a long way. Both d'Ablancourt in 1654 (in Robinson 2002:158) and G.H. Lewes in 1855, for example (1855:27), stress the importance of considering how the effect is to be kept.

Effect in translation has often been judged (e.g. by Chesterman 1997:35) too tenuous a thing to measure and comment on because of different readers' contexts. Cognitive poetics is particularly useful here, as it allows us to describe precisely how the effect of (1.29) interacts with different possible cognitive contexts, so that the different possibilities of translating it can be seen more clearly.

The above examples illustrate several possible ways of achieving closeness – linguistic, cultural and cognitive – between source and target text. But the very notion that what translation does is to establish such closeness or equivalence, though intuitively it seems reasonable, cannot just be taken for granted. This is a point to which we shall return in Chapter 2. For the moment, it is enough to note that there are different degrees of such equivalence; this is the difficulty behind interpreting scales such as that in (1.20) as well as scales such as that given in Munday (2009:8), which map different strategies.

But even taking equivalence (of whatever degree and type) for granted, there are clearly other factors than textual ones, even in an extended sense, that affect the source-target relationship. We could also consider such influences on the translator's practice as ethics, ideology, loyalty and so on. Venuti (2008:15), discussing Berman (see 2004), suggests that the translator has an ethical duty not to lose the foreignness of the source text. Though one of the tenets of postcolonial translation theory is that this is particularly the case when the source text is in a language embodying less power than will the target text, one could argue that the preservation of what is foreign, other, different, in the source text is a consideration for any translation, as indeed many earlier theorists, and especially Schleiermacher (1992:152), have pointed out. Thus we might consider ourselves ethically bound to show that, for example, French links crying and raining phonetically. This is also true in cases such as the word for summer and the various tenses of the verb '*être*' in French. Here the lexicon, or mental dictionary, or a speaker of French might show a phonological link (- one of sound -), but not a semantic link (- one of meaning). Consider the following example from Claude de Burine (Sorrell 2001:76–77):

> (1.32) Mon été étincelant et tendre
> C'était toi

Martin Sorrell translates these lines as

> (1.33) My sparkling and tender summer
> Was you

because, as he says in his Translator's Preface, the sound repetition in (1.32) is 'accidental' (2001:12). But might not the fact that French uses the same word for 'summer' and the past participle of the verb 'to be' (as in *j'ai été*, 'I have been / I was') be significant? That it is significant for this particular poet is suggested by de Burine's frequent use of the word '*été*' in her poems, and its close juxtaposition with images of time (see e.g. Sorrell 2001:24;34;56). But the play on its meanings is also used by Apollinaire in '*Carte Postale*' (2003:306). To treat it as accidental, then, seems to risk losing some of the essence of the French language exploited by its poets. But to try to retain echoes of the French, assuming that the poet's usage is a matter of choice rather than accident, is only one way of interpreting Venuti's 'call to action' (2008:265) and he himself was careful to say that he was not necessarily speaking of actual mimicry of the source text (2008:252). His term 'foreignisation' (2008:97), much used since he first introduced it in his 2005 book, is sometimes taken to mean 'echoing the foreign (i.e. source) text' and this was indeed the sense in which Berman, originally writing in 1985, but translated into English by Venuti (as Berman

2004), used it. Venuti himself uses 'foreignization' for a broader set of strategies than Berman: making the target text foreign *per se* (2008:263). This brings his concept of foreignization closer to terms such as 'foregrounding', used first in Garvin's (1964) translation of the work of the Prague Circle of Linguists. Foregrounding, which has since then become an important term in stylistics (see e.g.van Peer 1986, Leech 2008), means drawing attention to something in the text. Thus Venuti's foreignization could be seen to mean drawing attention to the foreign – which is also, in Prague Circle terms, the literary – nature of the target text, irrespective of the actual linguistic elements of the source text. On the broadest view of foreignization, then, (1.33) would be a foreignizing translation because the syntax (- the sentence structure -), by swapping the expected positions of the noun phrases 'my sparkling and tender summer' and 'you' in the sentence, foregrounds them both, just as 'What a piece of work is a man' (Shakespeare 1956:873) draws attention to both elements of the comparison in a way that 'A man is a piece of work' would not. On a narrower, more mimetic interpretation, (1.33) does not echo the *été* – *était* link.

We can understand translation ethics in terms of doing justice to the source text, and thus link the concept to such notions as Dryden's concept of 'paraphrase', which he described in 1680 as the ideal, and which always keeps the author in view (992:17), as well as to Nord's 'loyalty' (1997:125). Venuti's ethics of foreignization (2008) are clearly about loyalty to the act of translation, rather than to the source text or author, but for Nord, though loyalty is felt to both source and target, it is to the people involved in the translation process rather than to the process itself or the texts. The point behind (1.32) might thus be seen as Burine's pun rather than an issue of French lexis, and a pun, rather than a link between being and summer, would be the focus of the translator. Thus in terms of loyalty to Burine one might translate it as Philip Wilson (p.m.) suggests:

(1.34)   That sparkling tender summer
           You summed it up.

This is a translation that aims to reproduce the play on words, as the assumed intention of the poet. If the translator of (1.34) had seen (1.32) as embodying a fact about the French language rather than an intentional play on words, he might have translated as follows:

(1.35)   The world sparkled softly that summer.
           You were there.

Issues such as ethics, loyalty and audience expectations and effects might seem to be both abstract and outside the remit of linguistics or stylistics. But in fact they have practical consequences, because they all express a fundamental question in translation, and it is this: should the source text be presented in translation on its own terms or those of the target language? Does the reader of Burine in translation want to get a sense of the French language, and the sort of lexical and semantic link a French reader would make, or to experience a similar link in English?

This is the question behind many translation theories, and was explicitly formulated by Schleiermacher in 1913 (see 1992:42), who said that the translator can either bring the source text towards the target reader (that is, make it easily readable on the target language's terms) or take the reader towards the source text (that is, translate so that the source text has to be understood on its own terms). It is also implicit in views such as Venuti's concern with foreignization (though less so in his concern with the translator's visibility) and in postcolonial theories of translation (see e.g. Bassnett and Trivedi 1999).

It could be argued that meeting the text on its own terms demands greater work on the part of the reader, and is therefore more compatible with the way literary texts work. This is, then, a question that relates to such issues as the role of creativity on both the translator's and the reader's part, and we will return to this in Chapter 3. It is also a question about the function of translation, sometimes expressed as the difference between 'documentary translation', which aims to give an accurate picture of the source text – such as example (1.22) – and 'instrumental translation' (see Nord 1997:50–52), which attempts to preserve function or text-type. Thus it might be argued that (1.28) aims to work as an advertisement slogan in its own right, rather than telling us what the original said, or that (1.33) is itself a poetic line, in the sense that the reader needs to engage with it, and that both are examples of instrumental translation. It is important not to confuse 'instrumental translation' (a translation that preserves function, including literary function) with 'instrumental text' (a text with a 'predetermined end' as Attridge (2004:7) puts it). One could argue, as Attridge does (2004:6–10), that the function of a literary text is not to have a function. An instrumental literary translation could, in this sense, be said to be exactly that which results in a non-instrumental text.

The question of documentary versus instrumental translation gives rise to another question. Whereas documentary translation could be seen as a report on the source text, as instrumental translation is something much more autonomous, and this raises the question of whether the aim and text-type of the translation need necessarily have any relation at all to those of the source text. Consider a well-known translation of a literary text, say the translation of Shakespeare's *Hamlet* by Schlegel and Thieck (1916). Clearly the German Schlegel-Thieck *Hamlet* is intended to be a play. It will be performed and audiences will go to see it. It has the same text-type as the original. If, however, Hamlet is translated for German schoolchildren, in order that they can study the text in class, the text-type of the translation is obviously a different one, though it will still have some characteristics of the original play-text: it will involve dialogue rather than narrative, and so on.

A translation can, then, clearly be of a different text-type from the source text. But it is also possible to maintain that translations are *per se* a different text-type from non-translated texts. If this is so then we need to reconsider whether the 'fundamental question' I gave above – does the translation aim to give the reader a view of the source text on its own terms or on those of the target language? – needs reformulating. We perhaps must instead ask: should we see a translation from neither source nor target perspective, but as a text with its own set of characteristics? This is a question likely to be fairly irrelevant in the case of many non-literary translations. A set of instructions for a camera or a brochure for tourists are likely to be translated in such a way that the translated text addresses whatever needs the target audience has: to operate the camera or to visit the region (c.f. Gutt 2000:47–54). The fact that the text read by the target audience is a translation is likely to be unimportant, and not even known by the audience. Even literary translations can sometimes work like this. A German translation of the children's book *The Tiger Who Came to Tea* (see Kerr 1968), for example, is not necessarily read as a translation. But the Schlegel-Thieck *Hamlet* or the translation of a Swedish crime novel are potentially different. Here the audience will almost certainly be aware that the text is a translation. This might be especially the case where a text has several roughly contemporaneous translations, such as Rilke's *Sonnets to Orpheus*, translated several times in the last 20 years, for example, by Kinnell and Liebmann (1999), Paterson (2006) and Arndt (1989). A reader might compare any particular translation with the others. She or he might also be aware of reading the work of Paterson, or Arndt, as much as Rilke. Some literary translations, such as Ted Hughes' *Tales from Ovid* (1997) are in fact often read specifically because of the importance of the translator.

In all these cases, it makes sense to see the translated text as demanding a different sort of reading from a non-translated text, suggested to the reader by the presence of a translator's name along with the original author's on the book cover, and, often, a translator's preface, footnotes and the original text on facing pages, especially in the case of poetry.

There have been many discussions about how the translated text is seen in terms of its difference from an untranslated text. For example, I have suggested (see Boase-Beier 2006:146–148) that a translated text multiplies the voices, implicatures and other poetic qualities of the source text. Other writers have argued that the two types of writing are different in that the ideas or content of the text are already given (Hamburger in Honig 1985:175), or that different creative processes are involved (Trask in Honig 1985:14).

We will come back to this issue in Chapter 4, and suggest that in fact the translated text is read as a blend of an existing source text and an imagined untranslated text in the target language. It will combine elements of both source and target languages and of source and target cultural situations, and demands of the reader that it be read with both contexts in mind and as the work of two authors.

Possible and Impossible in Translation **2**

2.1 Translation and Linguistic Relativity

The discussion in Chapter 1 showed that a clear definition of translation is difficult: some things are clearly translations, some are not and many are somewhere in between. Translation is also constrained by what is possible, and it is to the question of what translation can and cannot do that we now turn.

Much has been said (see, for example Heidegger 1957:163; Barnstone 1993:18) about the possibility or impossibility of translation. There are two main reasons why translation might be considered impossible:

(i) in literary texts, meaning and form are assumed to be closely linked, so an act that threatens to separate them seems doomed to failure
(ii) languages might represent the world in incompatible ways

The first point has to do specifically with literary translation, and it will be the contention of this book that understanding the nature of the form-meaning link in language – understanding how style works – is one of the prerequisites for translation, especially of literary texts. I return to this issue in the next section.

It is to the second question that I wish to turn now. If languages do represent the world differently, then it seems there can never be complete equivalence of meaning in two languages. If complete equivalence of meaning is the aim of translation, then (ii) suggests it might be impossible.

One way out of the dilemma is to argue that translation is not about absolute equivalence of meaning. Catford said we replace a source-language meaning with a different one in the target-language which functions in the same way in a given situation (1965:20). Many studies of translation have been concerned with whether or not it creates equivalence of function, of effect, of connotation, or of communicative intent (see Munday 2008:36–53 for discussion). The perception that older, linguistically based, studies have a naïve view of what constitutes equivalence is a common one, and was expressed particularly by Snell-Hornby (1988:22). But in fact such older studies were very aware of the lack of equivalence between languages, as linguistic and anthropological works of the time (e.g. Whorf 1956) suggested. This led to the notion that there were different types of equivalence. Nida (1964:159), for example, used the term formal equivalence to mean that the form in the target language was similar to that in the source language, and dynamic equivalence (1964:159), later functional equivalence (de Waard and Nida 1986:vii), to mean that the function was similar.

In Nida's later work it becomes clear that the distinction between formal and functional equivalence is not easy to maintain. Though still working (as was Jakobson, whom we met in Chapter 1) broadly within what is known as a 'code-model' of language, in which 'communication is achieved by encoding and decoding messages' (see Sperber and Wilson 1995:1–64 for discussion), Nida and de Waard (1986: 13) place emphasis on the fact that 'the form itself so frequently carries significant meaning'. In this they reflect a more pragmatic understanding of language, as do Sperber and Wilson, who argue that a code-model must be supplemented – though not replaced – by an inferential model (1995:3) which allows us to focus on intended inferences (implicatures) in texts, and to see style as a set of weak implicatures, as suggested (see 1.11) in the previous chapter. A move from seeing meaning as encoded in the text to seeing meaning as left open for the reader to make inferences about has potentially profound effects on the notion of equivalence in translation, and how we describe it, as Tymoczko (2007:7) points out.

As pragmatic theories of language and communication such as Sperber and Wilson (1995), which first appeared in 1986, have had direct or indirect effects on translation studies, so the question of equivalence has largely been avoided.

Since Holmes (1988) mapped out the interaction between descriptive and theoretical research in translation, the focus has been on the types of translation that are actually observed. Toury (e.g. 1980) had by then already begun to initiate what is now called Descriptive Translation Studies, focusing on 'facts of real life' (1995:1). This broad descriptive basis makes it possible to say that equivalence has to be determined by what people regard as equivalent in a particular case or genre or historical period (Toury 1995:37,61; see also Malmkjær 2005:15). For Pym (2010:64), it is a useful idea that became less popular with the advent of functional and descriptive theories, remaining, however, a necessary illusion (2010:165).

But redefining equivalence so that it does not mean 'having exactly the same meaning' is only one way of solving the problem in (ii). If languages do not represent the world in equivalent ways, the other way to solve the problem is to split (ii) into a strong and a weak form, rejecting the strong and accepting the weak, as the latter is compatible with translation. These are the two views as applied to translation:

(iia) languages represent the world differently and thus make speakers of different languages think differently, so translation is not possible

or

(iib) languages represent the world differently but we can in principle think anything, so speakers of one language can both grasp and express a meaning habitually only expressed in the other.

(iia) is what one might call the translator's version of Strong Linguistic Relativity (with strong Determinism), while (iib) is the translator's version of Weak Linguistic Relativity (without strong Determinism). Note that Linguistic Determinism – the view that language affects thought – is, as Gumperz and Levison (1996:23) and Crystal (2003:15) also point out, always a prerequisite for Linguistic Relativity: people who speak different languages presumably only think differently (Relativity) if the language is causing the difference (Determinism). However, as (iia) and (iib) show, Determinism itself, like Relativity, also tends to have stronger and weaker forms: the strong form in (iia) suggests that we cannot be free from what our language makes us think, whereas a weaker form, as in (iib), only accepts that language influences thought. Confusingly, and wrongly, it is often maintained that Linguistic

Determinism is a strong form of Linguistic Relativity; this seems to be the view of Pinker (2007). From a translator's point of view the important thing is that (iia) and (iib) are strong and weak versions of a view that complete equivalence is not possible.

There has been much controversy and confusion surrounding the terms Linguistic Determinism and Linguistic Relativity, which are usually seen to derive from the work of Sapir and Whorf (see, for example Whorf 1956), anthropologist – linguists who studied the languages spoken by American Indians. As Malmkjær (2005:48–50) explains, Sapir and Whorf were motivated by a desire not to impose Anglo-American categories on the thinking of another culture. This was of course a laudable aim, and it is exactly the aim that forms the basis of much recent and current thinking in literary criticism and translation, often expressed using the term 'otherness'. It is the notion behind Venuti's foreignization, Kristeva's feminist criticism or Attridge's view of the special nature of the literary text, to give just three examples (see Venuti 2009:97; Kristeva 1986:252; Attridge 2004:123). It is in fact not just a laudable aim, but a common-sense one: it is unlikely that one's own view of the world is intrinsically better than others (see also Tymoczko 2007:15–53).

Conflicts arise both in the degree to which Linguistic Relativity and Linguistic Determinism are seen to obtain, and in the question of their interdependence. As Gumperz and Levinson (1996:24), point out, Linguistic Relativity is not the same as linguistic difference: the latter can be taken for granted.

Conflicts around Linguistic Relativity and Determinism have arisen particularly in linguistics and literary theory, usually for ideological reasons. Generative linguistics, based on the work of Chomsky (for example 1957, 2000) and others, such as Pinker (2007), mentioned above, is concerned to demonstrate universal language structures, realized differently in different languages. Much modern literary theory (for example post-structuralism), on the other hand, is keen to focus on the differences in cultures, world views and languages. However, most scholars of any area reject strong Linguistic Determinism, the view that language determines (rather than influences) the way we think.

What can seem particularly strange to theorists of translation is the need so many people apparently feel to be in either the relativity camp or the universalist camp, but it helps to remember that different researchers have different aims: a psychologist will want to know what linguistic determinism or relativity might tell us about the brain, a pragmatic linguist will be particularly concerned with the effects of context, and a translation studies researcher will be interested in many additional factors that affect the process and reception of translation. Pinker, for example, who is a psychologist, argues that Linguistic Determinism is wrong and Linguistic Relativity is right but 'mundane' (2007:135). In fact, one would expect a psychologist to find the effect of language on thought more interesting than language itself. For a translation scholar, on the other hand, such interactions are far from mundane. Even weak linguistic relativity (as an observation, rather than as a theory, hence no capitals) is highly interesting, partly because it is almost certainly true to some degree (as even Pinker admits) and partly because communication, and therefore translation, are concerned with differences in tendencies, with likely ways of interpreting, likely connotations, with inferences and with such things, in literary translation, as poetic effects.

Also from a linguist's point of view, as indeed must be the case for any theory that deems both stability and adaptability to be essential (see e.g. Spolsky 2002), it is exactly in the interaction of what is universal and what is language-specific, or culture-specific or context-specific, that one finds explanations for the way language works. Relativist linguists like Gumperz and Levinson (1996), rather than adopting a position midway between universalism and relativity, as Malmkjær (2005:48) suggests, and as even they themselves suggest (1996:3), are simply accepting the likelihood of interaction. For the translator and the translation specialist it is the nature of the universal-specific interaction that makes translation both possible and interesting (see e.g. Tabakowska 1993:128).

To take a concrete example, Boroditsky (2004) shows that languages with different grammatical genders for objects are strongly correlated with different perceptions of whether the objects in question are 'masculine' or 'feminine'. She describes tests which found that Spanish speakers, whose language classifies bridges as grammatically masculine, describe them as 'big, dangerous, long, strong, sturdy and towering' whereas German speakers, whose language classifies them as feminine, typically describe them as 'beautiful, elegant, fragile, peaceful, pretty, and slender' (2004:920).

Pinker would presumably say that, because a Spanish speaker is *able* to see a bridge as pretty or slender, this shows that Linguistic Determinism is nonsense, and there is nothing more to be said, because there is never anything to be said about Linguistic Relativity. However, as Gumperz and Levinson point out (1996:7–8) we can still ask whether gender differences merely reflect cultural distinctions or whether they influence them. A translation scholar will want to know more about the circumstances under which such differences might influence thinking, if they do. Supposing one were to consider the translation of French '*la lune*' and '*le soleil*', the moon (f.) and the sun (m.), into German, where the moon is grammatically masculine and the sun feminine. What differences and difficulties does this cause? How can German gender be made to fit the gender of the classical deities and in fact that in many ancient religions the moon was portrayed as the wife of the sun (Biedermann 1992:224)?

The reason a psychologist such as Pinker finds such problems uninteresting has to do with what one expects of theory. If theory (whether linguistic, literary, or about translation) is measured against real examples in order to judge whether the theory – one's mental picture of the world – needs adjusting, then some events and situations will not provide any evidence that such adjustment is necessary, and so they will be uninteresting. But there are other things one can do with the relation between theory and what it describes. The experiment with Spanish and German speakers might not tell us anything radically new about existing models of the mind, but it does tell the translator that connotations might be quite unconscious for most speakers, yet still play a role in the way an entity or a text is perceived. For the theorist of translation it would be very interesting to know whether translators unconsciously take such connotations into account. In other words, a theory such as Linguistic Relativity might tell us about language use in context (Gumperz and Levinson 1996:8) and therefore also in the context of actual translation.

There is, though, a further reason for the confusion surrounding the Sapir-Whorf Hypothesis, especially when consequences for translation are drawn from it. Malmkjær (2005:46) suggests that theorists such as Halliday (1978:185) said it was not possible to say the same thing in different registers of a language. And yet, close reading of Halliday makes it seem more likely that what he was actually saying was that 'the same thing' *can* be said in different registers but means something different. For example, we might say 'snicket' or 'passageway' and feel they mean the same but are just put differently. Halliday's suggestion, as I understand it, is that they are different in meaning to the extent that the first is talking about a specific kind of passageway which perhaps only exists in the areas in which the term is used and the other about a much less specific type of passageway. This observation, if taken also to apply at the level of languages, is particularly interesting for translation, because it suggests that what appear to be equivalents might not actually have the same meaning. It is not that it is impossible to imagine a Spanish bridge with feminine qualities, or to talk about it, but that the word '*Brücke*' in German and the word '*puente*' in Spanish do not mean quite the same to speakers of the respective languages.

This is what Jakobson said, too (2004:139). To say that if you say the same thing in Spanish and German, or English and German, you mean something slightly different, does not have as a logical consequence that you cannot say the same thing in both languages. In other words, if the examples in Chapter 1 '*Es ist gehüpft wie gesprungen*' (1.21) and 'It's as broad as long' (1.23) do not have exactly the same connotations for their respective native speakers, this is not at all the same as saying that an English speaker cannot picture and talk about the image of jumping and leaping nor the German speaker imagine breadth and width compared. Neither strong Linguistic Determinism nor strong Linguistic Relativity nor the impossibility of translation follow from the linguistic difference. What does follow is that the translator does not have a straightforward task. This misapprehension – that from 'the same thing' in two languages meaning something different follows that one cannot translate – is the worst of the several confusions surrounding the Sapir-Whorf Hypothesis.

2.2 Literary and non-literary translation

The existence of linguistic and cultural difference is one of the reasons some people might think translation impossible. The other reason given at the start of this chapter – (i) on p. 20 – is the close connection between form and meaning in literary translation. If the act of translation separates form and meaning, preserving only the latter, then literary translation (and the translation of any other type of text in which the form and meaning are closely connected) will be impossible.

Again, there are a number of issues to consider here: is the meaning of a text to be found in its representation of the world (or any world) or do its formal features carry (non-representational) meaning in their own right? In what sense is the meaning of a literary (and therefore fictional) text true?

A moment's thought will allow us to see that literary texts do not, or do not solely, represent the world. To some extent they can be said to represent different worlds, which may be merely fictional or even actually impossible, when measured against the world we know (cf. Gavins 2007:12). They may contain talking animals, thinking plants, or travel through time. But it is not just that the worlds they represent are not recognisable as what we call the 'real' world. Authors such as Samuel Beckett have tried hard to make their writing not represent anything else, that is, not conjure up a world the text refers to. If the forms in the following examples do not represent anything in the usual sense, then a translator needs to ask what they mean, because some idea of what things mean seems essential, in a practical sense, in order to translate:

> (2.1) Longing the so-said mind long lost to longing
>> (Beckett 1999:36)

> (2.2) Kroklokwafzi ? Semem̃emi !
> Seiokronto – prafriplo.
>> (Morgenstern 1965:226)

In (2.1) it is unclear what the grammatical subject of the first 'longing' is, assuming it is used verbally. The lack of clear syntax tends to reduce the meaning to the lexical meanings of the verb 'to long' and the adjective 'long'. It could be argued that in this sense (2.1) is not a description of a possible event, but merely a series of sounds. However, it is unlikely that most translators would feel it is sufficient simply to preserve sound, as in:

> (2.3) Locke den sosagten Geist lang gelockt in Locken.

There seem to be elements of meaning in (2.3) – 'entice' (*locken*) and 'curl' (*Locke*) – that are not in (2.1). And elements of meaning in (2.1) – perhaps the connotations of sadness, boredom and frustration that 'long' suggests – are missing. Example (2.2) is translated by Anthea Bell (1992:n.p.) as:

> (2.4) Kroklokwoffzie ? Seemimeemi !
> Siyokronto – prufliplo

Bell describes Morgenstern's poem as 'pure sound' (1992:n.p.), based on his own statement, but here again it could be argued that her translation shows it is more than this. The punctuation of the first line, which she preserves, tells us that it is a question and (probably) an answer. We cannot help but visualize whatever objects the sounds suggest in the world we know, based on the meanings of words we know. The first word sounds (to me) like a concrete object, perhaps an animal that is a cross between a crocodile and a dog, in both German and English, whereas the second appears to answer that it is something abstract that combines appearance and mimicry (a stronger connotation in the English than in the German). These images will be different for every reader and it is thus possible to see the poem as a representation of the way poems work: by embodying connotations that readers will contextualize in various ways.

What these examples suggest is that sounds, syntax, and other formal features of a text always draw part of their meaning from reference to something in the real world outside the text, even if the reader has great freedom in constructing this world.

From a translator's point of view, then, even where forms do not 'mean' in an iconic fashion, that is, directly represent sounds, as in the examples in (1.14), they do still carry meaning. This suggests that a translation that ignored meaning in (2.1), as (2.3) does, is as bad a translation as one like the following that ignores the sound:

> (2.5) Sehnsucht der sogenannte Geist längst der Sehnsucht verloren.
> longing the so-called mind long to-the longing lost

(Readers who do not have German should bear in mind that its pronunciation closely follows its written form.)

But even accepting that sound alone rarely carries meaning, the importance of keeping sound gives rise to a further question: should a translation echo the sound of the original text, as (2.3) does, or use sounds that in the target language have the same connotations, as (2.6) does?

> (2.6) Verlangen der sogenannte Geist lang in Verlangen verloren.

The different answers represented by (2.3), (2.5) and (2.6) to the question of how to represent the sounds of (2.1) will exactly reflect the answer one gives to the central question of translation mentioned in the previous section: does the translator of Beckett want her readers to understand Beckett on his terms or their own, in terms of the language he spoke or the language they speak? And the answer one gives to this question will depend on one's view of the translator's allegiance, to which we shall return in Chapter 3.

It seems we can thus say that formal features do carry meaning in literary texts, but that there is always also a representative element even in such texts. How, then, do literary texts represent the world? In what sense are they true?

While there is probably little disagreement about the meaning of the word 'true' – a true statement maintains that what is, is (see O'Hear 1985:88) – what is interesting in questions of meaning and representation is how one decides what is true. There are various views on this, that involve measuring statements against the world (as in what is known as truth-conditional semantics), or measuring their consistency with a set of beliefs, or even taking to be true anything that changes what we think (O'Hear 1985:88–97). In the case of literary texts, we do not expect them to be demonstrably true in relation to the real world, and in fact being demonstrably true in this sense has often been seen as inimical to the aesthetic (see e.g. Attridge 2004:14) but we do expect them to be consistent in the fictional world (or set of sub-worlds; see Semino 1997:71–77) that the text sets up.

Sperber and Wilson (1995:265) are concerned with the relevance, rather than the truth, of what is actually said. 'Relevance' in the technical sense used in Relevance Theory means the extent to which the work invested in understanding something rewards the reader with cognitive gains (1995:265). These might be increases in knowledge (for example by processing a non-literary text) or 'the reorganisation of existing knowledge' (1995:266), and so on.

For literary texts, the cognitive effects can be assumed to be poetic effects: effects such as activating assumptions that relate to a particular area of knowledge in the reader's mind (Pilkington 2000:134) or causing particular feelings in the reader (Pilkington 2000:164), causing pleasure as the reader searches for meaning (Boase-Beier 2006:88–89; Grandin 2005:96), physical reactions (Richards 1970:28–31) or the ordering of one's thoughts in the absence of the situation described so that one may be better able to cope with the situation when it does arise (Richards 1970:29).

Concerning ourselves with poetic effect rather than simply truth or falsehood (- though it could be argued that what is true in the world of the literary text, and might conceivably be true in the real world, is more likely to have such effects than what is demonstrably false; see Sperber and Wilson 1995:264 -) allows us to consider that what is transferred in the translation of literary texts is related to such poetic effects. Consider the following example, where the narrator describes looking out on a garden at dawn:

> (2.7) No moonshine mixed into the grey of morning,
>
> . . .
>
> And no more mine in this light than in dream
> (Hamburger 2000:64)

The word 'moonshine' has a number of poetic effects. It has at least three meanings: 'moonlight', 'foolish talk' (the meaning given by the *Concise Oxford Dictionary* 2008:927), or 'visionary talk or ideas' (the meaning given in the earlier edition, 1976:707). In conjunction with 'grey of morning' and 'dream' it suggests a contrast to the real world, and its parallel position and similar sound to 'no more mine' suggests a link between reality and dispossession (and between dream and possession). The processing of these different meanings (and particularly of the older and more recent colloquial meanings of 'moonshine', if we are aware of them) makes us mentally re-enact some of the confusion that 'this light' makes the narrator in the poem feel, while at the same time we feel that the meaning, though slippery, ought to be clear, as the narrator, looking out onto the garden in the morning, also feels: he comments that the dream carries on even into the approaching daylight.

Such effects are not, of course, as many scholars such as Pilkington (2000) or Turner (1996) have pointed out, confined to literary texts. For example, the following headline might also make us feel confused:

(2.8) Dead veterans happy to rock again for Obama (Reuters, July 2 2008)

It is in fact a well-known characteristic of headlines that they use ambiguity to cause uncertainty and to urge the reader to read on: here she will find that 'dead' is not an adjective but a noun: what is meant is surviving members of the Grateful Dead (see Boase-Beier 2006:86–7 for further examples).

The example (2.7) from a poem by Michael Hamburger has been translated by Franz Wurm (Dove 2004:104) as:

(2.9) Kein Mondlicht ins Morgengrauen gemischt
     no   moonlight into morning-grey   mixed

     Und mein in diesem Licht so wenig
     and mine in this   light so little

     Wie es im   Traum . . . war
     as it in-the dream . . . was

It could be argued that some of the poetic effect is lost in this translation. It will not make us feel any uncertainty about the meaning of '*Mondlicht*' (moonlight) and there is no parallelism to suggest the uncertainty of possession. Similarly, if (2.8) is translated as:

(2.10) Veteranen des Dead freuen sich, wieder für Obama zu rocken

the effects will be lost because 'Dead' is unambiguously a noun. In the literary example (2.9), the translation loss will lead to a less satisfactory experience of reading, and, if such losses occur throughout a whole collection, might affect sales of the translated book. In the headline in (2.10), the interest of readers might be affected. These might be tangible effects of texts which have nothing to do with 'truth' in its usual sense, but only with the way a reader's mind is affected.

These are fairly simple examples of loss of effect, something which, as discussed in Chapter 1, theories have often considered essential. Particularly in the case of literary texts, poetic effects can be complex and subtle and it is important for the translator to understand them. We shall focus on the question of poetic effects in Part II.

Formal features are clearly important to literary texts, and for this reason Gutt (2000:132–133) argues that the sort of translation involved in literary texts is 'direct translation', similar to direct quotation in that it depends on resemblance to the form of the original utterance and not just its content. Another way of putting this is to say, as Attridge does (2004:75), that the formal features in literary texts are so significant that they can be imitated in translation, and thus literature is by definition that which is translatable. What this means is that a literary text is translatable, not by representing the same truth but by keeping as far as possible both 'formal features' and its 'openness to new contexts' (ibid.).

Gutt also makes the point (2000:47–68) that some translations, especially of non-literary texts, are not really translations at all because they do not tell us what the original text said in terms of form and effect but simply describe the same situation in a different language. Gutt's example is the translation of a tourist brochure. It does not much matter that, or whether, it resembles the original brochure in keeping its form as long as it describes the same place. In Attridge's terms, a text like this does not have the 'singularity' (2004:25) that marks it out as literary and is the basis for translation proper.

Taking these various observations together, we notice a potentially very large difference between literary and non-literary translation, which could be expressed, with reference to point (i) at the start of this chapter, as follows:

(ia) non-literary translation aims to describe the same situation in target- and source-texts, but formal resemblance between the two is not important;

(ib) literary translation aims to tell us what the source text said, including recreating its particular formal features and stylistic effects.

However, the difference is not just a difference in the type of translation appropriate; there is also a difference in the text itself, and this is reflected in the second part of (ib) above. It is not just that literary translations tend to be seen in relation to their source text, but they are also translations of style and poetic effect. The difference is linked, then, to the understanding of style as a set of weak implicatures which achieve their effects by making the reader work, as discussed in Chapter 1 (see (1.11) and the discussion that follows it). The difference could also be linked to the notion of function introduced in Chapter 1. If the function of the advertisement is to cause its reader to buy a product, then the success of translation can be measured by the degree to which the translated text fulfils the same function. The function of literature can be understood as having poetic effects: to cause uncertainty, make the reader rethink something, or feel fear, for example. A functional view of literature, which has the specific aim of causing the reader to engage with it and experience poetic effects, suggests both that equivalence cannot be measured in terms of linguistic closeness (something we have already seen to be the case) and also that equivalence cannot be measured in terms of preserving meaning and implicatures. There are two reasons for this. As Gutt (2000:118) argues, the cognitive context of the reader is always of the utmost importance, and we cannot know what it is, but only make assumptions about it. As a Bible translator, Gutt focuses on the uncertainty about the audience's cognitive state rather than uncertainty about the cognitive state embodied in the source text. But this second uncertainty exists too, and crucially, in literary texts. Many literary critical studies, especially recent ones (see e.g. Iser 1971, 1974, 2006) make it clear that we cannot know the intention of the author, or the message of the text. Yet as translators we have to have some meaning to convey. I called this 'the pretence of translation' in my 2006 book (108–110). By this I meant a 'pretence' on the part of the translator that she or he knows the author's intention, in order to have a starting point for conveying it in translation. In having to have a sense of what meaning is conveyed by a literary text, translators are no different from any other readers of the source text: they create a meaning which, if they are experienced literary readers, they will tend to see as open-ended (cf. Attridge 2004:75). Because we all, according to conceptual metaphor theory, structure our worlds according to the metaphor EVENTS ARE ACTIONS (Lakoff and Turner 1989:36–37, Kövecses 2002:49–50), we will reconstruct an author. But it is the very openness of the style of a literary text, consisting of weak implicatures, that makes literary reading the creative venture it is (cf. also Carey 2005: Chapter 7) and makes literary translation itself a creative activity. Consider the following example, the final stanza of a poem by Celan (Hamburger 2007:380) in (2.11) and two possible translations:

(2.11) Schweigewütiges
silent-angry

sternt
stars

(2.12) and a body that rages for silence
stars

(2.13) the silent-angry
will star

(2.12) gives one particular meaning of (2.11), but there are many implicatures that are not preserved. In fact the verb in each stanza of the poem, including the verb coined by Celan in this final line 'to star', is dependent on the first phrase of the poem, which is '*Erst wenn*' (not until). The verbs could thus be in the future, rather than the present tense: (2.13) takes the parallel use of a verb phrase in each stanza to suggest all are future tenses, whereas Hamburger's translation (2007:381), from which (2.12) is taken, changes to present after the first stanza. Furthermore, the poem appears to be about a time after death: there are many words in the poem such as '*Schatten*' (shade or shadow), '*droben*' ('on the other side'), and '*Engel*' (angels) which suggest this. So the deadjectival noun '*Schweigewütiges*' has been translated by Hamburger as 'a body that . . .', and, to follow this subject, the verb 'rages' has been added. (2.13) presents an alternative translation which follows a different strategy. Rather than try to work out what Celan meant, it simply leaves it open.

If, along with Iser, Attridge and others, we accept that literary texts contain gaps that need to be filled by the reader, then a text like (2.11), which could be said to lack a clear subject, as well as a relation between '*schweige*' (silent) and '*wütig*' (angry), has weak implicatures which are potentially unlimited in number. And the weaker the implicatures, the more work a reader will have to do in constructing meaning. Leaving out the relation in a compound such as *Schweigewütiges* is one way of leaving a gap for the reader. Possible meanings, given as translations here, are:

(2.14) that which is angry about silence

(2.15) that which is raging to achieve silence

(2.16) that which is angry that silence cannot be achieved

and so on. Each could be said to be implicated by something earlier in the text, or in Celan's life, or his other poetry. Hamburger expresses ambivalence about disambiguating the original when he says on the one hand that study of Celan's life and poetry is necessary and on the other that it can lead to unproductive 'entanglement' (2007:410).

We therefore need to see the sort of equivalence that literary translation aims for not in the preservation of meaning and implicatures, nor just implicatures, but in the preservation of open-endedness, the possibility of reader engagement and the recreating of the effects often triggered by formal elements of the text.

Up to now I have been using the terms 'literary translation' and 'nonliterary translation' as though it were clear what they mean. But, as suggested in the previous chapter, they are ambiguous. In fact, we can distinguish four meanings of 'literary translation':

(i)   the act of translating a literary text
(ii) the act of translating any text in a literary way
(iii) the result of (i)
(iv) the result of (ii)

For (i), we could think of any number of examples, because what is meant is simply the act or process, irrespective of whether it is documentary or instrumental, successful or unsuccessful, direct or indirect, of translating a literary text, such as Ibsen's *Hedda Gabler* (1962), into a foreign language, such as English.

As an example of (ii) we might consider the process of translating an advertisement so that its stylistic features are kept, irrespective of whether the resulting translation actually sells the product. Consider the following

(2.17) Goodyear OptiGrip
       20% better braking in wet conditions
       100% better prepared for other people's off days

A translation into German that was concerned to get across both the measured fact, in the advert in question backed up by a footnote with exact details, of the twenty percent braking improvement and the idea that the tyres in question prepare you for the mistakes others make, might conceivably translate (2.17) as:

(2.18) Goodyear Optigrip
20% besseres Bremsen
Und 100% besser auf schlechte Tage anderer gefasst

This would keep the important, verifiable fact of the braking improvement with these tyres and would suggest the unverifiable fact that no other tyres give one such a sense of security, just like the original. But a literary translation in sense (ii) of this text might be:

(2.19) Goodyear Optigrip
20% besseres Bremsen
100% bessere Vorbereitung auf die Fehler anderer

The reason for seeing this as an example of (ii) is that here the parallels *'besseres Bremsen – bessere Vorbereitung'* are clearer, both because of the layout and because the syntax itself is parallel. The fact that the original has 'better braking – better prepared', that is, two different syntactic structures, might be considered immaterial, because a literary translation might want to focus on parallelism as a literary phenomenon more than to echo the original. (2.19) might not sell the tyres better than (2.18); the equivalence to (2.17) is stylistic rather than functional.

As for (iii), a literary translation in this sense is the English version of *Hedda Gabler* (e.g. Arup 1981). And for (iv), (2.19) would qualify. Even though it is not a literary text, because it has arisen as a result of a strategy of stylistic rather than functional equivalence, it is translated in a literary way.

These distinctions are extremely important, because they have consequences for how (and where) translation is taught, what sort of translator is employed by businesses and other bodies for what task and so on.

In general, it can be assumed that a literary source text will require a translation practice that takes the literary nature of the text into account and produces something that is itself a literary text. Senses (i) and (ii) will therefore often come together when we are talking about the process and senses (iii) and (iv) when we are talking about the product.

Throughout this book, I will generally take literary translation to encompass both senses (i) and (ii) and sometimes, as in 'a literary translation' (iii) and (iv), but this will be clear from the context. Much of what I say in the rest of the book will focus on literary, as opposed to non-literary translation, and the reason for this was suggested in Chapter 1. There we saw that the view of cognitive theorists such as Turner (1996) or Lakoff and Johnson (1980), and other writers on conceptual metaphor, is that what we sometimes regard as literary processes are fundamental to how we think. If literary thinking under-lies all thinking, that is, if we create new meanings in language by using such processes as metaphor and parable, then one might want to argue that all texts are in a sense literary texts. And yet there does seem to be a difference between (2.17) and (2.7) or between a thesis about evolution and a poem about it.

This is because, though literary thinking may be at the root of all thinking, literary texts do in fact differ from non-literary texts in their more frequent use of stylistic devices such as innovative metaphor, iconicity, ambiguity and so on. Though all these phenomena might underlie our thinking, their textual mani-festation is different in different types of text. Consider the following texts:

(2.20) Half a league, half a league,
      Half a league onward,
      All in the valley of Death
      Rode the six hundred
           (Tennyson 1894:222)

(2.21) At 11.00 our Light Cavalry Brigade rushed to the front . . . They swept
      proudly past, glittering in the morning sun . . .
                  (*Times*, 14 Nov 1854)

From the point of view of the translator, the distinction can easily be seen in the degree of importance that will be placed on the parallelism in (2.20), but not in (2.21), the *Times* report that is reputedly the source of Tennyson's poem (cf. Tennyson 1897:381). Yet the *Times* report also contains repetition: the alliteration of 'proudly past' is surely important. The difference is that the alliteration in the *Times* report serves to make the text more attractive, more striking and to emphasize the beauty of the scene that is soon to become one of destruction and defeat, whereas Tennyson's repetition, it could be argued, serves to iconically represent the movement of horses, the hopelessness of the situation, the pointlessness of orders and the blindness of obedience. The report recounts events; the poem leads the reader to question.

But there are other differences. The world created by literary texts is fic-tional, and in addition it may also be very different from the real world, con-taining elements not possible there (see Semino 1997:4–9). For the translator, this means that there is not, with literary texts, the possibility of rewriting that we mentioned above in respect of tourist brochures or advertisements. Literary texts are not merely representing a reality and so rewriting (2.20) in another language, in what Gutt (2000:61) calls an act of nontranslational interlingual communication, will not result in an equivalent (in any sense) literary text. And, as discussed above, literary texts are different in the amount of engagement they require or allow on the part of the reader, so a translation must allow similar engagement on the part of the new readers, if it is to fulfil the requirements of being itself a literary text. A literary text, because of the presence of weak implicatures, gaps, ambiguities and other elements that demand a search for meaning, will need to be translated so that a similarly creative reading is possible.

A further difference, discussed in my 2006 book (75–82) is that literary texts could be seen to embody a state of mind to a far greater extent than non-literary texts. The poem 'The Charge of the Light Brigade', from which (2.20) is taken could be said not just to convey the state of mind of an observer (wonder at the valour of the men) but also the state of mind of the men themselves, through the repetitions, which occur in most stanzas, and which suggest also the fear of battle and its hopelessness. A literary translation of (2.20) will need to take account of such states of mind.

Literary translation, then, can be seen in general as translation that takes into account the literary nature of literary texts, and creates a literary text as target text, that is also documentary in its relationship with the source text. It will generally do justice to the following aspects of the text:

  (i) stylistic figures such as iconicity or metaphor
  (ii) the fictional world created by the text
  (iii) the opportunities for the reader's engagement with the text
  (iv) the cognitive state embodied in the text

The degree to which these points are taken into account is likely to determine the degree to which the resulting translation is regarded as successful. In general there seems little reason why points (i) to (iv) should be preserved for non-literary texts, as function is likely to be more important. As we have seen, such translations often have little documentary relationship to the source text. In general, there is far less of interest to say about non-literary translations with no documentary relation to the source-text, as they are not translations in the strict sense. For this reason, they will not form the main focus of the discussion in this book.

Allegiance and Creativity

3

Chapter Outline

3.1 The allegiances of the translator

In Chapter 2 we considered the extent to which translation is possible in terms of Linguistic Relativity and in terms of differences in notions of form and meaning relevant in literary and non-literary translation.

It is important to remember that questions of what is possible, how we relate to the world outside the text, and especially questions of the effects of texts on the reader are all closely connected with what translation is considered to involve. As we saw in Chapter 2, though there is a general sense in which translation creates a target text equivalent to a source text, we always have to be aware that there are different views of what constitutes equivalence. Another way of approaching these differences is to ask: equivalent on whose terms? As has often been pointed out there are a number of players (human and non-human) involved in an act of translation, and they will have different expectations, requirements and effects (cf. Nord 1997:140). Jones (2009: 303–305) captures this situation by speaking of translation in terms of a 'network' that includes objects such as written texts, conditions such as time-pressures, modes of communication such as email or letter, and types of text such as poetry or drama, as well as the various people involved, such as patrons, readers and publishers. To see some of these elements, consider the translation of the following title from German news and current affairs magazine *Focus* (June 2004:137):

> (3.1) Umschlungen von Engelszungen
>   surrounded   by   angel-tongues

This is the title of an article about American singer Norah Jones, and refers to the 'melodies as gentle as children's songs' (ibid.; my translation). Possible translations of this title might be:

> (3.2) Surrounded with heavenly sound
>
> (3.3) Surrounded by the voice of an angel
>
> (3.4) Sung by an angel's tongue

The first translation reproduces to some degree the internal rhyme of the title, but changes the sense quite substantially. The second translation does not reproduce the sound repetition, and, though it keeps the broad image of angels, does not reproduce the image of angels' tongues, which in German suggests persuasiveness. It recalls Luther's translation of 1 Corinthians 13: 1 in the Bible, which is 'the eloquence of angels' in the King James Version, in a passage that says such eloquence, without love, leads to emptiness. Hence the implicature of '*Engelszungen*' could be said to be beguiling sound devoid of meaning. The third translation, in (3.4), loses the connotations of 'umschlungen', from the verb 'umschlingen', to surround, which suggests the embrace of a lover, or the pernicious effects of bindweed, or even, possibly, of snakes, a connotation slightly underlined by the use of 'tongues', and the suggestion of deception. As we saw in Chapter 1, linguistic or cultural closeness to the original is often described as 'faithfulness'. But this term suggests something more akin to allegiance, that is, something broader than mere linguistic or cultural closeness (see also Tymoczko 2007). If we consider the possible players in the translation of (3.1), we see that the translator might feel allegiance to:

> (i) the text itself, including its syntax, meaning and sound
> (ii) the writer of the original piece, who is given as Sven F. Goergens
> (iii) the reader of the original text in German
> (iv) the subject of the piece, the singer Norah Jones
> (v) the publisher of the English journal in which the piece is to appear
> (vi) the reader of the article in English

In terms of allegiance to the text itself, the translator might argue that it is important to keep a phrase with a past participle (like *umschlungen*), a preposition (like *von*) and a compound noun (like *Engelszungen*), and that furthermore it must rhyme, while not changing the meaning too much. So (3.2) would only be in part faithful to the text itself. Measured in these terms, any translation can be regarded as a compromise, because it is not possible to be faithful to syntax, phonology and semantics all at once. But a translation is also a compromise in that, if (i) to (vi) represent different allegiances, then not all are possible.

One could alternatively take the view that allegiance is owed to Sven F. Goergens, the writer. While this is much less likely to be a consideration here than in the case of, say, a novel or play by a well-known author, nevertheless the writer of any text has a particular voice. To say that a translation loses the voice of the original author could be considered a negative judgement, though not, as Hermans (2007:53) suggests, if the original author is someone generally reviled. His example is the translation of Hitler, and here the translator might feel no allegiance to the author. In terms of (iii), the translator who felt allegiance to the reader would argue that the original reader felt such-and-such an effect (for example, a wariness about the possibly vacuous beauty of the music) and that therefore none of the translations satisfy this requirement.

In terms of (iv), allegiance to the subject of the piece, we could argue that the connotations of the title relate also to Norah Jones' especially melodic voice, and even to her innocent, youthful and engaging appearance. Thus the translation in (3.2) does not, one could argue, give a true picture of the singer.

As far as (v) is concerned, we might note that many translations have a commissioner, who is often not the intended audience (see e.g. Nord 1997:30). Thus the translator of the article under the headline in (3.1) will have to consider the particular policy of the English version of the magazine, which might include making headlines especially short, preferring word-play or allusion over sound repetition, and so on. If allusion is preferred, a title such as 'Wings of Song' might be used and words in the text such as *Beschwingtheit* (elation, in German etymologically related to *Schwinge* (wing)) translated in such a way as to pick the title up.

With respect to (vi), when a translator feels most allegiance to the reader of the translated text this is of course generally a hypothetical reader, and has much in common with the implied reader that literary critics such as Fish (1980) or Iser (2006:57) have spoken about. The implied reader of the English version of a report on Norah Jones' new album might be different depending on whether the article is published in a music journal or is aimed at a general readership like the original German magazine *Focus*.

With respect to the sort of allegiances (i) to (vi) express, Nord (1997:125) distinguishes between 'faithfulness', which she regards as the relationship between texts, and 'loyalty', which she defines as the 'social relationship between *people*' [Nord's italics]. The main problem with this is that the difference between real people, imagined people, implied people, and impersonal elements of the translation process is never clear. Take, for example, a translation of an untitled poem by Thomas Bernhard (Reidel 2006:20). Here are five lines from the original poem:

(3.5) (1) Wann Herr   wird   mein Fleisch
           when lord   will-become my   flesh

      (2) und dieser kalte   Tod im Winter
          and   this   cold death in-the winter

      (3) Nacht und Mühsal
          night and   toil

      (4) steinig und erfroren
          stony   and frozen

      (5) zu den Blüten reinen Winds
          (to) the flowers of-pure wind

There are at least two ways of interpreting these five lines; these are roughly:

(i) When will my flesh and this cold death in winter – night and toil, stony and frozen – become the flowers of pure wind

(ii) When will my flesh and this cold death in winter – night and toil – become, in a manner both stony and frozen, the flowers of pure wind

(i) suggests these lines are about redemption: what is now cold and hard and full of suffering might become flower-like. But (ii) suggests something quite different: that the redemption itself is frozen and stony. The translation by James Reidel (2006) adopts the second position, and there are reasons for this: later in the poem there is the mention of '*starre Engel*', literally stiff or frozen angels.

But does Reidel's translation, which interprets redemption as tempered with an ironical distancing from its own coldness, take this position out of loyalty to the original author? And if a translator translated the lines in (3.5) to give a meaning similar to that in (i) – which in fact syntactically seems closer to the German – is she or he then merely being faithful to a perceived text? The fact is that, in order to decide which interpretation to base translation on, most translators will read up on Bernhard, his concerns, his other literary output, his reception. That Reidel has done this is suggested by his 'Translator's Preface'; he says he has spent 'many years' (2006:xv) on the work. He is clearly aiming to translate in a way that expresses Bernhard's ironical view of Catholicism. But one could also argue that Reidel's loyalty is not to Thomas Bernhard the person, nor even to Thomas Bernhard the poet, but to the persona in this and the other poems he has translated. And this persona is always a reconstruction on the part of the reader, and therefore also of the translator (see Boase-Beier 2006:108–110).

Loyalty is thus a difficult notion. In the sense of loyalty to the original writer, it is always loyalty to a reconstructed figure. Some translators of contemporary authors try to make their loyalty more concrete by asking the writer what they meant (see e.g. Clancy 2006:6–12) but there is still no guarantee that the writer will know or be willing to say. Similarly, loyalty to the reader is, as suggested above, always aimed at a hypothetical figure. It could be argued that the translator is herself a reader, and thus can speak authoritatively of the reader's role. But if literary texts are by nature open to different readings by different readers, and also to different effects, depending on each reader's cognitive context, then the readers, like the author, are always only possible or imagined readers.

The notion of loyalty as a relationship with the people involved in a translation thus always depends on the translator's imagination and interpretation as much as does the relationship with the text. For this reason the distinction between persons and things, or between author and text, or reader and effect, seems an artificial one; it makes sense to envisage allegiance as a relationship that is possible with *all* the determiners involved in the translation, as in Jones' model discussed above (see Jones 2009), and in other theories that use 'actor networks' (Pym 2010:154–156).

Central to the question of allegiance is an issue we have met before in both Chapter 1 and Chapter 2, when discussing faithfulness versus freedom, documentary versus instrumental translation, and foreignizing versus domesticating translation, as well as in the discussion of relativity. It is this: is the source text conveyed to the target readers on its own terms or those of the target language and culture? In other words, do the angels' tongues in (3.1) need to be kept in English translation because this is what Germans say, or replaced by something the English might say, as in (3.2 and 3.3)? Another way to consider this problem is in terms of context. Recent studies in linguistics and stylistics, as well as in literature, generally take context into account, in terms of the culture surrounding a text, and the actual situation in which it has arisen, is read, or is communicated. Barlow (2009:ix), for example, points out that there has been a 'new emphasis' on context in the teaching of English Literature, especially in schools, since 1999. And Bex, Burke and Stockwell (2000) point to the 'rejection of a purely formal description of linguistic features' in a text as now typical of 'the state of the art in literary stylistics' (2000:ii, iv). Context, for the linguist, the stylistician, the critic, and, above all, for the translator, is everything that surrounds an expression, a passage or a text. This may be a sentence (the immediate linguistic context), a book (the physical context in which a passage occurs) or the historical and cultural background against which a text is written, read, understood, translated, or bought. Context, history, and culture also determine the type of theory one subscribes to.

Context is particularly important in non-literary texts. If an Italian advertisement for a car is to be translated into English, it is less likely to be the context of Italian cars and more likely to be that of the English market that determines how the car in question is viewed and therefore how the advertisement translated. If a Swedish text on conservation is translated into English, we might possibly want to view it in the Swedish context (to see how Sweden approaches conservation issues, for example) but it is more likely that the translation will already adapt it to the English context. And in Bible translating, as the many examples by Nida (1964) or Gutt (2005) show, we might want to see parables in their original context, to tell us something about the way of life of Jesus of Nazareth and his disciples, or in our own context, where their applicability to readers' lives is clearer. In each of these cases, if the translated text sees things in the original context, the reader has to do more work in terms of applying it to his or her own context than if the translation has already undertaken some of the work. With literary texts, one could argue that there is always an interplay of specific and universal, as many critics (e.g. Vogler 2007:ix; Heaney 1955:4) have said. In this case, there is no need to adapt the text to the reader's context, as part of literary reading will be to understand the context of the original text both in general terms and in terms of its specific differences from the target culture. An English child reading of an African boy's village life, a German man reading of an American soldier's guilt, an English teacher reading the story of an Italian teacher's trials, will all be able both to assess the relevance for their own situation and will possess enough shared experience to understand the differences between their own situation and the original. For translation critics such as Berman (2004) or Venuti (2008) who are influenced by poststructuralist literary theory with its focus on context, relativity and difference and also by postcolonial theory and its concern not to see our own culture as the measure or vantage point on everyone else's, only the view that we translate the text on its own terms will be acceptable.

What is emerging from this discussion, then, is a further distinction between non-literary translations and literary ones; we have seen several in Chapters 1 and 2. Seen in terms of allegiance, we can add that a non-literary translation is more likely to show allegiance to the target context and a literary translation to the source context. A consequence of this is that the literary translation tends to leave the work of target-context application to the reader.

3.2 Translation and creativity

A translation of an Ibsen play or a Tolstoy novel is at least in part a text that tells us what the original said. On the other hand, as Gutt argues, no text can merely or even in substantial degree report neutrally on another, because it always involves an element of interpretation. For this reason, Gutt (2000: 127–129) refers to translation as 'interlingual interpretative use'. His point is that a translator has to make decisions about how the source text is to be understood, and every translation involves an often implicit comment on how the original has been interpreted. Sometimes this comment might also be explicit (see Hermans 2007:52–85). Just as all translation, and especially literary translation, involves interpretation by the translator, so all translation, and especially literary translation, involves creativity on the part of the translator, because interpretation is itself a creative act. That this is so can be seen in many discussions of the nature of the mind, which describe its processes as creative rather than merely neutral. Memory is a good example. It is simply not efficient to remember with no creative adaptation to our needs, and therefore it is not possible (see McCrone 1990:90–91).

Because creativity and imagination, as Turner (1996) and Fauconnier (1994) have also shown, are thus central to the way we think and make decisions, it is impossible to conceive of translation, or any other sort of writing, as merely reproducing or representing without creative interference. One might expect creative translation and documentary (or reporting) translation to be mutually exclusive, but in fact the opposite is true: literary translations are both more creative than non-literary and they also involve less rewriting of meaning, and more documenting of the source text. There appears to be a paradox here: if a documentary translation documents a source text and an instrumental translation might simply be a rewriting of content for the fulfilling of textual aims, and therefore need not be a translation at all, this seems to suggest that it is the instrumental translation – typically the translation of a non-literary text – that allows the greater latitude to the translator and therefore involves the greater degree of creativity.

One way to address the paradox is to consider how we define creativity. Pope (2005) and Carter (2004) have devoted whole books to this question. As both point out, according to Chomsky (e.g. 1972:100), linguistic creativity could be said to be a natural result of the 'infinite productivity' of language, that is, the fact that its finite resources are made infinite by an unlimited ability to form new combinations, as a direct result of the human capacity for creative mental processes. In this sense the rewriting of a set of washing machine instructions and the translation of a poem are both creative. And because rewriting does not provide a linguistic replica in a strict sense – what is being preserved is the instrumental functioning of the text – then it could be argued that non-literary translation is the more creative.

However, the creativity of translation is not just a matter of linguistic but also literary creativity. Attridge explains this difference by saying that non-literary texts are just as inventive as literary texts but less 'singular' (2004:73), because they typically do not give rise to the sort of creative reading seen in literary texts. Creativity for Attridge is not just an aspect of literary writing, but also of literary reading, signalled by the literary text (Attridge 2004:111). Given that translation involves the creative reading (by the translator) of the source text and allows the creative reading (by the audience) of the target text, it is clear that the product of a literary translation allows for a far more open-ended reading than a non-literary translation. Creativity on the part of the translator is always linked to the possibilities for creative reading by the reader of the translation.

It would be wrong to see such creative possibilities for the translator and the reader merely as an absence of constraint. As Michael Holman and I argue elsewhere (Boase-Beier and Holman 1999:1–17), constraints of themselves actually enhance creativity, both for the original writer, the translator, and the readers. There are a number of reasons for this. One is that, as suggested by many studies of interpretation and the mind (e.g. Spolsky 1993), what motivates the mind to creative thinking is the need to overcome limitation. This may happen in terms of new meanings created (for example, by blending) where a meaning did not before exist. In Chapter 1 I suggested that we need to regard a translated text as a blend of elements of the source and target languages and contexts; this idea is explored further in Chapter 4. A blend always results in an end product which has meanings that go beyond just those of the two inputs. We see examples of this in the way translated texts use words from the original language almost like target language words:

> (3.6) First I was allowed to choose a cake in the *Konditorei* opposite.
>
> (Osers 2001:18)

There is no corresponding word in the target language, so the reader's image is a blend of the original German *Konditorei* and similar concepts (café, cake-shop, tea-shop), in English. Such blending processes also happen within languages, resulting in what are usually called lexical blends (Bolinger 1968:102) or 'portmanteau words' (Thurner 1993), as in 'snood' a scarf-hood. Portmanteau words are also possible products of the crossing of language boundaries, for example, the word 'Denglish', meaning the use of English words in the German language. 'Denglish' is an English word, but it uses the first letter of '*Deutsch*', which is the German word for German.

But in (3.6) what happens is that the concept associated with the German word '*Konditorei*' needs to be seen in the context of the rest of the English sentence. It arises directly from the need to convey in the translated text something that, rather than taking the place of a café, teashop or cake-shop in English culture, is actually an element of German culture. Such examples as (3.6) result from a constraint of translation: the need to see the other on its own terms rather than those of the target culture, as discussed earlier in Chapter 2. This very complex type of blending allows us to imagine having a '*Konditorei*' with all its German connotations in an English version of Berlin.

Another reason for the positive effect of constraints on creativity becomes clear when the constraints are not to do with translation so much as with the nature of the literary itself. Thus literary constraints such as rhyme or the elements of a crime novel, when combined with the need to translate, will lead to different solutions in the target text such as slant-rhyme or the particular local adaptation of universal elements of crime fiction we find in crime novels set in England, Norway, Sweden or France.

In a sense, literary constraints function much like the constraints we see in censorship of one type or another (see Boase-Beier and Holman 1999:1–17): they encourage innovative ways of avoiding them. Tourniaire (in Boase-Beier and Holman 1999:73) argues that the 'secret poems' of Rhea Galanaki, written while Greece was under military dictatorship, should, in translation, keep the examples of the ellipsis and 'truncated syntax' (often with verbs missing) of the original because 'the creation of the poems is inextricably linked to the constraints that are brought to bear on them' (ibid.).

The enabling of creative reading by the reader of a translation can particularly be seen in the translation of gaps and silences in the text, an issue to which we shall return in Chapter 8. It is thus just illustrated briefly here. Consider the following example, from a poem by Peter Huchel (Hamburger 2004:196):

> (3.7) Im   Namen dessen –
> in-the name   of-him
>
> Bis ans   Ende der Tage
> until at-the end of-the days

The reader of the German text has to fill the gap in the text and is syntactically constrained to add a verb phrase, which might be active or passive. But the actual verb to be imagined in the gap is semantically only constrained by the context the poem gives: of the dead, of nature, of memory. This is thus a good example of how a fairly constrained gap in the text causes the reader to engage creatively (see also Iser 1974:275–277). Translators seem to be sensitive to the reader's engagement. Michael Hamburger (2004:197), for example, translates (3.7) like this:

> (3.8) In his name who –
> to the end of time

In fact in the German in (3.7) there is nothing corresponding to 'who', but it is the word order '*im Namen dessen*' rather than '*in dessen Namen*' that suggests the incompleteness of the sentence, an incompleteness Hamburger suggests by introducing the start of a relative clause with 'who'. This ensures that the reader does not see the line as complete, but works out what might possibly come next.

Because literary texts in particular demand creativity on the part of the reader, not just in exploring ambiguities or filling gaps, as in (3.7), but in the search for meaning that, it can be argued, all literary texts involve (see Attridge 2004:59–64), it is helpful to consider this demand in terms of Relevance Theory, as suggested in Chapter 2. What is relevant to the reader – that is, whatever produces contextual effects without demanding an unrewarded effort – will lead to the enhanced creativity of the reading process. It is important to see literary relevance as the maximization of relevance (see Boase-Beier 2006:39–43; MacKenzie 2002:31; Trotter 1992:11) rather than its optimization, as discussed by Sperber and Wilson (1995:158). That is, creative engagement with a literary text does not cease when a meaning is arrived at, because literary reading involves a search for a meaning that is not fixed (see MacKenzie 2002:45). Because literary texts contain a large number of weak implicatures in the style (as we saw in Chapter 1), the meaning that can be derived from them is individually varied and open-ended.

The creativity involved in writing and reading a literary text is enhanced when it is translated, not only because more constraints are involved, and constraints lead to creativity, as we have seen, but also because a literary translation multiplies the voices of the text, by adding the translator's voice (see Boase-Beier 2006:148). Thus Hamburger in example (3.8) has added his own particular style of very precise and slightly archaic English to the rather more colloquial voice of the original poet. As Attridge puts it, a translated text evokes a more complicated response because we see both original and translation (Attridge 2004:73).

Because literary translation is both documentary and instrumental, its documentary nature will serve to keep the source-text constraints on it (as in the case of Galanaki) and its instrumental nature will allow for the creativity of the reader. In practice, this will mean that the non-literary translator, though she may think of alternative translations, will at some point feel an optimum translation has been reached, but this might not be the case for a literary translator. Consider, for example, the following alternative translations for the lines of poetry (in 3.9) by Rose Ausländer (1977:73):

(3.9) Weltraum / überfüllt mit / Körpern und Katastrophen

(3.10) Universe / chockfull of corpses and catastrophes

(3.11) Universe / crammed with corpses and catastrophes

(3.12) Universe / overfull of / corpses and catastrophes

All of these translations are versions of the same line of the poem by the same translators. (3.10) was the earlier published version (see Boase-Beier and Vivis 1995:48) and (3.11) was the revised version (in press); (3.12) is an earlier draft. Further revisions might also be made; a later revision might even go back to the wording in the draft in (3.12). These translations show different interpretations and priorities, in terms of register and alliteration, but it is hard to say that one is better or more definitive than the other. This difficulty in evaluating literary translations has been noted by many scholars (e.g. Ricœur 2006:22) and statements by many translators (e.g. Bassnett 2002:18) bear out the view that in literary translation, and especially in the translation of poetry, there is unlikely to be what the translators consider a definitive translation. This is not because they see the translation of poetry as especially difficult, or because translated works mysteriously date more than originals, but because the transfer of meaning, style, effect and opportunity for engagement is 'always incomplete' in Attridge's terms (2004:74). Incompleteness cannot be equated with loss; it is the (positive) characteristic of a literary text that distinguishes it from a non-literary text. If a poem has only one translation, it is not a poem (cf. Boase-Beier 2010c:32; Chesterman and Wagner 2002:8).

In terms of the interplay of allegiance and creativity, then, it seems reasonable to say that allegiance to any of the partners in translation, given as (i) to (vi) at the start of this chapter, will be necessary, but that the degrees to which allegiance is felt towards different partners may differ from case to case. Allegiance to these partners is always balanced, in literary translation, by the translator's freedom to be creative, and a consideration of the reader's possibility for creative engagement with the text – point (vi) above – is central. This, it could be argued, is what is meant by capturing the 'spirit' of the source text (see Boase-Beier 2006:6–12). Being faithful to the spirit of the text means ensuring that the target text is both a translation in that it maintains its relation to the source text, and that it is literary in the sense that it engages the reader.

The focus on the reader, and the translator's concern for the reader's engagement, depend upon the text-type of the translated text, and it is to this that I turn in the next chapter.

The Translated Text

4.1 The text-type of the translated text

We have considered the process of translation in terms of what it involves, to what extent it is possible and in terms of the translator's allegiance. But I have not so far said very much, except in passing, about the nature of the translated text itself. To consider the nature of the translated text is to focus more closely on the reader's involvement with the text. Discussion in the previous chapter suggested the particular importance of the reader for literary texts and thus for literary translation, but in fact, as we saw in Chapter 1, the reader always has a greater or lesser involvement in the making of meaning from a text, and will need to expend a greater or lesser effort to understand it. A scientific report (if it reaches its intended audience) will demand less work of the reader than a poem, and an advertisement will be somewhere in between. Such considerations rest on a notion of different text-types with different characteristics, something that cannot be disregarded in a discussion of translation, as Reiß and Vermeer pointed out in their influential book on translation theory (1984), discussed briefly in Chapter 1 (see also Nord 1997:37–38). Newmark (1995) also sees the role of the text-type as central; he regards the author as central to literary texts, the 'truth' (which he writes with inverted commas) as central to informative texts such as reports, and the reader as central to notices and instructions (1995:40). While this is not the view taken here (- I have just argued, for example, that the reader is in fact central to literary texts -) it is an interesting attempt to determine how a translation works based on the function and type of the source text.

One obvious question, in the light of the concept of text-types, is to ask what text-type a translated text belongs to. In particular, we might consider the following two questions:

(i) Is a translation always of the same text-type as the source text?
(ii) If 'literary text' is a text-type, is 'literary translation' a different text-type?

The first question is fairly easy to answer; a few examples will show that translation can change the text-type of the original text. This is true in obvious cases of intersemiotic translation (see Chapter 1 and Jakobson 2004:139) such as the translation of a novel into a film, but also might be true in less obvious cases. Consider, for example, the translation of advertisements discussed in Chapter 2. Looking at example (2.17), the Goodyear Optigrip advertisement, we saw that we could translate it as a 'literary' text, paying special attention to parallelism of various types, or we could concentrate on the information it contains, taking it to be Newmark's 'informative' text-type (1995:40). But there are also other ways we could approach the possible translation of an advertisement. Consider the following example:

(4.1) Have company and companionship when you want it or privacy and peace when you don't.

This is part of an advertisement for a retirement flat in a large complex. From the point of view of its alliterative style and parallelism, (4.1) has much in common with literary texts, as we saw in the case of (2.17). We might think that the repetition here is merely for embellishment, unlike literary repetition which, as we have seen in our consideration of literary style in examples like (1.7), is always closely tied with meaning, but in fact this is not the case. There is reason to suppose that repetition has many functions: it contributes to foregrounding and so draws attention to the text, it is memorable and, most importantly, it is perceived as attractive, and there is some evidence that we are more inclined to believe what we perceive to be beautiful (McCully 1998:23). Put rather crudely, because (4.1) sounds good we think the flat will be good, too, and so will the way of life it offers. A translation of the advertisement into German which aims to have similar effects might run:

(4.2) Gesellig oder geruhsam, freundlich oder friedlich – gestalten Sie Ihr Leben ganz wie Sie wollen.

The form has changed to be more suitable to a German advertisement and the German language, but the notion that parallelism suggests truth has been maintained. (4.2), besides being a translation of (4.1), is itself an advertisement (or could be). However, supposing that (4.1) is a particularly successful English advertisement, and succeeds in improving sales of retirement flats for the company concerned. A German company might then request a translation of (4.1) to see what had worked so well with the English advertisement. This translation might be identical to (4.2) but never be itself used as an advertisement. Or (4.2) might be used as an illustration in an academic book, as it is here.

In both these latter cases, even a fairly close translation of the advertisement has resulted in something not itself an advertisement. So the answer to (i) is clearly 'no'. One can think of many similar examples, where the translation is documentary, but does not preserve the text-type. It should be noted that, although an instrumental translation by definition preserves at least the functional aspects of text-type, according to Nord (1997:50–52), a documentary one does not always change it, as shown by the fact that (4.2) could work as an advertisement. (See Chapter 1 for discussion of documentary and instrumental translation.)

The second question, which relates specifically to literary texts, is much more difficult to answer. Part of the reason for this is that, as mentioned in Chapter 1, literary texts themselves might be considered not to be instrumental in a functional sense. That is, they do not have a clear aim, such as to inform, to instruct, or to make someone buy a product, but could be said to be defined by their '*resistance* to such thinking' (Attridge 2004:7). When function is not seen as part of what characterizes a literary text, describing it as a particular text-type becomes more difficult. This is one of the reasons that various attempts have been made to characterize literary texts by their language, rather than by their function, as the Prague Circle Linguists in particular did with their notion of Poetic Language (e.g. Mukařovský 1964). Yet, as many scholars such as Fowler (1996) or Stockwell (2002) have argued, and as the discussion in the first three chapters of this book has suggested, language of itself will not distinguish a literary text: example (4.1) demonstrates this. For this reason, when I refer to 'poetic language' in this book, as the discussion in Chapter 1 suggests, I mean language in which style is especially important as a set of weak implicatures that are interpreted by the reader with resulting poetic effects. The type of reading that leads to such creative engagement and such effects is triggered largely by formal aspects of the text.

In Chapter 3, and especially in Section 3.2, I in fact suggested that translation enhances literary characteristics, leading to a translated text being more creative, and demanding more creative reading, than an untranslated text. This means that in literary translation there are differences between target text and source text that we do not see in the translation of other text-types. Does this mean that 'literary translation' should be seen as a separate text-type from 'literary text'?

The discussion in the previous three chapters (and see also Boase-Beier 2006:56) leads to the conclusion that a literary translation is always both documentary and instrumental: both a translation which documents for its reader its source and a literary text which manifests the characteristics and effects on the reader so central to the way literature works. It will always possess characteristics which differ from those of the original text. For example, as noted in discussion of example (3.8), it will add to the voice of the original author that of the translator. This is a characteristic noted by several earlier writers on translation, such as Baker (2000:261) or Hermans (1996:9); see also Boase-Beier (2006:148). But we need to consider what the addition of the translator's voice really means. (4.3) is a short passage from a novel by W.G. Sebald (1990:41) and (4.4) its translation by Michael Hulse (1993:33):

> (4.3) Ich war damals, im Oktober 1980 ist es gewesen, von England aus, wo
>   I was at-that-time in-the October 1980 has it been from England out where
>
>   ich nun seit nahezu fünfundzwanzig Jahren in einer meist grau
>   I now since nearly   five-and-twenty years in a   mostly grey
>
>   überwölkten Grafschaft lebe, nach Wien gefahren . . .
>   overcast   county   live to Vienna travelled
>
> (4.4) In October 1980 I travelled from England, where I had then been living for
>   nearly twenty-five years in a county which was almost always under grey
>   skies, to Vienna . . . .

This translation by Hulse appears to have been seen by critics and readers as embodying only the voice of Sebald: Susan Sontag speaks of the 'preternatural authority of Sebald's voice: its gravity, its sinuosity, its precision' (2000), and Robert McCrum (1999) describes Sebald's writing as 'wrapping itself, wrath-like, round your imagination'. Yet the versions by the two writers, Sebald and

Hulse, are very different. Part of what makes Sebald's voice so distinctive is his use of successive main clauses in the same sentence, divided only by commas, such as '*im Oktober 1980 ist es gewesen*' ('it was in October 1980'). This is not possible in English, where it is generally necessary to subordinate clauses to one another in a sentence unless they are coordinatively joined by a conjunction such as 'and' or 'but'. The succession of short main clauses allows Sebald to form very long sentences without greatly increasing their grammatical complexity. The effect of this style of writing is that the reader is forced to perform a feat of memory, but little complex syntactic processing. Furthermore, although commas indicate syntactic relationships, they also cause the reader to pause, in both German and English (Crystal 2003:283; though see Greenbaum 1996:507–509). So using successive main clauses can lead to the effect critics describe as 'mesmerising' (McCrum 1999), and it could also be seen as iconic of the way memory can give us a (false) sense of passivity, as though we did not have to work at the process of reconstruction. Hulse's version compresses Sebald's main clause '*im Oktober 1980 ist es gewesen*' into a prepositional phrase 'in October 1980', which modifies the following verb phrase 'I travelled from England'. He also uses the simple verb form 'travelled' where Sebald uses the compound one '*war gefahren*', literally 'had travelled'. The use of compound forms in German permits splitting of the verb, so that '*war*' is near the start of the sentence and '*gefahren*' comes much later, with the various other clauses in-between. Like the use of successive main clauses, this characteristic of German grammar gives a peculiar rhythm to the German prose, which also adds to the sense of its being mesmerizing. In English the effect is different, because the second main clause is turned into a prepositional phrase and put at the start, which reduces the number of pauses. Nevertheless, the long sentences typical of German prose, and untypical of contemporary English prose are also present in Hulse's version. For this and other reasons, too numerous to examine in detail here, Hulse's translation has a somewhat German feel, even though it is overlaid with the compression and tighter word order which is natural in English, where the poorer morphology cannot so readily carry grammatical function. What readers of Hulse's translation read is thus a combination of Sebald's and Hulse's styles, and the voice in the text – the voice of the 'I' speaking – is a combination of two voices.

This phenomenon is not, however, just a result of differences in the structure (in this case the effects of morphology on sentence structure) of different languages. It is also to some extent the result of personal writing style. For this reason it is often possible to recognize the work of a particular translator, especially when the translated text is contrasted with other translations from the work of the same writer. Consider the following examples, a line from the poet Hölderlin and its translation by Michael Hamburger (1966: 686–687):

(4.5) Das Leben ist aus Thaten und verwegen
　　　 the　 life　 is　of　 deeds　and　 bold

(4.6) Life comes from deeds and is daring, bold

The translation in (4.6) has a feature typical of Hamburger's own poetry, the repetition of adjectives, verbs or nouns without a coordinating conjunction, sometimes known, especially in traditional rhetoric, as asyndeton (which, incidentally is also how we might label Sebald's successive main clauses). Here are examples from Hamburger's own poetry in (4.7) and (4.8) and, in (4.9), his Celan translations:

(4.7) . . . when I say you've gone, moved out
　　　　　　　 (Hamburger 1995:250)

(4.8) Have never known the place, the day
　　　　　　　 (Hamburger 1995:111)

(4.9) and beds itself
　　　 in fragrances, nestlings
　　　　　　　 (Hamburger 2007:311)

The original of the Celan lines in (4.9) also has this construction: '. . . *und betten sich / in Gerüche, Geräusche*' (Hamburger 2007:310), and it is quite likely that the voice of Hamburger the poet (as in the previous two examples) was influenced by the original poets, including Celan, whose work he translated. This characteristic use of asyndeton in Hamburger's writing (whatever its source) allows readers and critics to distinguish his translation of Celan from that of other translators, such as Fairley's, whose translation of the lines in (4.9) is:

(4.10) and makes its bed amid
　　　　 stench and stir.
　　　　　　　 (Fairley 2001:85)

Fairley supplies the coordinator and loses the pause, so the line has a very different feel from Hamburger's version.

In (4.6) the addition of the second adjective 'daring' by Hamburger in his Hölderlin translation arises for several reasons, such as the need to add more syllables to the English, and perhaps the need to convey more completely the sense of '*verwegen*'. But it is instantly recognizable as Hamburger's translation.

Here, as in Hulse's translation of Sebald in (4.4), we see something that is peculiar to translated texts: a multiplication of the voices present in the text when it is compared with the original (see also Munday 2008:13–19).

The notion of voice has been much discussed in literary criticism (see e.g. Bennett and Royle 2004:68–76). It is sometimes used to mean what in linguistics is called 'register', that is 'a variety of language defined according to the situation'. In this sense we may speak of 'the confiding, colloquial voice' (Bennett and Royle 2004:18) of writer J.D. Salinger (1987), for example, and mean a voice that is common to many situations of colloquial, intimate conversation. 'Voice' can also mean the act of speaking itself: when Bennett and Royle mention 'the voice of a fictional speaker' (2004:19), they mean not so much the way the fictional speaker speaks as the fact *that* someone speaks. In this latter sense, voice is an index, in Peirce's sense (see Peirce 1960:160–165) of a person, in the same way as smoke is an index of fire. The sense of voice in a text is thus one of the elements which makes us assume the text is actually spoken. Because we always, according to conceptual metaphor theory, envisage that EVENTS ARE ACTIONS (see e.g. Lakoff and Turner 1989:37), we supply the actor for an event. This is true whether we are personifying death (1989:15–17), attributing personality or motive to the weather ('the weather turned nasty', 'the sun was trying to come out') positing that there is a God, or imagining an author. Though recent criticism, at least since the New Critics formulated what was known as the 'intentional fallacy' (Wimsatt 1954b:3–18), expressed later by Barthes as 'the death of the author' (Barthes 1977), has tended to refocus attention away from facts of the author's life to the text itself or the creative involvement of the reader (cf. Burke 2007:20–61), the author is a constant presence in literary discussions (see Burke 2007). This is not surprising, given that voice in a text leads the reader to construct a speaker, who is likely to be seen as the author, irrespective of whether the reader actually knows anything about the author. A reader of (4.4), (4.6) or (4.10) posits the voice of both the translator and of the original author.

The reader's need to process voices in the text is just one way in which the translated text is more complex for the reader than the original. But it also requires a greater activation of the reader's cognitive context. This is also true of non-literary translations: a tourist brochure about Dresden translated into English will require more effort to understand than would be needed by a German reader of the original. Consider the following example:

(4.11) Surrounded by the sandstone cliffs of Saxony's Switzerland, the city on the Elbe is a good base for days out, and its Karl May Museum provides an escape to the Wild West.

An English reader will possibly (just) be able to understand that 'Switzerland' is used metaphorically, as it sometimes is in England, and that 'the city on the Elbe' is Dresden, and that Karl May must have written Westerns, but in fact it is likely that at least some of these references will cause difficulty. This is unlikely to be a problem for the reader of the German original, even if he or she does not know Dresden.

In a literary text, though, even more additional effort on the part of the reader will be required. Consider the following example from another poem by Celan that Hamburger has translated:

(4.12) Oaken door, who lifted you off your hinges?
My gentle mother cannot return.
(Hamburger 2007:49)

This is the penultimate line in a poem which juxtaposes statements and questions about natural phenomena with statements about the speaker's mother, who was killed by the Nazis. An English reader of this translated poem will need to see in (4.12) the German expression '*die Tür aus den Angeln heben*', literally 'to lift the door off its hinges', to fully realize the sense of chaos or inversion the line suggests, though of course she will be able to process (4.12) as a metaphor and arrive at a possible meaning. The English reader will also need to make the connection with Goethe's oak (see Felstiner 1995:36), the oak the Nazis, in a grotesque act of recontextualization, left standing in the concentration camp at Buchenwald (which means beech forest), as a link to Germany's past.

One way that the difference in such effects between original and translated literary texts is sometimes described is in terms of translation loss (cf. Bassnett 2002:36). But it could equally be said that such loss is a translation gain if greater engagement on the part of the reader is needed, for, as we have seen, creative reading is a typical characteristic of literature.

The above discussion suggests that a literary translation does differ from a non-translated literary text. There seems good reason to consider it at least a sub-type of literature, as in fact polysystem theory, the theory that all literature, including translated literature, is part of a complex system, has suggested (see Even-Zohar 1978:117–127).

4.2 Translation as a conceptual blend

In the previous section we saw that a translated literary text differs in several ways from an untranslated one. One way to explain this difference which accounts for both its existence as an instrumental literary text in the language translated into, and the presence of a source text to which it stands in a documentary relation, is to see a translated text as a conceptual blend. The notion of a conceptual blend in cognitive linguistics and cognitive stylistics rests on the notion of mental space. A mental space is the counterpart of a 'possible world' in truth-conditional semantics (that measures meaning against the world rather than what people think; see Chapter 2). A mental space, then, is a cognitive referential structure that allows us to think about events or states (see Croft and Cruse 2004:32–39; Fauconnier 1994). In a conceptual blend, two or more mental spaces (the input spaces) that have something in common are combined in a creative mental process, blending so that some elements of all the input spaces are there but so that the new mental space (the blend) contains elements (the emergent structure) not in any of the basic ones (see Stockwell 2002:96–98; Gavins 2007:148; Fauconnier and Turner 2002). A blend is therefore not a possible world, but is usually an impossible one, with 'fantastic aspects' (Fauconnier and Turner 2002:21). A typical example of such a conceptual blend is the representation of a unicorn, which, in the way we think of it, combines elements of an imagined real horse and a mythical beast. The resulting image we have of a unicorn is itself a mythical beast, but it still has some resemblance to a horse, and characteristics of mythical animals (such as its enormous strength and magical powers). It should be remembered that a blend is a creative cognitive structure, not a thing. This is obviously so in the case of a unicorn, but the case of a teddy bear, another conceptual blend, is more difficult, because there might also be a real teddy bear. And yet even a real teddy bear (and especially a real teddy bear) has in our minds some human characteristics which it does not have as a real thing. One could try poking a teddy bear in the eye in the company of others to test that this is so.

For both the translator, producing a target text, and the reader, reading the translated text, it makes sense to explain the way they think of this text as a conceptual blend. If we imagine a translation of a novel by Henning Mankell, the Swedish crime writer, into English, the English translation is in some sense represented in the translator's or reader's mind as the Swedish book itself. People say 'I have read the latest Mankell novel', not 'I have read the latest Seberberg novel' (Ebba Seberberg is the translator; see e.g. Mankell (2002)). On the other hand, they also know that they have read a translation, even if they do not know the name of the translator. So the book is also represented in their mind (and perhaps in the mind of the translator more than in the mind of the reader) as an English book, which has an English publisher and is paid for in English currency. It is characteristic of a blend to contain elements that are in neither of its input spaces, and, as we have seen, the translation will have effects on the minds of both its writer and its reader as a result of the combination of voices, languages, styles and cultures in the translated work, that are neither in the original work itself nor would be in an original work by the English translator. It is important to remember that the input spaces to a blend are mental spaces, as is the blend itself, so it makes no difference that one of them has no real counterpart. The source text in the mind of reader and translator does have a counterpart in the real world – the real Swedish novel by Mankell – and the blend (of an original and an English book) also has a counterpart in the book by Seberberg, but the imagined English book itself which is one of the inputs to the blend does not exist in reality. Unfortunately, the non-existent non-blended English book is more strongly represented in the minds of some readers, and especially of critics and publishers, than the blend itself; they thus might speak of the translation as though it were that non-existent English book, as quotations from Sebald's English critics in the previous section suggest.

The fact that a translation is a blend has many consequences, some of which have been noted by other translation scholars when they refer to a translation as a hybrid (Barnstone 1993:88), a term originally used in postcolonial studies to describe the space 'in between' (Mehrez 1992:121) the traditional culture and the former colonizer; see also Bhabha (1994:224) and Bassnett and Trivedi (1999:1–18). Studies of the translation as a hybrid include references to its multicultural background and its blended linguistics (see also Snell-Hornby 2006:95, 99–100). Seeing translation as a blend explains why readers are unsure how to refer to its author, unless they simply see the translation as the work of the original writer ('I have read the latest Mankell novel'). The cognitive spaces can vary in strength, according to what we know about them. Thus Hamburger's translation of Hölderlin (Hamburger 1966) may have, in a reader's view of the text, a stronger element of Hamburger's authorship than is the case with the Mankell novel and Seberberg's authorship, as the bibliographical entries for these two works at the back of this book suggest. An English publisher, trying to sell Hamburger's Hölderlin to a reading public will probably have a mental representation of the work that has quite strong affinities with Hamburger's other work. But a Hölderlin expert whose German is poor might see Hamburger's Hölderlin simply as Hölderlin.

Because the translation is a blend, readers also get a sense, just as scholars such as Snell-Hornby point out (2006:99), of a language not quite the usual English. In the case of Hamburger's Hölderlin this is partly because the real-world translated Hölderlin combines the original German with Hamburger's English to a degree that allows the German to influence the English more than would have been the case had Hamburger not been born in Germany. But it is also because, as readers, we conceive of the translated book as a blend. And because the translator's name sounds (and of course is) German, we are open to the German nuances of his English when reading his translation.

Blends generally involve clashes at some level. In the example of a philosopher in 2006 saying 'Kant disagrees with me' (Fauconnier and Turner 2002:59) Kant spoke German, so the imagined debate (assuming the other philosopher to be an English speaker) either has to have Kant speaking English, 'me' speaking German (Fauconnier and Turner 2002:125) or each person speaking their own language but understanding one another. It also has to have Kant living at the same time as the philosopher who is speaking in 2006. Blends which involve such impossible situations are known as counterfactuals (see Fauconnier 1994:109–142). The clashes they involve are generally managed by our minds because the whole point of a blend is that it allows different times, situations, or even parts of different animals (as in a chimera) to co-exist and interact smoothly. In the translation of the Mankell novel, this is seen when we have, for example, characters speaking English but suddenly referring to aspects of the Swedish language. These clashes did not of course exist in the source text, and nor do they exist in the blended mental space that represents the world of the book: we simply suspend disbelief as though encountering a talking animal. In reading the translation we manage such clashes effortlessly unless we suddenly become aware that the book is a translation, perhaps because we are studying it, or reviewing it, or reading it as a work of art rather than a story. Then we are likely to see the whole act of translation and its problems suddenly brought into focus, and to wonder why Swedes speak English to one another.

Blending also explains how such connections as 'false friends' come into being. The translator (speaking or writing) erroneously maps their mental representation of a word in one language onto that of a similar-sounding word in the other language, even though the meaning of the words (seen in mental space semantics as the cognitive space they occupy in the mind) is not the same in all details. Thus a German speaking English may say she has bought new pumps (meaning high-heeled shoes) for a wedding or an English person speaking French might use the word *curé* to mean a 'curate', whereas it means a parish priest. I have even heard several English speakers who habitually speak German, refer to preservatives as 'conservatives' in a blend of the mental representation of *Konservierungsmittel* (preservatives) with that of the English word preservatives. Most examples that happen in translation are of course more subtle. Consider the following, from Michael Hamburger's autobiography (1991:153):

> (4.13) In any case, we fell in love

This sentence occurs after Hamburger describes meeting a pianist 'somewhere' and taking her to a recital that 'somebody' had arranged. He has forgotten the details, but in any event they fell in love. The phrase 'in any case' in (4.13) sounds odd, because we usually use it in structures relating to the future:

> (4.14) I will go to town in any case

or to a contradiction of an actual state of affairs:

> (4.15) In any case I think you should have won the prize

We do not usually use it to refer to uncertain past events when we mean that, whatever the actual circumstances, this was the result: here we would generally use 'in any event'. 'In any case' in (4.13) is a mixture of '*jedenfalls*' or '*auf jeden Fall*' ('be that as it may') and '*in jedem Fall*' ('come what may') in German and the phrase 'in any event' in English. It is a false friend, though an extremely subtle one: '*jedenfalls*' or '*in jedem Fall*' or '*auf jeden Fall*' in German are expressions that mean not quite the same as 'in any case', even though '*Fall*' can often be translated as 'case'. The effect of the phrase in (4.13) is to add a curious unreality to the statement, because the phrase takes on some of the connotations of non-present time or virtual reality as in (4.14) and (4.15).This is not to say that (4.13) is impossible, or even highly strange, but just that it is not quite the conventional meaning. (4.13) is not a translation in the narrow sense; Hamburger wrote his autobiography in English. But it is translation in the broader sense, just as I suggested in Chapter 1 that the label on a Chinese iron (1.2) might be a translation of a Chinese speaker's thoughts. Example (4.13) shows how the very act of translating between languages, in this broader sense, can lead to enhanced cognitive effects for the reader. Here they are the effects of unreality and uncertainty. This multiplying of effect is behind the notion discussed in this and the previous chapter that a literary translation is in an important sense more 'literary' than a non-translated text. Not only is our conception of a translated text a conceptual blend but each individual expression in it, as well as the world it describes, is to a greater or lesser extent a conceptual blend, and has greater potential for cognitive effects, especially as a blend has, in its emergent structure, elements that were not present in each of the original inputs.

Non-literary translations are not blends in this sense. This is what scholars like Gutt (2000:57) have noticed, when describing non-literary translations as rewriting, that is as bearing no necessary relationship to the source text. However, all writing is itself a blend of the physical book or page or sheet of paper and what it represents (cf. Fauconnier and Turner 2002:211), and to the extent that we read the non-literary translation as a text about the world, it, too, is a blend. Even if it is a descriptive rather than an interpretative text (Gutt 2000:56–68), it is still a blend in the sense that every description is a representation. However, literary texts add more input spaces into the blend, because they represent both the world of the text and what we have called the cognitive state embodied in the style, which may be the author's, narrator's or character's attitude, or view, or take on the world of the text. Though a non-literary text may also include this element, it is only of marginal importance: the cognitive state of the writer of a set of instructions, the label on the Chinese iron, or the brochure about Dresden is rarely part of our understanding of the text. This fact is noted by Newmark (1988:39–40) when he says that 'the mind of the speaker' is the core of an expressive text but plays virtually no role in the informative text. The literary translation also adds yet another input space: that of the translator's world, culture, beliefs and attitudes. Again, this aspect is only marginal in a non-literary translation, because the translation itself will be, in Newmark's terms, informative. A translation of a literary work can thus be seen as an exceptionally complex conceptual blend; this is the reason for the many metaphors of translation that regard it as a painting or theatrical performance (Tan 2006:47); like books, all works and instances of art are complex conceptual blends. It is also the reason for discussions of translation that involve counterfactual blended situations such as the observation that the translator writes as the author 'would have done, had he lived in our age, and in our country' (Dryden 1992:19), an unreal situation rather like the imagined conversation with Kant mentioned above. Furthermore, it is the reason for the use of such terms as 'pretence' (Boase-Beier 2006:108–110) used to describe translation or 'social illusion' (Pym 2010:164) used to describe equivalence. As Fauconnier and Turner put it (2002:233), a pretence or illusion involves living in a blend. What I have just been arguing is that both the translator and the reader of a translation are living in a blend where many fictions exist, the main one being that the original author wrote the translation.

Describing translation as a blend can thus explain many of its characteristics, but it is still not clear whether such a description can affect the way we translate. It is to the relation between theoretical pronouncement and actual practice that we turn in the next chapter.

Theories and Practices 5

5.1 What is a theory?

In the preceding four chapters we have examined a number of questions about the nature of translation, its relation to the world outside the text, and whether there are different types of translation. Some of these questions, such as those about what constitutes a language and what sort of content we translate, cannot be answered in a straightforward way. They give rise to further questions which will be answered differently depending on one's theory. For example, as suggested at the start of Chapter 1, if you subscribe to a theory that a dialect is a language, then translation from Yorkshire dialect into standard English will be interlingual, not intralingual translation. Many questions are open in this way and giving a particular answer presupposes a theory, not necessarily of the exact area the question is about (interlingual versus intralingual translation in this case) but often of another area (here the language-dialect demarcation) that will affect the one in question.

Theories are not static models of the world: they partly determine the answers to such questions but they are also determined by the answers. For example, the language – dialect question might lead me to suggest refinements to Jakobson's tripartite division into interlingual, intralingual and intersemiotic translation (2004:139).

Theories are adjusted whenever the answers they give seem unsatisfactory either because other theories can be seen to interact with them, modifying or contradicting them or the evidence for them, or because they do not themselves seem to explain the evidence properly. For example, if I happen to hold the theory that the same translator will translate a medical report on a drug trial, a newspaper account of a drug trial, and a novel about a drug trial in the same way, I might apply it directly to the evidence. If the evidence contradicts it, I will discard or adjust that theory. A possible adjustment might be to say that some characteristics of an individual translator persist across text-types but some do not, just as different text-types themselves overlap in some characteristics.

Theories, then, are pictures of the world, regularly readjusted as they come up against answers, from real-world evidence and from other theories, to the question they pose. These other theories might themselves be adjusted: I might decide that text-type theory needs refining to account for translation similarities better. Or perhaps my own theory might be adjusted: I might adjust my theory of the language-dialect demarcation by saying they are the same from a linguistic point of view but different from the translator's point of view. We have seen something rather like this in the case of Linguistic Relativity and Determinism in Section 2.1. Some scholars, such as Slobin (1987:435), would see a difference between strict determinism, which they maintain does not exist, and a deterministic element in the language when we are about to speak. Other scholars (e.g. Pinker 2007:135) may scoff at this sort of 'featherbeddish' theory but in fact it is exactly where theories interact that the most interesting explanations come about. If everything were black and white we would probably not need to theorize at all.

When I say that one's theory interacts with both evidence and with other theories, it sounds as though one were in the world and the other in the mind. Yet we cannot really separate them so clearly. For one thing, other theories are themselves based on evidence and are constantly adjusted to the world in the same way one's own theory is. So to some extent we use theories as evidence. In the first four chapters of this book I have taken many theories as evidence-based in this way: Slobin's theory of thinking for speaking (1987), Jakobson's tripartite theory of translation (2004), Fauconnier and Turner's theory of blending (2002) are just three examples and I assume all to be based on evidence which is potentially valuable. Secondly, evidence is taken to be evidence in relation to a particular theory; it is the theory that tells us what the facts are and which ones are important. And thirdly, other theories are not just other people's theories. I will myself hold many theories at any given time, and some of them will lead to conflict. I might, for example, theorize that there is a God, because I accept the theory that people see events as actions, and need a God in the world as much as they need an author in the text. I might equally subscribe, like Bertrand Russell did (1957) to the theory that there is no God because I can find no evidence that there is one. It is quite possible to hold both theories at once, as we saw with the language-dialect demarcation.

So far, then, it seems clear that theories are fluid mental constructs. They vary among different people and across different times for the same person. And it is even possible to hold conflicting theories at the same time. It is even possible to hold a theory and not hold it at the same time. I might, for example, hold the theory that the world is coming to an end, and yet I might most of the time not hold it in any real sense because I will repress it in order to get on with life.

Sometimes people use 'theory' and 'belief' interchangeably; the view that there is a God might be seen as a theory or as a belief. It is possible to distinguish a theory as something that can potentially be tested against evidence from a belief, which cannot. But in fact theories and beliefs are both mental pictures of the way the world is. One way of evaluating what people say about the world is to be aware of the theory (or world-view or ideology) behind it. Fowler (1977:17) defines world-view as the 'modes of representation of reality' held by an individual or society, or embodied in a text, and Simpson defines ideology as 'the ways in which what we say and think interacts with society' (1993:5). World-views and ideologies, like theories and beliefs, are pictures of the world.

Everything we do involves our having a picture of the world, and most actions we perform, unless they are reflexes, or happen without consciousness (see Ratey 2001:110–111), are preceded or accompanied by a theory of how the action is to be performed, and what its consequences will be.

The above discussion is important in several ways for the examination of translation in this book. First, the reader must be aware of my theory in order to understand why I describe translation in the terms I do. Throughout the course of Chapters 1 to 4 my theory should have become clear, and it is also summarized at the end of this chapter.

Secondly, we need to be aware that the theories of translation we read about in works with titles such as *The Translator's Invisibility* (Venuti 2008) or *Translation and Relevance* (Gutt 2000), also represent descriptions and explanations of the field of Translation Studies against the background of a particular scholar's theory, whether or not that theory is explicit. For example, Gutt's view of the importance of the 'cognitive environment' of the audience being addressed (2000:128) might seem like common sense, but it is based on his theory that translation is a form of communication and communication follows the principles of Relevance given by Sperber and Wilson (1995; see also Chapters 2 and 3 in this book). Furthermore, Gutt's view that the Bible is a religious rather than a historical document is important for his description of translating it. Gutt makes things easy for his reader by being explicit about his theory. Similarly, Diaz-Diocaretz (1985) tells us that she is using theories of reading to explore the translation of a feminist poet. Other writers are less explicit: Venuti (2008) describes his study, first published more than ten years earlier, as 'frankly polemical' (2008:viii) and tells us his motive was 'to question the marginal position of translation in Anglo-American culture' (ibid.), but leaves the reader to work out his theoretical background. The reader arrives at a picture of this theory – which one might characterize as a theory that, in the tradition of Poststructuralism and Postcolonialism, emphasizes difference over universality – through reading Venuti's works. Whether the underlying theory is explicit or implicit, it is important that the reader of such works sees it as the context against which every statement in the work is to be read. It is also important to be aware of the historical situation of every theory; for example, Diaz-Diocaretz, in 1985, did not have the benefit of later refinements of theories of reading, such as Scott (2000), and Gutt (2000), also first published a decade before this, could not use later studies of Relevance Theory as applied to literature, such as Pilkington (2000).

Thirdly, a theory is a mental picture, not a set of instructions on how to do something. Gutt (2000:107–111), for example, explains why Scott Moncrieff translated 'tu' as 'thou' in his 1929 translation of Stendhal, and why the critic Adams (1973:14) disapproves. He also says that most readers would share Adams' view. But he does not actually say we should or should not translate 'tu' as 'thou' in this case.

Fourthly, theory affects the way practice is described. Adams' rejection of Scott Moncrieff's rendering of 'tu' is evidence, in Gutt's eyes, for his own view (as well as his view that Adams intuitively feels) that what takes too much effort to process will be rejected. Such descriptions as 'its recovery involves considerable processing effort' (Gutt 2000:111) are determined by the use of Relevance Theory, which measures effects obtained against effort invested.

Fifthly, practice affects theory by providing evidence against which to test it; Gutt (2000:111–118) looks at the actual translation of the poet Morgenstern by Max Knight (1963) in order to consider whether Levý's theory of a 'functional hierarchy' of aspects of word-meaning will offer a good explanation, deciding that the theory, when tested against the facts, is 'doubtful' (2000:116).

A sixth consequence is that, taking on board all the above points, we need to ask ourselves whether theory also affects practice in terms of how we carry out practices, as well as in terms of how we describe them. I have just said that Gutt tells us what people do rather than what we must do, but this still does not rule out the possibility that theory in some circumstances might affect practice, and we need to know what those circumstances are and what the effects are.

There are two possible views about this. One is that a theory is prescriptive. This view leads readers to imagine, for example, that Gutt endorses a particular way of translating and rejects others. His mention of Adams' rejection of Scott Moncrieff might be seen as his own. We might expect him, having weighed up the effort the reader needs to invest to see the French '*tu*' behind the English 'thou' in the Stendhal translation, to translate it differently himself. The other extreme would be to say that theory describes practice but does not directly affect it. This could be seen as a basic tenet of Descriptive Translation Studies (see e.g. Toury 1995:2). But in fact Toury, while careful to see theory as non-prescriptive, suggests that it does affect practice, pointing out that critics and teachers (rather than actual translators), might draw from descriptions of practice useful conclusions about the best way to judge or to teach translation (1995:17–20). In this sense, theory affects practice because it is a known and often agreed way of describing the world, and people will act accordingly. We are often confronted with such effects: if a government has a theory, abstracted from a few cases, that all adults are potential paedophiles, it will issue regulations that prevent any adult from taking photographs of a school play. Similarly, if we subscribe to a theory that a translation should not invisibly replace the original, because we can describe cases – or read Venuti's (2008) description of them – in which this happens, we can influence publishers and they might in turn instruct their translators (and indirectly influence reviewers) to behave in a particular way.

In a general sense, then, it seems that a theory is not a prescription or set of rules, but that it cannot be just a description either. A description of any practice, in translation or elsewhere, will affect the way people see things, and this, in turn, will affect practice.

But a further question is to do with what happens in the case of the individual translator. If a translator takes theories to be descriptions of what people do, and not instructions, does this mean that they have no effect on what that translator does? In a general sense, this cannot be the case, because collective knowledge will affect each individual translator. Translators who have not read Venuti or Gutt will still be indirectly influenced by what they have said, through publishers, editors, critics, academics, and audiences.

The effect of collective knowledge seems clear enough, but there is a possible stronger view of the theory-practice link. This is that in any particular instance the theory that a particular translator entertains will to some extent determine how they act. A translator who has read Venuti's views on foreignization in his 1995 book, reissued in 2008, or his translation of Berman's article (2004), might try to translate '*Es ist gehüpft wie gesprungen*' (see example (1.21)) in a character's speech in a novel as 'It's the same whether you jump or leap' (see (1.22)), as a way of indicating either that the speaker was speaking German or that this is a German speaker of English. Someone who has read Nord's views on instrumental and documentary translation (Nord 1997:47–52) might do the same, or might alternatively take the view that in a literary text an instrumental translation is more appropriate, and thus translate the German expression with 'it's all the same' (see (1.24)), losing either of the above suggestions of the original expression (in the fictional world of the novel or in the speaker's mind within that world). This example suggests how difficult it is to convert a theory directly into a practice or method, as Iser (2006: 10) puts it. The same theory could easily result in opposing practices or methods. Toury suggests (1995:17) that the translator is less likely to be directly influenced by theory in this way than the critic or teacher, because the latter 'indulge in the *applied* activities themselves' whereas the former is not necessarily undergoing training. To some extent this must be true, though such a view rather ignores the fact that translators, as we saw above, all hold theories, and that these are subject to influences in the culture around them, whether or not they consciously wish to train. In fact Newmark (1993:15) maintains that no choices could be made without at least an unconscious theory to follow; this link is examined in the next section.

5.2 Theories and strategies

Strategies are sometimes confused with theories, but they are something quite different. A theory is a picture of the world and a strategy is a translation of this picture into a plan of action. It may be acted upon or may remain a mental construct. For example, the theory that was first put forward by Schleiermacher in a talk in 1813 is that a translator 'either leaves the writer alone as much as possible and moves the reader toward the writer, or [. . .] leaves the reader alone as much as possible and moves the writer toward the reader' (1992:42). This gives us a picture of two people, writer and reader, with the translator making the one or the other actually move in the other direction. It is possible for a later critic to take Schleiermacher's view of the two ways of translating and interpret it in accordance with other theories of translation; thus Venuti (1998:17–20) interprets Schleiermacher in accordance with a view that translation is an act of violence. Venuti's conclusion is that violence is a bad thing, and can be avoided by foreignizing translation (20). One way of translating (foreignizing) is better than another (domesticating), in Venuti's clearly argued view, and this evaluation leads, logically, to a 'call to action', a strategy involving 'cultural resistence' to the appropriation of the source text by the target language and culture (1998: Chapter 7). Venuti's argument provides a good example of the extent to which a theory, once it involves evaluation, always tends towards prescription. This is because of the link between theories and ethics. In Chapter 3 we looked at the notion of allegiance, which already carries a suggestion of moral considerations: if we feel allegiance to an actor in the network of translation, as we put it there following Jones (2009), such as the original author or our publisher, then this allegiance will determine what we see as the right course of translational action. Ethics is a difficult term, suggesting the right way to think, or to act, or even 'a threatening denial of thought' (Badiou 2001:3). Translational ethics could be defined as a set of principles (often with a moral dimension) that inform action; there is a right way to do a translation, based on right thinking. When scholars speak of the ethics of translation (see, for example, Hermans 2009), they are usually speaking of what is right in this broader sense, rather than what might be right in terms of linguistic or textual equivalence. If a practice is evaluated as right in this way, the theory that gives rise to it could be regarded as prescriptive. But just because it is a prescriptive theory it is not automatically a strategy; strategies are further developments of the theory. In Venuti's case, he himself suggests these in the course of his works; they are strategies such as 'choosing to translate marginal texts' (1995:267) or using dialect instead of standard forms or keeping mimetically close to the original (1995:167–181). Other translators may develop other strategies and use practices such as presenting translation in bilingual versions (such as the 'Visible Poets' series), or 'leaving a word untranslated' (Elsworth 2000:12).

To adapt Iser's view again, strategies are particular ways of translating, that relate to one's view of what translation is and how it works; a theory seeks to generalize (e.g. to explain that, and why, there is a tendency for translations to be fluent and disguise their sources) whereas methods tend to apply in individual cases (e.g. Elsworth's use of foreign words; see Iser 2006:10). Thus Venuti's theory of domesticating and foreignizing can be converted into a number of methods or strategies that will produce a foreignizing effect, the effect which Schleiermacher was describing when he spoke of taking the reader to see the foreign author (1992:42).

Some theories are very simple, in that they consist only of a metaphor. A translation is a window, according to Sayers Peden (1989:13), or an ice cube, according to Trask (Honig 1985:14) or, as we saw at the end of the previous chapter, a theatrical performance (Wechsler 1998). With such theories it is especially clear that they cannot be applied unless they have first been converted into a method. For example, the theory that a translation is a pane of glass through which we can see the original could lead to a literal method of translation, which aims to closely follow the obvious lexical, syntactic and phonetic properties of the original but does not represent what cannot immediately be seen, such as the cognitive impact of metaphors, the effect on the reader's emotions or the state of mind a particular type of iconicity conveys. The window or pane of glass metaphor, also criticized by Venuti (2008:1), thus only works if a particular view of the text is subscribed to: a view that the text as physical object is all we need to worry about. Such things as attitudes, emotions and effects are assumed to be irrelevant to the source text and remain so in the target text and for the translator. Some of the dangers of thus converting such simple metaphor-theories into strategies are explored in my article 'Who Needs Theory' (Boase-Beier 2010a). In that article I argue that what goes on behind a text, in the state of mind conveyed, and in the mind of the reader engaging with it, is central to how a text works. The theory I argue for there is not specifically a translation theory but a theory of cognitive stylistics. Indeed, I argue there that theories from outside translation (or any area that forms the object of a study) are more useful than theories of translation itself: they tend to have been tested independently of translation and they avoid the reductiveness of simple metaphors. But, once a theory from outside, such as cognitive stylistic theory, is combined with a view of translation, it in fact becomes a translation theory.

5.3 The theory here

In the 2010 article I have just mentioned, as well as in several other articles and my 2006 book, the theory I am arguing for, as I am here, is a combination of cognitive poetics with a view of translation as essentially creative, literary reading as essentially creative. Like many other translation theories, in fact possibly most, this theory, as I have just suggested, is not specifically a translation theory in a limited sense: it does not arise merely from observation of translation. It shares this feature with others we have discussed: Gutt (2000) uses Relevance Theory and Tabakowska (1993) uses Cognitive Linguistics. In fact Gutt even goes so far as to argue that we do not need a translation theory because a theory of communication – Relevance Theory – is sufficient. This is not an argument I accept because, once Relevance Theory interacts with one's views of translation, as I suggested at the end of the previous section, it becomes a theory of translation.

The theory of translation that has arisen out of the discussion so far in the first five chapters of this book and which will be further explored in the remaining four chapters, is based on the following points:

(i) Translation can aim either to resemble its source text (documentary translation) or to fulfil a particular function as a text (instrumental translation). Literary translation usually does both but non-literary translation is often just instrumental.

(ii) Some (usually non-literary) translation is not really translation but rewriting as it only aims to represent the same (usually non-fictional) world as the source text and does not need to have any other relation to the source text.

(iii) Translation is more than transfer of content. Literary translation is also, and especially, the transfer of style from one language (however understood), or medium, to another.

(iv) Style is central to all translation. It is important in all types of text, but literary translation is largely the translation of style.

(v) Style is a cognitive entity, not just a linguistic one. So to translate style is to translate poetic effect, implicature, state of mind, attitude, and so on.

(vi) All texts make readers work but literary texts make readers work much more, and translation aims to transfer this characteristic and to allow the poetic effects that result from the work that readers do.

(vii) Translated literary texts make readers work more and have more cognitive effects on them than untranslated literary texts.

(viii) Literary translation is both the translation of literary texts and the translation of texts in a literary way (i.e. that treats them as literary texts in that they are seen as fictional and that a greater importance is placed on style).

(ix) Translated literary texts are conceived of as blends of a real source text and an (imagined) original target-language text.

(x) Translation involves creativity, more so in the case of literary translation.

(xi) A translator will always have to decide whether more allegiance is owed to the source text, or the audience, or the publisher, or any of the other elements involved. This will affect the way the translation is done.

(xii) Theory describes how translation works but also – directly or indirectly – affects how it is done.

One of the things that should have become clear from this summary, if not before, is that literary translation involves more complex processes and actions than non-literary, both for translator and reader. Its relationships to its source text and to the world are both more complex.

As Turner (1996) points out, the literary mind is not substantially different from the non-literary mind. All the mental processes such as metaphor, ambiguity, constructing fictional worlds and so on that we encounter in the writing and reading of literary texts are also at work in non-literary communication. However, their presence is more marked in literary texts, and they play a greater role in literary translation than in non-literary.

And we have also seen that literary translation is always translation whereas non-literary translation is often just rewriting.

For these three reasons, most of what can be said about translation can be illustrated best with literary translation, and this will be the focus of the second part of the book, though I will continue to discuss examples from all types of text.

Part II
A Poetics of Translation

Literary Translation as the Translation of Mind

6

Chapter Outline

6.1 The literary mind and the role of the translator

Part I of this book considered the basic questions involved in translation: its definition and remit, its relationship with such difficult issues as truth and allegiance, voice, style and the way its theory and practice interact. The answers and partial answers have all tended to suggest a new way both of considering translation *per se* and of seeing the relationship between literary and non-literary translation. These answers emphasize the importance of the mind in the text and beyond the text. In this chapter, and throughout Part II, we consider further what it means to see literary translation as essentially the translation of mind. Poetics (as in the title) is not just the study of poetry, though it is sometimes understood in this way: Tsur (2002:281) for example, uses it like this. Stockwell (2002), as we saw in Chapter 1, sees cognitive poetics as a discipline that describes the 'process by which intuitive interpretations are formed into expressible readings' (2002:8) and uses 'poetics', as I do here, in its broad sense of both 'theory or system' and the 'practical creativity' involved in literary texts in general (2002:7–8).

The idea we first came across in Chapter 3 that 'the literary mind is the fundamental mind' (Turner 1996:v) has profound consequences for both cognitive poetics and translation studies. If the mind is by nature literary, then we have to consider the way the mind works in order to understand how literature works, and therefore to understand what literary translation involves. But the converse must also apply: we can best see how the mind works by studying literature, and we can best see what translation is by studying literary translation. This book thus takes the position of cognitive views like that propounded by Turner, and also by Stockwell (2002) or Johnson (1987) that when we read a text what we are reading is not just words and meaning in the sense of representation, but also a particular mental state embodied in the text (see Turner and Fauconnier 1999:409). And what the reader experiences are also not just textual effects, but poetic effects, which are cognitive, that is, they are effects on the mind and imagination, and even, as this chapter will suggest, on the body.

Style, in other words, is always mind-style. Fowler (1977) speaks of mind-style as 'the distinctive linguistic presentation of a distinctive mental self' (1977:103) that manifests itself particularly in repeated patterns in the text. Fowler was writing before the development of cognitive poetics, but now that more research has been done into the cognitive aspects of texts, it makes sense to take Fowler's view together with views of meaning, style, and poetic effects discussed in the previous chapters and to see all style as representing the mind behind the text. This can be a distinctive individual mind, as Fowler suggests, or it can be a conventional collective mind, such as that behind many types of non-literary text, and called by Fowler 'world-view' (1977:17). This is the notion of mind that informs register. The register of a legal text or a sports commentary, or a *Sun* article, could be said to embody a particular attitude or state of mind or world-view we all recognize. Such states of mind can be implied in the use of register in literary texts: we recognize the innocent view of Benjy in Faulkner's *The Sound and the Fury* (1993) or the ambivalence of Hardy's *Ruined Maid* (1977:195) from their register, and consideration of the state of mind or attitude we would attribute to these characters can be an important issue for translators: do we want a French Benjy or an American one, for example, in a French translation of *The Sound and the Fury*? But a cognitive approach to style and the text involves more than just recreating minds and attitudes in the source text. It affects even apparently straightforward issues of micro-textual style such as lexis.

To see how a cognitive approach to meaning affects the lexical level we might consider features of lexical semantics such as polysemy and homonymy, as in the following:

(6.1) The child gave a little skip of pleasure

(6.2) Don't skip classes

(6.3) We hired a skip as we were clearing out the shed

Most speakers of English would have no difficulty in saying that (6.1) and (6.2) are two meanings of the same word, and (6.2) and (6.3) are two different words that just happen, by an accident of language history, to be the same. In linguistic terms, then, the first relation is one of polysemy and the second homonymy. Cognitively, there is a major difference between polysemy and homonymy. As Johnson points out, polysemy involves the imagination in that it is 'the extension of a central sense of a word to other senses' (1987:xii). This is not the case with homonymy, because there is no extension of meaning: 'skip' as in 'container' is, according to the dictionary (*Concise Oxford* 1976:1070) a variant of 'skep' (used in English for a wicker bee-hive) which comes from Old Norse '*skeppa*', meaning a measure of volume or a container; it has nothing to do with 'skip' in the other two examples above. However, 'extension of meaning' in the sense in which Johnson discusses it, as an example of an underlying metaphorical cognitive process (1987:107), may have been a historical process, rather than something speakers of today do consciously. In other words, the modern-day speaker of English may treat (6.1) and (6.2) as homonyms, and so no cognitive act of meaning extension is involved. There are many cases in the language where speakers may not feel that an extension of meaning is involved. For example, 'cross' as in the religious symbol and 'cross', an adjective meaning 'annoyed', will often be seen as separate words, related only by homonymy. The fact that they originally both come from Latin '*crux*' is irrelevant to most speakers. It is important to note, though, that individual speakers may differ in this. Some may relate 'cross' as an adjective meaning 'annoyed' to 'to be at cross purposes with someone', 'to cross swords' or 'to cross someone' and therefore always make the imaginative leap that recreates what happened more gradually in the history of the language. For others, this will be a lexical quirk rather than a connection that involves imaginative extension. In other words, the difference between polysemy as involving a cognitive process and homonymy as just a linguistic accident depends on how an individual speaker treats the words and not on how the dictionary categorizes them, or history explains them.

The above examples primarily serve to illustrate that behind linguistic descriptions of language there are cognitive processes. But we need to think about whether this sort of distinction has consequences for translation. Consider a further set of examples:

(6.4) Our quarry gave us the slip

(6.5) The wood was full of cowslips

If I wish to translate these examples into Japanese, or German, or Spanish, I will have to consider such questions as whether, in the case of (6.4), 'to give someone the slip' exists as an idiom in these languages and, in the case of (6.5), what the flower is called that we call in English a cowslip. If (6.5) occurs in a scientific report on the healing properties of cowslips, I will have to translate it as *kibananokurinzakura* in Japanese, *Schlüsselblume* in German and *primula* in Spanish. But if (6.4) and (6.5) are two lines in the same poem, I might change the flower in (6.5) in order to pick up the repetition of 'slip', for example in German:

(6.6) Unsere Beute ist uns entkommen
      Und der Wald war voll mit Anemonen

The question a translator has to ask here is what is important: is it just the fact that 'slip' in (6.4) and 'cowslip' in (6.5) contain a repeated element of sound? This may be enough if we assume that for most speakers cowslip is actually 'cow's-lip' (because they know that a larger form of cowslip is called an ox-lip). A translator might then treat the connection as phonological but not as involving lexical cognitive extension. The dictionary is no help for the translator here, because, although it understands cowslip as cow-slip (and not cow's-lip), it says that 'slip', meaning 'slime', is not etymologically connected with 'to slip', but is from Old English 'slyppe', slimy substance, whereas 'to slip' is from Middle High German '*slipfen*', as in modern day '*schlüpfen*', to slip into something. The reason etymology does not help the translator here is because it does not reflect what is available to our cognitive processes, and in any case seems doubtful in this instance: most people would assume a slimy substance and the verb to slip must be related, whatever the dictionary says. This might all seem merely an uninteresting digression, but in fact how to link 'slip' in (6.4) and '–slip' in (6.5) in literary language is exactly what a literary translator will need to know. Is phonological repetition as in (6.6) enough or do we need to consider thought processes? And to what extent do the thought processes of most actual readers reflect the idealized thought processes behind such notions as 'historically related', 'etymologically connected', 'cognate', and so on, as given in dictionaries? We saw another instance where cognitive process may not echo actual etymology in Chapter 1, when we discussed '*pleurer*' and '*pleuvoir*' in examples where the reader might relate the words though etymological study does not: the first is from Latin '*plorare*' (to utter cries of pain) and the second from '*plovere*' (to agitate water) (see Picoche 1994). The difference between textual information, historical linguistic knowledge and individual cognitive processing is crucial in deciding both what style is and what translation needs to do. The difference also suggests that a literary translator must be more of a linguist than a non-literary translator. Literature is concerned with our thought-processes and so is linguistics; active linguistic context is always potentially separated from collective historical linguistic context (see Crystal 2003:191).

Seeing style in literary texts as mind-style involves an awareness that textual devices always correspond in some way to cognitive processes. There are always two aspects to this awareness. The first is that style in the text represents – however indirectly – a cognitive state and the second is that it has cognitive effects. If we take the sentences in (6.4) and (6.5) to be two lines of the same poem, they are, first of all, conveying a particular attitude or state of mind – perhaps, for example, a link between the human quarry and the natural world – and, secondly, they are making the reader go through the various mental processes involved in the linking of *slip* and *–slip* such as extending the meaning of the first to include the second, and seeing the physical sound-link as an analogy for a link of meaning.

The first aspect – awareness of the mind behind the text – rests on an inference by the reader on the basis of the interpretation of evidence in the text, and on the fact that we all possess a 'Theory of Mind', that is, we view other humans (and possibly animals) as intentional beings (Carston 2002:7–8); this view is linked to the conceptual metaphor, discussed in Section 2.2, that EVENTS ARE ACTIONS. In literary criticism, as discussed in Chapter 4, the emphasis has shifted from a focus on the author as the sole repository of meaning, at least since Wimsatt described the 'intentional fallacy' (1954) and Barthes the 'death of the author' (1977), to a focus on the reader (e.g. Iser 1979). But the process of writing that has created the text and the process of reading the text are closely linked: the writer writes with a reader in mind and the reader reads with a recreated writer in mind; this writer is a cognitive construct that only in part is the same as the real author.

Yet the tendency of pragmatic studies such as Sperber and Wilson (1995) or Gutt (2000), which have gone beyond a code-model of communication to look at implicatures, attitudes and half-conveyed meanings, has always been to envisage some actual meaning intended by the speaker. While post-structuralist criticism has emphasized that we cannot assume a simple meaning to be got from the text, put there by a writer – in other words, it has taught us the insufficiency of both the code-model of language and the view that a writer's intention is apprehendable – it is nevertheless the case that readers want to know who the writer is, and translators have to know what they think the writer meant. Fortunately, there are at least three recent strands within literary criticism in its broadest sense in which revived interest in the writer has become a focus. The first is in studies of creativity, such as those by Pope (1995:2005). Though the act of writing is here often used as a means to under-standing texts (Pope 1995:1), such books nevertheless place great importance on how texts come to be written. The second is in more philosophically orien-tated critical studies such as that of Burke (2007), who argues that, if we can-not know what the author was thinking, we equally cannot regard the question of authorship is something that can be ignored; his intention is thus to ques-tion closely the very discourse of the death of authors. And the third is in approaches within cognitive poetics, which can be seen, as mentioned in 1.1, as being situated at the intersection between literary and linguistic studies.

In cognitive poetics, the writer or author can be seen as someone recon-structed from the text in a variety of ways. For example, if literature is seen as a particular type of discourse, then the author is one participant in the world of the discourse (see Gavins 2007:129), and readers may equate him or her with the narrator, in an extension of the Proxy Principle discussed in the previ-ous chapter. In Relevance Theory, an author may be viewed as the initiator of a text as part of an act of communication, leaving the text open to a variety of interpretations among which may well be the 'inferred authorial communi-cative intention' (MacKenzie 2002:61). It is not so much implied by the text as inferred by the reader.

In translation studies, this relationship between reading and writing is crucial, and has been much discussed. Eco (1981), for example, sees the trans-lator as a model reader. The translator Michael Hamburger says there are 'two distinct functions and processes . . . reading and writing' whereby he sees reading as including 'intuitive grasp of the original text as well as more conscious grappling' with problems, and writing as 'the capacity to reconstitute the text in another language' (2007:405).

But there are always two writers and two sets of readers involved in the process of translation, and it this fact that makes the reading of a translation different. First, there is the writer of the original text, who will be concerned to write a text which engages its readers. This will be the case especially with literary texts and some other types of text such as advertisements and philosophical texts, but the potential reader will play a much smaller role in other non-literary texts such as weather reports, instructions and so on. Secondly, there is the reader of the original text, who will, especially if it is a literary text, reconstruct its imagined writer, often through the narrator or one of its characters. Thirdly, there is the writer of the target text, the translator, who is also one of the readers of the source text and who will take the reader of the target text into account in writing it. And fourthly, there is the reader of the target text, who will reconstruct the writer of both that text and of the original text to varying degrees.

The second aspect of our awareness that the text has cognitive counterparts – the text's effects on the mind – is central to our understanding of literary texts and also, according to scholars such as Johnson (1987) and Turner (1996), to our understanding of the mind. The move from a sound-link to a semantic link in (6.4) and (6.5), when they are considered as lines in the same poem, is not just a question of a distinction between homonymy and polysemy, but it is in fact an instance of a much more general process. For illustration, consider another example, that of the two modal verbs 'can':

(6.7) You can't read French

(6.8) You can't drop litter in the park

This link is also, according to Johnson (1987:55–56) not merely a sound-link, one of homonymy, but it involves an extension from physical ability in (6.7) to permission in (6.8), and is part of our conceptual metaphor of 'understanding the rational in terms of the physical' (1987:50). We understand morality in the simpler terms of ability, in the same way as we understand semantic links in the simpler terms of phonological links. In other words, we do not only link these two meanings of 'can' because they have the same form but because one is seen as a more abstract, 'moral' version of the other more concrete one. And this cognitive process of moving from concrete to abstract can be even further generalized. Most cognitive linguists and cognitive poetics scholars would say that our thought processes are determined to a large extent by our physical presence in the world. This is sometimes referred to as 'embodiment' (e.g. Stockwell 2009:4–5). I will come back to this in the next section, but in the rest of this section I want to look at other types of stylistic features besides just lexical links and repetitions, in order that we can see the cognitive counterparts of these lexical features and the effects of such cognitive counterparts on the translator's reading of a source text.

Works on cognitive linguistics and conceptual metaphor argue for the importance of thought processes such as blending, analogy and metaphor in understanding, exploring and creating meaning (e.g. Fauconnier and Turner 2002:20–21; Lakoff and Turner 1989). If we use an expression such as:

(6.9) That was a black deed

we are using 'black' to mean 'bad', and this is done on the basis of a conceptual metaphor that structures the way we think, sometimes written as BAD IS BLACK. This conceptual metaphor is the cognitive counterpart of the linguistic metaphor in (6.9), and other such expressions. Conceptual metaphors are often seen as likely to be universal; thus the English version (6.9) could be translated into German as

(6.10) Das war eine schwarze Tat

However, even though the notion of representing something bad as black might be present in several languages, it is not the case in every language. Some German speakers are hesitant about (6.10). And in Italian or Turkish you would have to say 'a bad deed' (*cattiva azione* or *kötü işler*, respectively). So, although a concept such as black might have a meaning common to many cultures (see Evans1970:115–119), individual languages might not express it in the same way.

Rather than seeing (6.10) as a translation of (6.9), we might want to regard both as 'translations' of the conceptual metaphor BAD IS BLACK. In literary texts, as in all writing and thinking, this conceptual metaphor will lead to negative connotations: Celan's '*schwarze Milch*' (black milk) uses these connotations, such as night, darkness, death and destruction, to call up and contrast with the connotations of whiteness – light, goodness, wholesomeness, healing – which the conceptual metaphor GOOD IS WHITE suggests. However, a translator needs to be aware that, besides having different linguistic manifestations, such conceptual metaphors are not common to every culture. Because they have an embodied basis, black will be associated with not being able to see or move about, and being vulnerable, and so it will be bad. But because metaphors are partly culturally determined, the badness of black might interact with its smartness (as in 'black tie') in an English context, its conservatism ('the blacks' in German are members of the Conservative *CDU* or *CSU*) or its wisdom (in Japanese culture), and so on. A particular connotation in English and many other European languages is mysterious (as in 'black arts'). This connotation can interact with notions of difference from oneself to pernicious effect in the sort of cultural stereotype many light-skinned people and cultures have associated with darked-skinned individuals or cultures. Consider the following extracts from Enid Blyton's children's novel *The Mountain of Adventure* (2007; first published in 1949):

> (6.11) David gave another yell and got to his feet . . . 'Come!', he cried, in Welsh, and then in English. 'Black, black, black!'. (2007:88)

> (6.12) She got a terrible shock. Looking down at her was a face – and it was black. . . . She saw that the face was topped by black, thick hair, and had bright eyes and a cheerful expression. (2007:112)

The German translation of this book, while keeping David's shout as '*Schwarz! Schwarz! Schwarz!*' (Ellsworth 2007:83), changes the second passage to say (in back translation):

> (6.13) . . . she saw that the face was framed in thick black hair, (and) intelligent eyes and had a friendly expression.

Ellsworth's translation alters the 2007 English version by replacing 'bright' with 'intelligent', presumably a response not to the 2007 version itself, but to Blyton's original 1949 version, which in fact says of the stranger's face that it was 'topped by black, woolly hair, and had very white teeth and thick lips.' What Blyton was indicating with her various uses of 'black' in 1949 was foreignness, mystery, potential danger (in 6.11) on the one hand, and she was then subverting these connotations with the sudden appearance of a friendly black man in (6.12). However, the description of the black man conforms closely to the stereotypes common in England in 1949 about black people.

The 2007 German translation keeps the mysterious connotations of '*schwarz*' in David's words (which also exist in Welsh *du*, and clearly existed in Blyton's view of a Welsh speaker), but goes even further than its modern English counterpart in trying to remove stereotypical connotations of the person whose black face the girl sees. For Ellsworth (or the publisher DTV) what was important was to preserve the frightening aspect of 'black' (this is after all an adventure story) but not its specific, culturally determined ones. And yet the replacing of 'bright eyes' with 'intelligent eyes' shows all too clearly in the comparison of the 2007 English and German texts that the translation, in attempting to eliminate possible stereotypes, merely emphasizes them, for behind 'intelligent' must be an assumed characteristic that the term is meant to counteract.

What examples (6.9) to (6.13) show is the extent to which 'universal' cognitive metaphors cannot be just assumed by a translator to be universal: they interact with cultural and historical context and with linguistic usage. The translator needs to be aware of this rich and complex cognitive context in reading the original and in considering the effects on the readers of the translation.

As noted above, metaphor is often seen as fundamental to the way we think and create new meanings, extending a basic meaning in a similar way to the process seen in polysemy (see Furniss and Bath 2007:187; Gibbs 1998:90). Thus 'black deed', 'black mood' and 'black Monday' all involve an extension of the conceptual metaphor BAD IS BLACK. The extension of meaning in metaphor often recruits the mental process of blending, as discussed in Chapter 4. Like polysemy and metaphor, a blend (which is often itself the result of a metaphorical process) has a linguistic manifestation and a cognitive counterpart. Consider the following:

(6.14) I am not yet born (MacNeice 2007:213)

(6.15) She had lost her ticket and her temper

(6.16) A colleague threw his keys in the bin and tried to open his office door with an empty joghurt pot

(6.14) is not linguistically odd at all but conceptually it involves two incompatible images: a foetus and someone speaking; (6.15) is an example of zeugma (like example (1.30)) and could be said to involve the sort of extension of meaning we saw above in examples (6.1) and (6.2). But it goes beyond this because both meanings – the concrete and the extended – are juxtaposed. It is only funny to the extent that we are aware of both the basic concrete meaning of 'to lose' and its extension at the same time. In other words, it is a cognitive joke rather than a linguistic one. (6.16) is an example of blending two actions, similar to many of those discussed by Fauconnier and Turner (2002). Again, there is nothing odd about the language, but the images they conjure up in this case both involve an action which blends two others: throwing the keys in the bin blends throwing away rubbish with holding a tool in one's hand and trying to open the door with a joghurt pot the same two images, though with the opposite result. (6.16) illustrates particularly well that a blend is not something fixed (though it can become a fixed concept such as a unicorn or a teddy-bear, whose lexical entry will define it implicitly as a blend) but something that is 'active in the moment of thinking' (Turner and Fauconnier 1999:398). The reader of (6.15), for example, has to actively blend to see why it is funny.

The fact that all the examples in (6.14) to (6.16) have a cognitive counterpart is what a translator would need to take into account. Because (6.14) describes an impossible, blended world, it is this world that the translator of MacNeice's poem needs to recreate. Anything that prevents this – such as translating the first person with a third person, for example – will reduce the cognitive complexity of the text-world. Because (6.15) is a cognitive and not a linguistic joke, a direct translation is likely to produce merely a linguistic anomaly, but none of the sense of concreteness that 'temper' takes on in the English from its pretended analogy to 'ticket'. (6.16), like (6.14) will cause few problems for the translator because it involves recreating a blended world in the mind of the person making the error. The only cultural adjustment necessary will be, possibly, to the actual objects involved, such as a joghurt pot.

All literary figures such as iconicity, ambiguity, repetition and metaphor have cognitive counterparts, and all involve cognitive processes whereby the meaning of one thing or image is extended to cover another. In the case of iconicity, examples such as those in (1.15) – words that begin with 'fl' such as 'fling' or 'flutter' – illustrate clearly the distinction between a writer's or reader's knowledge of morphology and the sort of knowledge that tells us this combination of sounds has a particular 'meaning'. For the translator, the latter, which is at the periphery of linguistic knowledge, is as important as the former. In other cases of iconicity, such as repetition in the text assumed to stand for repetition in the world the text creates, we seem to be dealing with a metaphor-like process. Consider the following example:

(6.17) Or its past permit
         The present to stir a torpor like a tomb's.
                    (Hardy 1977:99)

Here it could be maintained that the alliterated [p] and [t], along with syntactic and lexical repetition earlier in the poem, are all examples of linguistic repetition which stands iconically for actual repetition, that is, the impossibility of moving on in a present that must always repeat the past. A translator will need to take into account what the repetition suggests, not just the sounds or words themselves, as discussed in Chapter 1. And it could be argued, as for example Hiraga (2005) does, that doing this involves a metaphorical process whereby the linguistic repetition is taken to stand for some other sort of repetition. This view of extension could be taken further; McCully (1998), for example, argues that what is beautiful (e.g. rhyme) is more likely to be taken to be true. When applied to advertisements such as that exemplified in (1.25), it is perhaps not just the memorability of the phrase used in that advert to describe a car that is important, but also its possible unconscious effects on the reader. As we saw above with ambiguity, a word with two meanings, as in the case of 'slip' in (6.4) and (6.5) or 'lost' in (6.15) actually conjures up two different images or frames. And it is the cognitive link in both cases – linking the quarry with nature in (6.4) and (6.5) seen as a poem, and linking frames of 'lose' in (6.15) – that is responsible for the cognitive effect.

In a similar way to the way our cognitive structures allow us to take the concrete meaning of ability in 'can' and extend it to morality, we also take the text and extend it to the mind. Fowler (1996:175) says we take action in a text to stand for 'internal states', but in fact we also take the text itself as a representative or proxy for a state of mind, as the following example shows:

(6.18) *L'assommoir* is a sad story

What we mean is that the story (see Zola 1995) describes a sad world-view or, more precisely, the world-view of an imaginary person (author or narrator) who is sad when she or he considers the world. It also means that its effect is to make its readers feel sad. Again, this example has parallels in several given by Fauconnier and Turner, such as the 'safe beach' example (2002:25). Furthermore, we take a translated text as a proxy for both the source text and the state of mind the source text embodies. In example (6.18), it is likely that the speaker has read the English translation, for example by Margaret Mauldon (Zola 1995), of the novel by Zola.

What determines the reader's perception that the target text is in fact the source text is something I will call the 'Proxy Principle', and it is just a specific case of the sort of conceptual extension we have seen at work in metaphor, or iconicity, or polysemy, or even transferred epithet, which is what (6.18) could be said to be. Using something as a proxy or an analogy is, according to Mithen (1996:171–210), one of the basic mental attributes that allowed early humans to develop art and religion. This principle allows us to appoint someone else to vote for us, it allows us to blame the messenger for unwelcome news, to worship an icon, to take credit for jokes not our own (even though we may acknowledge that they are someone else's) and to say we have read Zola even though it was Mauldon. When we read literary texts, it encourages us to see the narrator as the author (cf. Gavins 2007:129), or, when watching a play, to see an actor as a character (cf. Fauconnier and Turner 2002:266). The Proxy Principle comes into play in translations as a direct result of the fact that a translation is a blend. Being a blend means, as we saw in Chapter 4, that it is both itself – a translated text – and its original. It does not supplant the original but shares some of its characteristics, while having some which are different. To be a proxy a person or thing has to be similar to what it is a proxy for: a child or a tape recorder cannot vote in my place; a letter is not a messenger, however bad the news it brings (though I may tear it up in anger or burn it in disgust); I cannot take credit for a joke unless I can tell it in a funny way; and a review of *L'assommoir* will not be referred to as 'Zola'. We see the principle at work in translation bibliographies; for example in Venuti's (2008) bibliography he gives his own 1995 translation of de Angelis as de Angelis 1995 (Venuti 2008:249), though consistency with his call for visibility should mean the translator Venuti is seen as the author, and the book therefore should be listed under Venuti. And Hermans (2002:10) says he cannot remember the name of Dostoevsky's English or Dutch translators, though he has obviously not forgotten Dostoevsky's name. Even translation specialists privilege the original by seeing the translation as a proxy.

Behind the Proxy Principle is conceptual extension, just as it is behind stylistic figures or metaphors. What the above discussion suggests is that the translator needs to be aware of such conceptual extension as the cognitive counterpart to whatever is in the text (besides being aware also of its contribution to the invisibility of translation). Any reading that fails to take the mind inhabiting the text into account is at best a half-reading, and not a good basis for translating the text into another language and culture.

6.2 The embodied mind

As we have seen, a translator needs to consider both the cognitive states a text represents, such as sadness in (6.17), and the cognitive effects a text might have, such as making us recreate an impossible blended world in (6.14), because both aspects are essential to the meaning of a literary text and both need to be conveyed by the translated text. If this does not happen, the translation will often be considered inadequate. Gutt (2000) has many examples where the negative criticism of a translation arises because the translator has failed to take cognitive aspects of the text into account (e.g. 2000:107–111).

The various mental processes the translator finds in the text, uses to read it, and aims to allow the reader of the translation to experience, and which include extending meaning, seeing one thing as a proxy for another, and blending, are, in cognitive poetic and linguistic theories, as the BAD IS BLACK metaphor suggested, assumed to be embodied. Johnson (1987:xxxviii) expresses embodiment like this:

> as animals we have bodies connected to the natural world, such that our consciousness and rationality are tied to our bodily orientations in and with our environment.

This means that the mind, including that inhabiting the source text, is constrained by what the body allows or encourages it to do. Even our view of the mind is partly determined by embodiment metaphors such as THE MIND IS A BODY (Lakoff and Johnson 1999:235–243); we conceptualize the abstract mind as the concrete body. It has been observed many times that the forms we see in literature are 'rooted in human experience' (Attridge 2004:109) to the extent that poetic rhythm is a way of 'harnessing the energies of the body' (Attridge 1995: 4) or narrative a process of using patterns that 'recur in our sensory and motor experience' (Turner 1996:16). It seems likely that the embodied nature of meaning and effect, used particularly in literary texts, explains why, according to Cook (1994:3–4), we would want to bother reading untrue information we already know. We find symmetry pleasurable because we are (outwardly at least) symmetrical (Turner 1991:68–73), and we think in the way we do because 'structures of bodily experience work their way up into abstract meanings and patterns of inference' (Johnson 1987:xix). Thus the processes we commonly think of as mental, such as interpretation, imagination and reasoning are based on our physical experience in and of the world (Freeman 2008), and the way we describe reality is not based on 'a value neutral, ahistorical framework' (Johnson 1987:xxi), because no such framework exists independently of human beings and human imagination. Johnson is here arguing against what is generally regarded as the Cartesian mind-body split, as is also Damasio in *Descartes' Error* (1994). The reader should note that to speak of the Cartesian split is always a form of shorthand; in fact, as many critics have pointed out, Descartes was careful to explain how 'the body acts on the mind' (Koch 2006:414; see also Hatfield 2003:330).

What all the above works have in common is that they place importance on the role of imagination, which supplements reason by making connections, drawing inferences and being alive to connotations, and which is crucially dependent upon the way human beings exist in the world. This central importance of imagination was borne out by almost all the views on reason in a recent *New Scientist* debate (26 July 2008): reason was seen by most thinkers represented there as dependent on imagination, which in turn depends on a sense of what it means to be a human being.

However, it is important to remember that, as the discussion of 'black' above showed, embodiment is not a notion free of culture and history. It is also important to see the discussion of embodiment and imagination in connection with ideas discussed in Chapters 1 and 2 about encoding, relativity, the theory of meaning and truth in general, and what is translatable. As discussed in Section 2.1, a code-model of language suggests a particular view of translation: that meaning is decoded and extracted out of the source text, to be re-encoded by the translator in the target text, and decoded again by the reader of this text. Pragmatic studies (such as Sperber and Wilson 1995; Carston 2002) show that the encoded meaning is only part of the meaning: the rest is in connotations, implicatures, and other means of expressing state of mind, point of view and attitude. It is especially in this part of meaning, which I am equating with style (see also Boase-Beier 2006:111–114), that questions of imagination come into play. This is not because literary style uses special cognitive processes: as we have seen, what happens in literature is what happens in the mind. But literary style exploits the imaginative to a greater extent than either everyday language or non-literary texts because it calls into play the reader's imagination. All studies based on cognitive linguistics and cognitive poetics assume that thought is 'richer' (Johnson 1987:1–17) than the straightforward encoded, propositional meanings that can be extracted from the text. It is up to the translator to be aware of the rich language of thought, both in the text, and in the thoughts the text gives rise to in the reader.

Burnshaw (1960:xiv), discussing how to translate poems, concludes that it 'would of course be impossible' to capture such effects not only on the mind but in evoking 'a physical response in the reader's body' (ibid.). His solution is to include the original poems as part of his translation, with an 'English approximation' (1960:xiv) and he comments that this procedure allows the reader to see' *what* the poem is saying and *how*. The essence of Burnshaw's argument seems to be that only the original poem can have such physical effects, but this is to take rather a dim view of what translation can achieve.

6.3 Recreating poetic effects

A translator reading a text to be translated thus needs to take into account the mind expressed there and its embodied basis, and the effects of the text on the mind of the reader, including the way they interact with our physical presence in the world. Traditionally, translation has often been assumed to be about conveying effect (see e.g. Chesterman 1997:35); we have already seen that this is not a simple matter, as the effects are different for each reader and potentially for each reading. But in order to recreate effects it is necessary first of all to notice them. For the translator, this means looking for the clues or 'signs of literariness' (Riffaterre 1992:205) in the text that trigger them. Literary texts, or texts read in a literary way, are texts with a particularly large scope for reader engagement and thus with the potential for a large number of cognitive effects on the reader. They are therefore texts with an especially large number of such clues; these are often very subtle, and this subtlety enhances the text's openness and the possibility of poetic effects. Such clues are referred to by Gutt as 'communicative clues' (2000:134) that indicate, in Gutt's Relevance Theory view, what the author of the source text meant. But what the author meant could also be taken to include poetic effects of stylistic features. Such clues, for the translator, might be stress patterns, use of different registers, repetition and so on; they are what are often referred to as stylistic devices (Stockwell 2002:14) or features (Short 1996:18). In a literary text, where meaning is not clearly fixed, it makes sense to see such devices both as clues to the way the text is to be read and also as clues to the sort of readerly engagement that will form part of its poetic effect. But some types of effect are more complicated than others. Let us consider five different types of effects which the translator needs to look for in the source text and recreate in the translation.

First, there are the types of effect we usually associate with the term 'response' (see e.g. Attridge 2004:89–92; Fabb 1995:144) or affect (Semino 1997:150–151). Consider the following examples:

> (6.19) Now she could hear . . . could she? Or was it her imagination? Footsteps, slow and quiet in the corridor outside. (Reah 2003:439)

(6.20) I've been feeling sleek and furry
      Since you came and made me whole (Harvey 2005:12)

(6.21) Ah! As the heart grows older
      It will come to such sights colder (Hopkins 1963:50)

In accordance with the Proxy Principle outlined above, we will attribute our own fear, joy or regret, triggered by the examples above, to the character presented. In other words, experiencing physical and mental feelings of fear when reading the novel from which (6.19) is taken, we will assume these are the feelings the heroine has when she hears the footsteps in the corridor. Similarly, we can feel 'sleek and furry' or experience the regret of losing the freshness of grief, and also sympathize with the characters in (6.20) and (6.21) feeling these things. We can see that even apparently straightforward feelings of fear, joy or regret have at least two aspects: the initial feeling, sometimes attributed to the limbic system, and the reflection upon it, assumed to be the product of consciousness (Taylor 2008:19–20), one of the effects of which is to attribute our feelings by proxy to the character or author. A translation which failed to give rise to these feelings in the reader would not work as a psychological thriller, or a poem. A distinction is traditionally made in the teaching of creative writing (e.g. Sansom 1994:40), and sometimes, not quite correctly, attributed to Henry James (see Booth 1983:23–25), between 'showing' and 'telling', with the former assumed to be more effective, but in fact 'showing' a character's feelings is no better than telling them, and may be less effective. What the text needs to do is to make the reader experience them and attribute them back to the relevant person in the text.

These responses or emotions caused by a text are discussed by Pilkington as 'non-propositional effects' (2000:163), located not in meaning in the narrow sense but in 'images, impressions and emotions' (Sperber and Wilson 1995:5), and a central concern of literature; Pilkington refers to such emotions collectively as 'affect', which he defines as 'phenomenal state attitudes' (2000:164). Literary translation, then, must also be centrally concerned with affect, possibly what was meant by theorists and translators such as Pope who have referred to the 'spirit' or 'fire' (Lefevere 1992:64f.) of the source text, to be preserved in the target text. Fabb (1995) argues that such instances of affect cannot easily be described, except perhaps in physical terms. Advances in science will gradually allow us to measure this sort of bodily and cognitive response according to Damasio (1999:9), and such bodily responses have potentially taken on more significance in cognitive theories of meaning, because of its embodied basis. The discussion of affect and response is closely related, as Pilkington observes (2000:170–176) to the philosophical debate about qualia, the way experiences feel; he calls states of mind that are characterized by feelings that a text gives rise to 'aesthetic qualia' (2000:177). These are complex feelings, as noted also by Fabb (2002:136;215–216), rather than the simple emotions of revulsion, or nostalgia, or anger, that non-literary texts or what Pilkington calls 'second-rate art' might give rise to; these he refers to as 'emotional qualia' (2000:177). In terms of the distinctions made in Chapters 1 and 2 between literary and non-literary texts and therefore between literary and non-literary translation, we can see that a literary text would typically give rise to aesthetic responses, whereas an advertisement or a rhyme in a birthday card would not. This is because it is characteristic of literariness to engage the reader in 'exploring extended contexts' (Pilkington 2000:177), whereas an advertisement or birthday card might aim for a simpler and more rapid response: a desire for a pair of shoes or a feeling of delight, both forgotten until some other trigger arouses the same feelings again.

Given this distinction between rapid emotional responses and those that have the characteristics of aesthetic responses or aesthetic qualia, it would seem wrong for a translator to elicit the wrong level of response just as much as to elicit the wrong type of response. Consider an advertisement for a charity that shows a clearly dying child, with a vulture waiting in the background, and asks for money. It appeals instantly, arousing feelings of guilt and the need to alleviate the child's suffering: to chase away the vulture, as it were. What it does not do is encourage the reader or viewer to think of the vulture returning, or, driven off, going to sit behind another dying child. If the original in (6.22) were translated to say something like (6.23)

(6.22) Save this child!
        Give now!

(6.23) They cannot all survive! Give this child a chance!

then the reader would be encouraged to think too much. The appeal would lose its point, which is to ensure rapid emotion and rapid action. Or, if the reader of (6.23) were to identify herself with the vulture and examine the reasons for the need to respond, such as guilt about voyeurism, for example, the effect of the appeal would be lost.

In a poem, the opposite is the case; the translation that gives rise to transient and immediate feelings is likely to be less satisfactory. Consider these two lines from the poet Rose Ausländer (1977:30)

(6.24) Es ist Zeit den
      it is time the

      Traum zu bauen in Grau
      dream to build   in grey

The most obviously striking thing about these lines is the assonance of '*Traum*', '*bauen*' and '*grau*' in the second one. In our first translation of Ausländer's poems, my co-translator and I translated the lines as:

(6.25) Now it is time / to shape a dream in shades of grey
                               (Boase-Beier and Vivis 1995:38)

This translation echoes the sound-repetition of the original, but the second line sounds curiously clichéd. Clichés are simply lexicalized phrases that have come to achieve some of their cognitive effect through familiarity (which is why people like them) but also to lose deeper, more lasting effects because their meaning does not have to be worked out (which is why people hate them). The expression in Ausländer's original poem does not have this effect at all: the effect it does have is to contrast '*Traum*' ('a dream, an imaginary world') with '*grau*' ('grey', suggesting the monotony of the everyday). (6.24) suggests many possibilities: an everyday, reachable dream; a hesitant, understated dream; a dream that transcends the everyday; a sad dream; a dream neither good nor bad, and so on. The effect of the translation in (6.25) is to cut off exploration because the expression sounds too familiar. There is no obvious contrast, because the phrase 'shades of grey' makes the connotations of 'grey' get lost. The translation in (6.25) certainly causes feeling, but it is a feeling of mild pleasure in the familiarity. For this reason, the second edition of the translation (in press) changes the lines to:

(6.26) Now it is time / to form my dream in grey

There is no cliché here, and thus the contrast of 'dream' and 'grey' invites further thought. It is a better instance of 'the active refusal to accept that which is pre-arranged and pre-ordained, pre-packaged' (Bartoloni 2009:71) that characterizes poetry than is (6.25).

A second type of effect is those that arise from the reader's search for meaning. Reading is frequently seen as an open-ended process, exactly because, in literary texts in particular, the reader engages most strongly with those parts of meaning that are not clear-cut in order to create further meanings, or give rise to further feelings. Kuiken (2008:53) describes this process as open-ness to the 'unsayable "more" that is implicit in the felt sense of a situation'. In literary texts, because such engagement is not a finite search for a meaning but rather an examination of one's own thoughts, and a search which is by nature without an end, what is searched for is what writers such as MacKenzie (2002:7–8) have called 'maximal relevance' (see also Boase-Beier 2006:42). By this is meant the pursuing of a search for meaning as long as new meanings can be found. It is this sense of searching that leads readers to reread and trans-lators to retranslate (see Hamburger 2007:39). Because such searches (and perhaps all searches; cf. Grandin 2005:96) are pleasurable, we do not want them to end. They are searches of the mind rather than of the text. There is plenty of evidence that we are cognitively geared towards searches with no necessary or useful end: games, poems, hunts, mazes and the like all suggest the search itself is what matters. As in the case of affect, which, as we have seen, is not merely felt by the reader but cognitively examined, so the process of completing a text, the different potential ways of doing it, will result in 'changes [to] an individual's mental world' (Attridge 2004:19). According to Attridge, it is the apprehension that one's current modes of thought are inadequate and need adjusting (2004:33) that leads to such mental examination, the basis for viewing reading as 'creative' (Attridge 2004:79–87). It could also be argued that creativity is what the brain is designed for. McCrone (1990) for example, says that storing is inefficient, and so even memory contains only enough informa-tion for creative reconstruction. Creativity is thus not only more pleasurable but also more efficient. Literary texts, and especially poetry, by combining their affective aspect with openness, lead to mental examination.

This process of creating meaning, besides being in itself pleasurable, has many further cognitive effects on the reader, such as the rethinking of 'old positions' (Attridge 2004:8). In Relevance-Theory terms, the search for further meaning will continue as long as cognitive effects are still being obtained (see Boase-Beier 2006:43–49). Consider the following example, which describes the appearance of a rower approaching across a lake as:

(6.27) Zuerst verschwommen, die Konturen fließend
(Strubel 2008:93)

A translator will want both to reproduce the immediate effects of the text and to allow for this open-ended process of searching for meaning that triggers further effects. *Fließend* in (6.27) is a word meaning indistinct, when used, as here, of contours, or permeable, fuzzy or unclear, but also flowing, as a stream or the water supply in a house. The author's choice of the word '*fließend*', in the context of an exploration, in the novel, of a summer spent on a lake, and of the effects of light and water on the way things appear, and the subtleties of male and female perceptions, and of homosexuality and heterosexuality, can be taken to be significant. A translation must therefore consider how the effect on the reader of exploring the connotations of '*fließend*' (perhaps not merely soft or unclear but also merging and overlapping) can be preserved.

Here we can read the term '*fließend*' as relating to the image of a figure approaching in a boat across a lake and also in relation to the connotations of '*verschwommen*', blurred, which is etymologically connected to the verb 'to swim' and literally means something like 'having been affected by a blurring caused by the eyes watering'. The fact that the passage occurs in a novel is a clue to the likelihood of such connotations having importance for the reading, and the link between the lake image, the word '*verschwommen*' and the word '*fließend*' acts as a cue for the translator to consider whether the whole scene is perhaps in some sense metaphorical for the relationships in the novel. In this sense clues to cognitive effects in the source text serve as cues to the translator to try and recreate such effects in the translation. A possible way to do this might be to translate the above passages as:

(6.28) Blurred at first, its contours fluid

which manages to suggest both uncertain vision (an important theme in the novel), and the instability of category-boundaries (the central theme) as well as linking the latter theme to images of water, though it loses the connotation of water in '*verschwommen*'.

Thirdly, effects in the reader, to be recreated by a translator, might go beyond both the immediate and the considered feelings of joy or regret, or the resulting effects from the search for meaning, to include all manner of changes to knowledge. Cook describes such changes as 'schema refreshing' (1994:10–11), that is, causing changes in schemata or mental representations. He regards it as a 'primary function of literature' (Cook 1994:191) to effect such changes. Philosophical texts, too, often actively encourage such rethinking, so that readers might develop different ideas about truth from reading Blackburn (2005) or evil from Vardy (1999) or fear from Nietzsche (1998).

Consider the following examples, taken from the same book as that in (6.27) and (6.28) by German author Antje Ravič Strubel:

> (6.29) Morgens lag der See unbewegt da wie Glas. Er spiegelte den Himmel, der klar und lichtblau war und seine Spiegelung im See wiederum zurückzuspiegeln schien . . .
>
> (Strubel 2008:39)

> (6.30) In the mornings the lake lay calm as glass. It reflected the sky, that was clear and light-blue and that appeared to reflect back its own image reflected in the lake . . .

> (6.31) In the mornings the lake lay calm as glass. It mirrored the sky, that was clear and blue as light and that seemed to mirror back its own image mirrored in the lake . . .

The difference between the second translation (6.30) and the first draft in (6.29) is only that the verb 'to reflect' has been replaced by 'to mirror'. It seems a small difference, and yet the difference is important in the context of the novel. As in the earlier example, nature here seems a metaphor for relationships. And relationships in this novel are not clearly heterosexual or homosexual: an apparently heterosexual man attempting to rape a woman is, we are told, really attracted by the woman's boyishness, and the lesbian relationship at the centre of the story begins when the main female character is mistaken for a man. There is a constant conflict between the way people see themselves and the clear categories others put them into. Looking into a mirror in men's clothes, the main character sees herself as others see her and becomes aware of her intermediate status between male and female. To reflect is what nature does, to mirror is what humans do. The link between the lake which mirrors the sky, which mirrors itself in the lake, and the way we are determined by how others see us is stronger in (6.31). The effect of this mirroring is more concrete, less natural, and more intentional than the reflection in (6.30). It is thus far more likely to make us think about the fact that how others see us is partly influenced by how we see them than is (6.30); the sort of 'schema refreshing' that Cook (1994:10) speaks of, with respect to the categorization of others as hetero- or homosexual is thus likely to be greater. In the same way the reader may develop new meanings of silence by reading the poem by Hardy from which example (6.17) came, or new meanings for 'time' in a postmodern novel or for 'loss' in a religious poem.

A fourth effect of reading texts is that they might actually change behaviour. This is an idea already discussed by I.A. Richards in 1929 (Richards 1964) and taken up by Attridge (2004:90). Richards argued that 'stock responses' (1964:235) in and to literary texts could be counteracted by an 'absence of self-deception' (p.28) and by humility which would allow us to 'become less easily imposed upon' (p.350) by convention or uncharitable attitudes. Consider the following two lines from a poem by von Törne (1981:56):

(6.32) Ich lese in der Zeitung, dass die Mörder
     I read in the newspaper that the murderers

     Von Mord und Totschlag nichts gewusst.
     of murder and manslaughter nothing known

This example is discussed at length in my 2006 book (Boase-Beier 2006: 122–127) and it is not my intention to discuss it in detail here. But, in the sense of changing behaviour, one might observe that translation (6.33) also attempts to do this:

(6.33) Butchers ignorant of slaughter
     - so at least the papers say.

The lines in (6.32) lack an auxiliary verb and the reader has to supply it; that verb could be either the indicative '*haben*', suggesting that the reader of the paper is sure the murderers (- Nazi perpetrators of genocide -) did not know what they were doing, or subjunctive '*hätten*', suggesting the reader thinks they did. (6.33) leaves out the main verb, thus making the reader of the poem work out whether the perpetrators were ignorant, or just said they were, and whether the reader of the paper thinks they were ignorant or knowing. Von Törne's poetry, one could argue, was clear in its aim: it meant its readers to be witnesses rather than bystanders, to speak out and act against injustice. Yet unlike some 'committed' poetry (- see Richardson 1983:7–11 for discussion -) its cognitive effects are extremely subtle and profound, and only a very careful examination of how they are achieved is likely to enable the translation to similarly at least have a chance of affecting behaviour.

A fifth possible response to literature, according to Attridge (2004:93), is to translate. Attridge echoes Benjamin (2004:76) in regarding translation as a response called forth by the text itself, rather than independent of it; translation (whether interlingual or intersemiotic) is on a par with the creation of meanings from a text. We could argue that many examples given in Chapter 1 show that this will always be true of good translations. Morrison's *The Cracked Pot* (1996), a translation from German of a Kleist play, was staged in 1995 by Northern Broadsides; Seberberg's translations of Henning Mankell have recently formed the basis for films on English television, and so on. Unsuccessful translations could be expected to end the process of translation: in the sense of Benjamin's phrase 'the afterlife of the text' (Benjamin 2004:76), that life comes to an end if the translation does not work as a literary text.

It is possible to discover many more such effects; the ones I have suggested above fall into five types: immediate feelings the reader experiences and attributes to a character in the text, mental effects that arise from the search for meaning; changes to knowledge; changes to behaviour; and, finally, the textual action of translation.

Preserving these five types of effect would guarantee an instrumental translation – one which was capable of being read as a literary text – but would not necessarily guarantee it was accepted in its documentary aspect. To do this, it must conform to the Proxy Principle. It must be seen as the work of Ausländer or Strubel or von Törne. That is, it must be possible to refer to the translation of Ausländer's poems (Boase-Beier and Vivis 1995) as 'Ausländer'. One of the ways translators make their translations viable as proxies is to find approximations for personal idiosyncracies of the original writer's style, as we saw in Hamburger's translation of Celan in example (4.6).

Another way the translator might echo the original poet is by having the same line-layout as the original poems (as for example Hamburger does) or having a picture of the original poet on the cover, as does Sarah Lawson's book of translations of Jacques Prévert (Lawson 2002).

The reader of the translated text will, as we have seen, always reconstruct an author for the text being read, and features such as the target language, the translator's name, and particular elements of the translator's voice (as mentioned in Chapter 4), will enable the reader to reconstruct the translator.

Although I have said that a translated text is a blend – in the case of Celan, it is a blend of an original German poem and an imaginary untranslated English poem – there is no reason to suppose that the reconstructed writer is a blend. It is not likely that the reader of Celan's poetry in English will attribute it to a Hamburger-Celan figure, or the reader of Lawson's Prévert will assume as the author a Lawson-Prévert blend. But for a translation to be accepted as a translation, it is essential that the reader is aware that it is one. Otherwise, one could argue, it has merely succeeded as a proxy, but not as a translation.

6.4 Cognitive context and the reader of the translation

In Chapter 3, I argued that the way a reader approaches the translated text is to an important extent a question of context. In cognitive linguistics and poetics, context is seen not as a fixed entity but as something that is constructed during the interpretation of utterances and texts (see e.g. Gavins 2007:35–44). Writers such as Blakemore (1987, 2002) or Sperber and Wilson (1995), and others who use the framework of Relevance Theory, see the construction of context as aiming to 'match that envisaged by the speaker' (Blakemore 1987:28). But as we have seen, a literary writer might in many cases envisage a context with no fixed form and an interpretation with no fixed end-point. As Attridge points out, the formal and the contextual always interact (2004:114) because context is always inherent in form. Such context might be the collective knowledge of the history of a word or its connotations, or the effect that rhyme has, and so on. From a cognitive point of view, collective elements of context form part of the cognitive context of the reader, as do cultural elements and individual experiences (cf. Semino 2002:97; Stockwell 2002:31–32).

For the translator, the translated text needs to take into account the cognitive context of the readers, both in terms of what shared elements this context is likely to contain before reading and in terms of the changes to context that reading will produce (see Cook 1994:23).

In cognitive stylistics, the reading of all texts is seen to involve the construction of text-worlds, using elements in the text in conjunction with the reader's own changing cognitive representation of that world (cf. Stockwell 2002: 137–143; Trotter 1992:13) to build up successively complex representations. It is in part the construction and reconstruction of such mental contexts that gives rise to poetic effects. Literary texts typically require and allow for mental representations that are extremely complex as well as open-ended. The various aspects of cognitive effect we have been looking at – feeling and speculating about feelings, searching for meaning, changing our views or behaviour – all involve changes to our cognitive context. This is true of any literary text, translated or not. Every writer, in order to achieve or make possible such changes to the cognitive context of his or her readers needs to construct an image of it and in doing so is constructing an image of the mind of the imagined reader, sometimes called the implied reader (Iser 1979:34). This process of envisaging a reader and constructing the text so that the reader can engage with it is sometimes referred to as 'positioning' (Montgomery et all 2000:271ff.) or 'manipulation' of the reader (Boase-Beier 2006:38–39). The positioning by the translator of the readers of the target text will carry over some elements of the positioning judged to exist in the source text, but will also have new elements. Consider the following examples:

(6.34) Wenn der Krieg beendet ist
　　　 if/when the war　　ended　is

　　　 . . . .　 . . . .

　　　 gehn wir wieder spazieren
　　　 go　 we　 again　 walking

(Ausländer 1977:266)

(6.35) When the war is over

　　　 . . . . . .

　　　 we'll walk once more

Both original and translation place the reader, like the speaker, in a time of war. The source text suggests uncertainty; it says that, if and when the war ever ends, the speaker and addressee might again go walking. The German phrasing could be taken as a question. We cannot tell, because the inversion of '*wir gehen*' in (6.34) both follows '*wenn*' and signals a question. The narrator in the translation says to the reader that the war *will* end, and that speaker and reader *will* go walking again. This is quite a striking example of the way the reader is placed in a different position (of reassurance rather than uncertainty) and may have to do with the translator's (unconscious?) desire to avoid the uncertainty of war or of the future in general (see Boase-Beier 2010b for a discussion of this poem). The implied reader in (6.35) seems less like someone with whom doubts are shared and more like someone in a possibly subservient position to the speaker, who needs to be reassured.

A literary text can be seen as conveying an act of literary communication. The author envisages a reader, to whom something is communicated, and the reader envisages a writer (who may be a character in a poem or novel) who does the communicating, on the basis of the universal cognitive metaphorical process that suggests EVENTS ARE ACTIONS. In every act of literary communication the context of the author and that of the reader will inevitably be different, because cognitive context includes the actual discourse world – the world surrounding the act of reading – and it will almost certainly not be the case that the writer and reader of a literary text are in the same place, time, or circumstances. In the case of translated texts, the writer of the original and the reader of its translation almost always have greater cultural and linguistic difference from one another than writer and reader of a non-translated text. But cognitive context includes, besides a mental representation of the actual discourse situation, different mental representations of the world described in the text: the text-world (cf. Werth 1999; Gavins 2007). These representations always differ from author to reader and among readers, because they are constructed in interaction with existing knowledge, and everyone's knowledge and experience is different. In a translation, not only does discourse situation differ greatly between source author and target reader, but so will the existing knowledge and representation of experience. Consider the following example:

(6.36) Die Öde wird Geschichte.
       the wasteland becomes history

                         (Huchel, in Hamburger 2004:82)

This can be translated in various ways:

(6.37) The barren land will be history.

(6.38) The desert now will be history.

(6.39) The wasteland is becoming history.

The translation in (6.37) might cause the reader to envisage farmland, which at some point will grow crops again, and is informed by a knowledge of Huchel's other poetry, often about the rural landscape in which he lived. (6.39), which is Michael Hamburger's translation of this line (Hamburger 2004:83), suggests a contrast between the present and the future, and is built partly on a knowledge of Huchel's philosophy of hope (see Hamburger's Introduction to this book, 2004:11–17). It is also the translation which departs furthest from the specificity of Huchel's own German landscape (where there are no deserts) to use a more universal image of barrenness, which would fit any landscape. And (6.39) takes another possible meaning of the German verb-form '*wird*' (which can be present or future) to suggest that change is already happening. It also suggests a landscape made barren by war or industry.

Not only is the translator's reconstructed cognitive context different in each of these three translations, but the text-world the reader builds up will be different. Even if 'desert' (in 6.38) is read as a metaphor, the mental image the reader has is likely to include sand, and be very different from that the other two give rise to. A literary translator needs to have some sense of the common elements in the audience's context (some image of uncultivated land), even while being aware that there is, and must be, individual variation. In fact it is exactly the interaction of individual contexts with a text that gives the text its literary effect of multiple meanings: in the case of (6.36) the universal desert and the particular uncultivated land one knows, the possibility of hope and the likeliness of its present or future realization, and so on.

This multiplicity of meaning and the possibility of individual changes to individual cognitive contexts will be greater in the case of literary texts than non-literary texts. Thus there is a danger that supplying too much information to the target audience, in the form of footnotes and the like, will lessen the literary effect. Consider the following possible footnotes to go with the line '*Die Öde wird Geschichte*' in (6.36):

> (6.40) Huchel lived in Wilhelmshorst, a rural village near Berlin at the time the poem was written.
>
> (6.41) Huchel had been publicly disgraced and sacked from his position as editor of an important literary journal at the time he wrote this poem.

The footnote in (6.40) positions the reader to see the '*Öde*' in the poem as representing actual barren land, perhaps local farmland (see 'Introduction' to Hamburger 2004), whereas (6.41) manipulates the reader to see '*Öde*' as a representation of a barren time. Either of them, just like the gloss in (6.36), not, of course, meant to be a literary text, and which uses one particular translation of '*Öde*' and one particular tense of the verb '*werden*', to become, closes off other possible meanings and lessens literary effect.

If it is the building of cognitive contexts by the reader that allows poetic effects, and therefore the possibility of such context-construction that makes a text literary, then a translation of a literary text will only be instrumental – that is, will only be itself a literary text – to the extent that it does not inhibit context-construction.

Translating the Special Shape of Poems

Chapter Outline

7.1 Shape as interaction and constraint

One of the issues that has recurred throughout this book is the notion of literary reading – a reading which is open-ended and involves the reader in changing his or her cognitive context in significant ways – and what it is in the text that signals and drives this type of reading. Every act of translation starts from a particular work and thus the sort of questions that need to be asked relate not only to the general nature of what is literary, and how literary texts work, but also to how the style of the author in question works.

In this second part of this book I am going to concentrate particularly upon poems and their translation. This is not because other literary texts are not poetic. The definition of poetry attributed to Frost as 'what gets lost in translation', and sometimes used to show that 'not every poem comes across equally well in another language' (Hartley Williams and Sweeney 2003:152) is rendered by Burnshaw (1960:xi) as 'that which gets lost from verse and prose in translation'. But poetry provides a particularly focused way of discussing what is poetic in texts (cf. Attridge 2004:71–72), because its lineation and rhythm create a sense of 'real-time unfolding' (ibid.), and because it is more concentrated. But the notion that it is not in essence different from prose is inherent in the use of the term 'poetics' in this book.

Jakobson (2008:141) said in his 1960 paper 'Linguistics and Poetics', that poetics set out to answer the question 'What makes a verbal message a work of art?' This is also the sense in which it is used by Stockwell; he calls it 'the craft of literature' (2002:1). Poetics is the study of the literariness of literature and a poetics of translation is the study of how the literariness of literature is translated. Because, as Chapter 6 suggested, literature is just an especially good example of how the mind works, a poetics of translation is also a study of translation which particularly takes account of the way our minds work, thus trying to explain that essential aspect of the study of translation embodied in both Pope's notion that we must capture the 'spirit' of the original author (see Lefevere 1992:64f.) and Constantine's view that translation is about the preservation of effect (2005:xxxix).

So what is it about poems that makes them a particularly good way of talking about literature, and that makes examining the translation of poems a particularly good way of looking at literary translation?

Most importantly, perhaps, poems have an obvious shape. Though it is often less obvious, all literary texts have shape: novels are divided into chapters or paragraphs, plays have dialogue interspersed with stage directions, and so on. Most have a finite length, so that the beginning and ending is clear. Some works signal the beginning with expressions such as 'Once upon a time', as does Joyce's *A Portrait of the Artist as a Young Man* (2000:5), and the end with 'The End', for example Grimmelshausen's *The Adventurous Simplicissimus*, which, in Goodrick's translation ends thus' 'God grant us all His grace that we may all alike obtain from Him what doth concern us most, namely a happy END' (Goodrick 1962:356). Other novels subvert these notions of the shape of a novel by beginning or ending mid-sentence, e.g. David Madsen's *A Box of Dreams*, which starts thus: '. . . when, suddenly, just as I was lifting a forkful of *filet de bœuf poêlé villette* to my mouth, the lights went out' (Madsen 2003:7). Subverting a norm in this way is only possible because such a norm exists, and gives rise to expectations in readers.

Poems, too, have conventional types of shape. One of the definitions of poetry that Furniss and Bath (2007:3) give (the other two are to do with its language and its difference from drama and narrative prose fiction) is that 'it is arranged differently on the page'. Furniss and Bath point out that the conventions of poetic shape change over time, but are also unstable at any given time. They suggest that we could question whether there is such a clearly definable category at all (2007:4). One obvious defining characteristic of poetry is that it is written in lines, a fact which has consequences for the way a poem is read; the lines interact with other structural patterns in the poem, in particular the metre and the syntax (Furniss and Bath 2007:14; 33–64), leading to Attridge's sense of 'real time unfolding' (2004:71). Because the division into lines encourages the reader to read quickly, while the concentration of stylistic features holds reading up (see Kuiken 2008:55, van Peer 2007:100); a conflict arises which, it could be argued, echoes the real-time experience of emotion, rather than just telling the reader a story about it. It is also a conflict typical of how literary texts work; there is a contradiction between different 'conclusions about the literary form of a text' (Fabb 2002:215), for example between syntax and lineation, as happens in enjambement, and this gives rise to a sense of the aesthetic.

If, then, we accept that it is 'the subtle interplay between poetic language and the poetic line' (Furniss and Bath 2007:64) that makes poetry distinctive, and we understand poetic language as being language in which the style is especially important (as described in Chapter 1 and Chapter 4) as a set of weak implicatures that demand reader involvement, then it seems reasonable to describe poetry as a type of literature with the added dimension of fore-grounded shape.

In Chapter 1 we saw that what we often consider to be characteristics of literary texts are in fact elements present in all language, but used in literature especially to engage the reader. Thus, in a literary text, metaphors, which characterize all our thinking, are often unusual or demand particular effort on the reader's part. Ambiguity will be used in a creative and complex way, that goes beyond merely the use of homophony or polysemy, and often leaves complex and very different interpretations open to the reader. Iconicity, a common characteristic of language, that exists whenever form is not in an arbitrary relationship with meaning, will be exploited to give poetry its characteristic feel of 'doing what it says' (see Ross 1982). All these elements of language are used in highly complex ways in poetry, which is what has led many poets and critics to regard poetic language as what Hopkins called 'the current language heightened' (Abbott 1955:89), or as 'literature in its most concentrated and (arguably) quintessential form' (Leech 2008:6).

What I want to consider in this chapter are some of the ways these various characteristics of literary language interact with the shape of poems – its arrangement in lines – to give the particular effects that poetry translation hopes to preserve. One way of characterizing poetry is to say that what is 'heightened' is the interaction of freedom and constraint which exists in language and communication in general. Chapter 3 suggests this interaction is at the heart of translation itself and this is the argument put forward in the 'Introduction' to *Practices of Literary Translation* (Boase-Beier and Holman 1999).

In poetry, where metaphor, or ambiguity, or the rhythms of speech serve to provide freedom of interpretation by involving readers in examining and reconfiguring their cognitive contexts, the repetition of semantic, syntactic and phonological elements creates strong patterns in the text, an especially important aspect of poetry (cf. Strachan and Terry 2000:10). This repetition (Kiparsky 1973:233), also discussed as cohesion (Leech 2008:29) or parallelism (Short 1996:14), serves to constrain the reader's interpretation and, through reiteration, to position the reader. This happens in non-literary texts, too. Consider the following example:

> (7.1) The City Council plans to put ugly phone masts at the end of our street. These masts are huge and ugly and will spoil the view. Protest against these ugly masts!

This text, taken from the local newsletter of a political party, by reiterating to the reader that the masts are aesthetically unacceptable suggests that they probably are in other ways, too. This is an interesting response to the legal situation in which local communities cannot protest against phone masts on grounds of health, but only on grounds of appearance (see www.mastaction. co.uk). Such texts pose few problems for translators because their effects, though interesting, are obvious.

In poetry, repetition can take many forms; besides the types of rhyme, common in prose such as alliteration and assonance, full rhyme is common in poetry, because the position in the line draws attention to it, whether it is end-rhyme or internal rhyme; the following example from a traditional ballad 'The Wraggle Taggle Gipsies' has both:

> (7.2) They sang so sweet, they sang so shrill,
>   That fast her tears began to flow.
>   And she laid down her silken gown,
>   Her golden rings, and all her show.

Repeated lexis or repeated syntactic structures, as in the following, are also common:

(7.3) Who is at my window? Who? Who?
       Go from my window! Go! Go!
                             (Anon)

Repetition can be a signal of a particular convention, such as a rhymed couplet at the end of a sonnet, or it can convey attitude. Consider the following:

(7.4) This is the last; the very, very last!
                         (Hardy 1977:81)

The repetition in this line can be taken to emphasize the fact that nothing more is to be said or done, and is similar in cognitive effect to that in the non-literary example (7.1).

In (7.2) and (7.3), as well as in examples such as the conventional rhyme scheme of sonnets or limericks, it is clear that the lineation of the poem underlines other characteristics of poetic language such as sound repetition ('down – gown' and 'flow – show' in (7.2)), or semantic or structural repetition as in (7.3). Besides such interactions, the shape of a poem can have meaning in its own right. George Herbert's famous 'Easter Wings' (Herbert 2007:147) is in the shape of wings, and Apollinaire's '*Il Pleut*' (2003:62) is written in the shape of falling rain. In both these cases, the layout of lines is iconic in what appears a very straightforward way; such poems are often referred to as 'pattern poems' (Westerweel 1984) or as 'figure poems' (Furniss and Bath 2007:86). These aspects of pattern poems, as well as the fairly straightforward effects in (7.2), (7.3) and (7.4), are not difficult to reproduce in another language. However, the real interest (and difficulty for the translator) in poetic shape lies in the way it interacts with other aspects of poetry.

Although it might intuitively seem that metaphor has nothing to do with position, the shape of a poem does constrain it. Consider the following example, discussed by Furniss and Bath (2007:157–8):

(7.5) *A nun takes the veil*
       And I have asked to be
       Where the green swell is in the havens dumb

The line is taken from G.M. Hopkins' early poem 'Heaven – Haven' (Hopkins 1963:5) and the italicized title in (7.5) is in fact the subtitle. Furniss and Bath point out how the similarity of sound between *heaven* and *haven* in the title strengthen the metaphor: heaven is seen as 'a haven from the storms of life' (Furniss and Bath 2007:158). The subtitle repeats this sequence: a nun takes the veil. The sequence is kept in the line in (7.5): the speaker has asked to go where the waves become muted. Elsewhere in the poem the same sequence occurs again. Thus 'I' in (7.5) is seen as the nun, verb-phrases such as 'asked to be' (or 'desired to go' earlier in the poem) are linked with 'takes' and 'havens dumb' linked with 'the veil'. In this way taking the veil is not just a conventional action but is read as a metaphor for finding haven. The potential freedom to assign other meanings to the lines in (7.5) is still there, but the parallelism of sequence between subtitle and other structures in the poem suggests a particular understanding of the 'Heaven – Haven' metaphor of the title.

In particular, the shape of a poem changes rhythm, which is present in all texts, into metre, or a particular 'pre-arranged template of beats and offbeats that are realized by a fixed number of stressed syllables and (sometimes), unstressed syllables per line' (Furniss and Bath 2007:583). The notion that such metre can be seen as 'pre-arranged' can be interpreted in two ways: either it is a constraint imposed by certain types of poetry upon the 'basic rhythms at the heart of all metrical poetry' (Carper and Attridge 2003:1) or it is itself a basic mechanism which is generated and understood by a 'specialized kind of "metrical cognition"' (Fabb 2002:13) that explains its invariant aspects. The difference between these two views of the rhythm-metre relationship will not concern us here. In any case, whether metre is seen as imposed by poetic constraint or whether it is seen as something more basic are not incompatible views, especially if we remember Turner's statement that 'the everyday mind is essentially literary' (1996:7).

It seems, then, that one thing the shape of a poem does is to create aesthetic tension with the freedoms that other aspects of literary texts such as metaphor or rhythm allow. Another thing it does is to convey its own meaning, as in pattern poems. And yet another thing it does is to cause effects of foregrounding. In the next section I will examine the latter in more detail, as a way of exploring what it means to translate poetic shape.

7.2 Shape, foregrounding and translation

Foregrounding has been mentioned many times in the earlier chapters of this book, as a characteristic of literary texts which has both a textual and a cognitive aspect. In its textual aspect, it was defined by Prague Circle structuralist Mukařovský (in Garvin's 1964 translation) as 'deautomatization' (1964:19) of linguistic elements of the text, not in order to convey content but to 'place in the foreground the act of expression . . . itself'. It was linked to deviation in the text (Leech 2008:15): what deviates from the expected can be determined linguistically, at least to some extent (van Peer 2007:101), and it signals both the author's choice and the effects on the reader. Poetry was seen as the 'maximum of foregrounding' (Garvin 1964:19). Mukařovský, who spoke of 'aktualisace', translated by Gavins as 'foregrounding' (1964:19), in poetic texts, and Havránek, who spoke of the same features in non-poetic texts (1964:9), were concerned especially with the textual aspect of foregrounding. But it was always described as also 'functional' (1964:19), because its effect on the reader – 'to attract the reader's (listener's) attention' (ibid.) was the reason for its use. And the Russian Formalist critic Shklovsky had in 1917 spoken of its function in creating a 'special perception' of objects (1965:18). At the time Shklovsky was writing, and even when Mukařovský and Havránek were originally writing, in 1932, the effects on the reader could not be explored beyond the notion of 'attention', which was a phenomenon understood by psychologists (see e.g. Wimms 1915:26–39), but was rarely the focus of literary or linguistic scholars. By the time Leech was writing about foregrounding in 1985 (reprinted in Leech 2008), he was describing it as 'an effect brought about in the reader by linguistic or other forms of deviation' (2008:61). Since the 1980s, much further work has been done to provide empirical evidence for the poetic effects on the reader of foregrounding (see van Peer 2007:99–104), Short, in 1996, refers to deviation as a linguistic phenomenon and foregrounding as its psychological effect (1996:11).

These effects go far beyond just having one's attention drawn to something in the text. Miall and Kuiken (1994b), for example, go back to the Russian Formalists and Prague Circle Linguists and pick up their notion of 'making strange' (Shklovsky's word was *ostraneniye*; see Shklovsky 1965:4), to discuss how it 'overcomes the barriers of customary perception' to 'evoke feelings'. In this sense it 'requires cognitive work' of the reader. This 'obliges the reader to slow down', so that the feelings can develop (1994:392). As I noted above, the slowing effect of foregrounding in a poem is one of the sources of tension in the reading of a poem, because it contradicts the apparent speed the shortness of poetic lines suggests. Miall (2007) describes the poetic effect of experiencing the sublime when reading literature as an effect of foregrounding, and Martindale (2007) suggests that the need to constantly create new foregrounding effects is what causes literature, and especially poetry, to develop and change.

For these reasons, foregrounding and deviation are often seen to be the 'keys to the stylistic explication of literature' (Leech 2008:181). What I have been arguing throughout this book is that the stylistic explication of literature must always be at the centre of what the translator does, and for that reason must be an important concern of translation studies scholars. I want, then, to consider the notion of 'shape' in its relation to foregrounding, as a way of examining poetic effect and its translation. The shape of a poem is not the same as the form of a poem. The latter term is often used to contrast with content, as it is by Furniss and Bath (2007) and could be said to be 'the shaping of the poem's contents in order to generate specific effects' (Furniss and Bath 2007:71). Form thus seems a wider term than shape: form means the way something is said as opposed to what is said, though it is a common view in literary theory (and in stylistic theory) that form and content cannot be separated (Furniss and Bath 2007:74). But form might include such things as the placing of adverbs at the start of sentences, the use of subjunctives, participles, or ambiguous syntax, or the variant and invariant aspects of metre (Fabb 2002:1–33). One way of separating form from style is to say that form is made up of the linguistic means used to say something, and style is the form plus its cognitive effects. Shape, however, is something at once more restricted, sometimes also more subtle than form, and is perceived by visual or auditory means. Examples of shape in a text might be:

   (i) the repeated word 'window' in example (7.3) above
   (ii) the number of chapters in a novel
   (iii) the look of an advert about storage systems that fits text into a box
   (iv) the lineation of a poem
   (v) the repetition of sound that creates end-rhyme in a poem, as in (7.2)

and so on. Later in this chapter, I will consider something known as 'the eye of the poem' (see Boase-Beier 2009:1–15), a spatially, semantically or stylistically central point in the poem, and its importance for translation.

If we consider the instances given above, we can see that, as suggested in the previous section, repetition often plays a role in creating a sense of shape: in (i) (iv), and (v), for example. Other instances of shape such as those in (ii) and (iii) are not so obviously concerned with repetition, but may interact with repetition. In all such examples, the shape of the text is foregrounded. This is particularly the case, as mentioned above, in pattern poems. Herbert's 'Easter Wings', echoing a Classical tradition of 'wing poems' (Westerweel 1984:73–76), is a poem with decreasing and then increasing line lengths in each of its two stanzas, so that its shape suggests (possibly two pairs of) wings when the page is turned round. No translator is likely to translate this poem without considering – and most probably preserving – the shape of the text. Yet such poems have aspects of shape the translator must consider that go beyond the obvious. For example, why are Herbert's wings lying on their side? It could be because a poem in which each stanza has decreasing and increasing line lengths, thus:

```
(7.6)  xxxxxx
         xxxx
           x
           x
         xxxx
        xxxxx
```

is able to suggest depletion and renewal, one of the poem's themes, more clearly when written in this 'hourglass' (Strachan and Terry 2000:29) form than if it were turned round to suggest wings more clearly. The poem's content, which has 'Most poore' in the centre of the first stanza and 'Most thinne' in the second, appears to underline this. Wilcox (2007:145) suggests a further reading is possible in the (7.6) format: the poem can be seen as representing a cross. And Strachan and Terry (2000:28) point out that almost every line ends in 'e', suggesting a (somewhat tenuous, in my view) link to Easter. They also stress the uncertainty of Herbert's original intention as to the shape of the poem (2000:29). What they do not suggest, but what I would think, were I translating the poem, is that a possible implicature of the sideways wings is that the holy can not be portrayed or received directly, but instead needs the intervention of its human reader, represented by the act of turning round of the page to get a pair of wings.

A translator of this poem is thus faced with many problems. For example, does Herbert's original intention matter? If research suggests that he actually meant it to be printed on its side, should the translator ensure the translation is printed thus (as indeed the German edition – see Leimberg 2002:78–82 – does)? Does the 'e' at the end of each line matter? Most translations (e.g. Leimberg into German; Najmias into Spanish: www.saltana.org/i/docus/0432. html) keep the shape of the poem, but do not keep the 'e'. Does the translator's reconstruction of Herbert's intention to require human intervention to create wings have any role to play? Every translator will have different answers to these questions; no translator can ignore them.

In most cases, the shape of a poem does not actually represent an object, or quality, as in pattern poems. But shape can be iconic in other ways, and is thus foregrounded. Consider the following stanza from a poem by Anise Koltz and its translation:

> (7.7) Le soleil tend des filets
> the sun   sets the nets
>
> aux   oiseaux
> for-the birds
>
> et les   dévore au soir
> and them   eats   in-the evening
>
> crachant   leurs ombres
> spitting-out their shadows

> (7.8) The sun sets a trap
> for the birds
> and devours them in the evening
> spitting out their shadows
> (Glasheen 2009:134–135)

The stanza starts with the sun and ends with the shadows. Because the sun is the subject of both '*tendre*' (to cast, e.g. a net) and '*crâcher*' (to spit), the stanza gives a strong sense of the sun actually casting the shadows, an interpretation underlined by the position of the verb '*tendre*' and the object '*ombres*'. There is also the sense of temporal unfolding that Attridge mentioned (2004:71) in this sequence. The translation keeps the position of all the elements of the original almost exactly, so that both the agency of the sun and the temporal sequence are similarly echoed.

The syntax of a poem itself can also serve to attract the reader's attention. Consider the first line of a poem by Ingeborg Bachmann:

(7.9) Aus der leichenwarmen Vorhalle   des Himmels tritt die Sonne
         out- of the corpse-warm antechamber of-the heavens steps the sun
                                                                        (Boland 2004:94)

I have discussed the syntax of this poem in more detail in an article (Boase-Beier 2010a), but here I am using this line to illustrate the importance of word-order and syntax. Because the sentence begins with a long prepositional phrase ('*aus der leichenwarmen Vorhalle des Himmels*'), the subject '*die Sonne*' is not mentioned until the end of the sentence. We do not know immediately that it is the sun that steps out of the antechamber. This postponing of the subject is made possible in German, as in English, by the freedom to put the subject after the verb when this is preceded by a prepositional phrase. This structure, though much less likely in English, is still possible and is sometimes used for dramatic effect, as in the following expressions:

(7.10) Out of the strong came forth sweetness

(7.11) Under the mountain lived a troll

But it is by no means the only possible way of expressing this content in German. As in English, the subject might come first:

(7.12) Die Sonne tritt aus   der leichenwarmen Vorhalle   des Himmels
          the sun steps out- of the corpse-warm antechamber of-the heavens

A translator could see the particular word-order in (7.9) as a result of Bachmann's conscious choice, or simply as the style of the text, whether Bachmann consciously intended it or merely unconsciously wrote it. One of the reasons stylistics developed in the 1960s as the application to literary texts of linguistic description was to say what was actually in the text, not because the author's intention was necessarily unimportant or did not exist, but because what can be observed in the text is there, as 'the facts of language' (Fowler 1975:91), whether the author intended it or not, and its effects on the reader might be independent of the author's intention. In translation, where it seems counter-intuitive to ignore the author's intention, pragmatically orientated theorists such as Gutt (2000), have said we aim to find out with reasonable certainty what it is, so that we might either go along with it or change it in the translation. In my 2006 book I argue that the reconstruction of author's intention by the translator is a 'pretence' (2006:108), but a necessary one based on clues in the text to possible implicatures. It is for this reason that I suggested above that a translator might wish to know about the questions surrounding Herbert's (possible) intentions for 'Easter Wings'.

The difference between the two following translations of the line in (7.9) is quite significant:

> (7.13) Out steps the sun
> out of the corpse-warmed entrance hall to the sky
> (Boland 2004: 95)

> (7.14) Out of the corpse-warm antechamber of the heavens steps the sun
> (Boase-Beier 2010a:34)

The first translation, by the poet Eavan Boland, has the advantage of a slightly more natural word-order, placing the verb at the beginning, as is quite common in expressions that suggest movement and use verbs with directional particles, such as 'Up goes the balloon', 'Down falls the rain' or 'In comes a clown'. It does have a slight oddity, though, in the expression 'entrance hall to the sky'. 'Entrance to the sky' would not be a problem, but words that are typically followed by a qualifier in a prepositional phrase do not work well as the first elements of nominal compounds; thus 'roadway to the isles' is strange and 'buyer-behaviour of gold' (behaviour of a buyer of gold) is impossible. The second translation (which was discussed briefly as (1.17) earlier) echoes more closely the deferring of the subject to the end. This deferring, in (7.4) and in the original (7.9), allows the reader to imagine, depending on their cognitive schemata, that something else – perhaps a corpse or a killer – steps out. In other words, it creates suspense. But it also places emphasis on 'the sun', and this is important because the poem is about resurrection, and alludes to the Christian symbolism of the sun, and its rising in the East (cf. Rahner 1983:125).

The particular shape of the line, as seen in (7.9), is not just a feature of poetry, as discussion at the start of this chapter will have suggested. Novels and stories of all types, adverts and many other texts, all use delay of this type to focus attention on the subject or object of a sentence, for example:

> (7.15) In your next issue: budget weddings.

(7.16) All he could see when he looked through the darkened windows was a tiny
light.

But there is an added dimension to (7.9) because it is a line of poetry. The syntactic structure and the sentence end where the line ends (this is known as end-stopping in poetry), on '*Sonne*', creating a pause before the next line. The next two lines of the poem are much shorter, thus placing even more emphasis on the final phrase '*tritt die Sonne*' or 'steps the sun' in (7.9), because it stands alone on the page at this point, with only space below it. The line could also be seen to represent iconically the movement of stepping, which is in fact the only action in the poem. The translation in (7.13), by making of this line two lines, reduces the visual impact of the long line. The use of lines is something we generally associate with poetry, but advertisements are often written in lines, too, as the following advertisement for Bathmate (an inflatable seat for the bath) illustrates:

(7.17) It's the bubble
that gets you
out of trouble.

In this example, the lines are used much as in poetry. And even advertisements for jobs, though they do not foreground individual words or concepts in the same way, are never written in long lines that take up a whole page. Visual impact is greater (and processing of information easier) when short lines are used. This is seen, too, in newspaper columns. The use of short lines in such cases suggests that the lines in poetry have a number of effects. They allow highly complex information to be taken in while reading. They are used for visual impact in their own right, as they are most obviously in a pattern poem, but also as they are in leaving 'the sun' isolated above an empty space in (7.9) and (7.14). And they allow other stylistic devices, such as repetition, to be used more obviously. In Bachmann's poem, from which the first line is quoted in (7.9), the pattern of a long first line followed by two shorter ones is repeated in the second stanza. Each stanza consists of three lines, and the third lines of the two stanzas are as follows:

(7.18) Stanza 1:
sondern die Gefallenen, vernehmen wir
but   the   fallen   observe   we
('but, we observe, the fallen')

Stanza 2:
aus dem   es keine Auferstehung gibt
from which it   no   resurrection gives
('from which there is no resurrection')

(Boland 2004:94)

The contrast between 'the fallen' and 'no resurrection' is made more notice-able by the fact that these two noun phrases occur in the third line of each stanza. In these and many other examples in this short poem, it seems, then, that the shape created by the lines along with the consequent aspect of posi-tion is crucial in carrying meaning.

It is often considered that such elements as syntax, rhyme, metre and allit-eration are formal elements while metaphor and metonymy are of a different order because they are figurative. Thus Furniss and Bath, for example, separate their discussion of the elements of poetry in *Reading Poetry* (2007) into Part One, which deals with these elments of form, and Part Two, in which figurative language, metaphor, voices and so on are discussed. What I suggested in the previous section, though, is that the shape of poems is important even for the understanding of metaphor, as example (7.5) above showed. Consider also the following lines:

(7.19) Beten will ich auf dem heißen Stein
       pray want I on the   hot stone

       und die Sterne zählen die   im   Blut
       and the   stars count which in-the blood

       mir schwimmen
       in-me   swim

These three lines, the first lines of a poem by Thomas Bernhard (Reidel 2006:36), contain adaptations of at least two German idioms. The first is '*(nur) ein Tropfen auf den heißen Stein*', meaning completely insufficient, literally '(just) a drop onto a hot stone'. The second is '*Sterne sehen*', 'to see stars'. In line 1, the inversion of the usual word-order '*ich will beten*', places the emphasis on '*beten*', to pray. Line 2 omits the finite verb and the subject which means that the reader automatically reads gapped verb-phrase '*will ich*' as being in the same position: '*und die Sterne zählen will ich*', according to the recovery principles of 'gapped' elements (see Greenbaum 1996:313). Thus to pray and to count stars are unexpected, foregrounded, emphasized elements. This fact has the effect of turning the idioms from the dead metaphors that idioms always are to active metaphors whose meaning is yet to be worked out by the reader. Now, one could argue that to write the three lines in (7.19) out as prose would still front both finite verb-phrases, thus creating the same emphasis and the same reviving of dead metaphors with all that this entails, and that is true, though the fronting would be less obvious if there were no lines. But, crucially, the passage in (7.19) also has the effect of spatially fronting '*mir*', 'in me', which the syntax of this sentence does not do. In fact, were (7.19) written as prose, '*mir*' would usually come before '*im Blut*'. When I said above that lineation in a poem works at cross-purposes to the usual rhythm of reading and thus rhythm and metre are in conflict, as the latter depends on the line, this was a fairly common observation (cf. Furniss and Bath 2007:583). And it is also a commonplace of poetry criticism to note a similar tension between syntax and line-endings, wherever the end of a line does not correspond to the end of the syntactic structure, as it does in (7.9); this is what causes syntactic run-on or enjambement (cf. Furniss and Bath 2007:574–5). But the point I am making about (7.19) is that the line-breaks emphasize the unusual syntax and its repetition, emphasize the turning of dead to live metaphor, and also, in line 3 of the example, create a further tension, first by spatially fronting 'in me', although syntactically it is postposed, and secondly by spatially fronting the 'in me' in contrast to the postposing of the 'I want' and the corresponding gapped 'I'-phrase in lines 1 and 2. A focus on the self is in conflict with a losing of the self. A losing of the self is further suggested by the idiom 'just a drop in the ocean' and the violence of self-loss in 'to see stars'. In fact, line 6 of this poem reads '*Ich will vergessen sein*' = 'I want to be forgotten' (Reidel 2006:36–37). Yet a foregrounding of self is suggested by Bernhard's writing of a vast number of poems in the first person, and his themes of guilt, ambivalence, one's place in history, and the nature of faith.

While a literary critic will make observations of the latter type, and a linguist those of the former – about the effects of gapping, for example – a translator must do both, because the effects of the style in Bernhard's poem are not interesting merely as effects, but also in terms of their linguistic cause. A translation might begin, as Reidel's does in the bilingual book from which (7.19) is taken, with 'I want to pray' but, taking the above linguistic and literary considerations into account, an alternative would be to front the verbs thus:

(7.20) To pray in drops upon the ocean
      and to count stars . . . .

What the above discussion shows is that shape is not merely a poetic characteristic that creates tension and carries meaning, but that it also leads to foregrounding effects which a translation, if its aim or *skopos* is to demonstrate allegiance to text, author, subject and reader, must take account of.

7.3 Shape and expectation

We have noted several times that repetition, which we saw to play a role not only in examples such as (7.19), but also in (7.3), (7.4), and many others, has been seen as one of the main characteristics of poetry (Kiparsky 1973; Strachan and Terry 2000:114) and one of the main devices for achieving foregrounding in texts in general. Leech calls repetition 'the sequential exploitation of sameness' (2008:148) and describes it as a feature 'which calls attention to itself'. Leech is examining, in this context, Virginia Woolf's story 'The Mark on the Wall' (1917), and he gives several instances of repetition, such as wh-questions (e.g. Where was I?) and the repetition of particular lexical items, e.g. 'mark'. Repetition clearly plays an important role in both prose and poetry as well as in non-literary texts, and is usually something a translator notices (see e.g. Zhu 2004). Translators typically keep notes or set up a database, but keeping repetition is not purely mechanical; it involves very subtle decisions. In examples (6.29), (6.30) and (6.31), we saw that the later translation (repeated here as (7.22)) made subtle alterations to the earlier draft in (7.21):

> (7.21) In the mornings the lake lay calm as glass. It reflected the sky, that was clear and light-blue and that appeared to reflect back its own image reflected in the lake, . . .

> (7.22) In the mornings the lake lay calm as glass. It mirrored the sky, that was clear and blue as light and that seemed to mirror back its own image mirrored in the lake, . . .

In the later version 'mirror' instead of 'reflect' for the German word '*spiegeln*' (to mirror or to reflect) is simply a word with a more obvious link to other scenes in the novel which involve mirrors. But the word 'appeared' has been replaced with 'seemed' largely to give more possibilities for a repetitive link with 'see', which occurs later in the passage and often throughout the book. 'See' and 'seem', though not etymologically connected, sound similar, and in a novel that revolves around seeing and seeming, this sound-connection is crucial, especially given that, in German, the same word '*scheinen*' means 'to shine' and 'to seem', providing a repetitive link to the concentrated light imagery in the novel. One could argue, on the basis of Weak Linguistic Relativity, that to seem is connected with light in German in a way it is not in English, but that connection can be suggested in English by the use of 'mirror'.

Repetition is thus very important in prose, and in the novel the examples above are taken from it adds to the mesmerizing effect, an effect we saw in Chapter 4 attributed to Sebald's work. In poetry, even elements that would not be considered to be repeated in prose are more noticeable, and more likely to be seen as a stylistic device. An obvious example of this is rhyme. In the following lines, 'lie' and 'untie' rhyme only *because* they are in the same position:

> (7.23) Lie down with me you hillwalkers and rest.
> Untie your boots and separate your toes,
>
> (Simmonds 1988:9)

It does not make sense to say these words rhyme in the following (invented) prose extract:

> (7.24) If hill-walkers were to lie down and untie their boots . . .

A translation of (7.23) would need to find some way of keeping the rhyme, whereas a translation of (7.24) would not. Even in the two lines in (7.23), the repetition has started a pattern, and patterns create expectation in the reader's mind.

But there are more subtle instances, especially where repetition is lexical and semantic rather than phonetic. When discussing Bachmann's poem '*Botschaft*' above, I noted that the position of 'the fallen' and 'no resurrection' in the final line of each stanza allowed us to make a link between them which would be less noticeable without the effect of lineation. If this were prose, it would still be a passage about the dead not being resurrected, but it is poetry, and the expectation of rising created by the fallen and the sun is thwarted; this thwarting of expectation is emphasized by having the dead not resurrected in the same position in which they lay in the previous stanza.

Rhythm, as mentioned in section 1 of this chapter, is another example of repetition, and metre is rhythm with added (possibly underlying; see Fabb (2002)) repetition: the repeated elements can be put together in groups which themselves repeat to form a pattern, where 'the units are countable, and the number is significant' (Attridge 1995:7), and the countability depends upon lineation. Attridge (1995:3–4) describes rhythm as 'a patterning of energy' which is related to 'evenness and predictability'; because a pattern is set up, it draws attention to itself, and is in this sense an instance of foregrounding, while variations in rhythm are themselves foregrounded against a regular pattern, as they overturn expectations. Consider the following poem by Edward Thomas (1997:46):

> (7.25) In Memoriam (Easter, 1915)
>   The flowers left thick at nightfall in the wood
>   This Eastertide call into mind the men,
>   Now far from home, who, with their sweethearts, should
>   Have gathered them and will do never again.

The first three lines have a regular metre of five stressed syllables, each preceded by an unstressed one, a metre known as iambic parameter. The *abab* rhyme of these lines leads us to expect a '*b*' rhyme in line 4, and the regular rhythm of the first three lines and the first 4 syllables of the final line lead us to expect the same rhythm throughout this line. But something happens at the phrase beginning 'and' in line 4. Because the line does rhyme with line 2, completing the *abab* pattern, an oral performance of the poem would tend to maintain the rhythm in the final line. This means that unwary students asked to read out this short poem invariably read the second half of the final line as 'and will never do again', thus managing both to maintain the beat of 5 stressed syllables, and also to follow the word order they feel the sense demands. But this is not what the line says. Invariably, too, when this is pointed out, students realize that the sudden stumble caused by the metrical and syntactic patterns conflicting is iconic of the change that has come into the lives of those left behind. A translation would need to capture the discomfort of this fourth line, perhaps with something like:

> (7.26)   . . . die
>   die Blumen sammeln sollten, doch nie werden sie es.

The shape of the poem, its division into lines, interacts with the rhythm to give a much stronger sense of metre than would be the case if the poem were rewritten as prose, where the effect would practically disappear. Though prose, too, can have rhythm, Attridge warns against finding other than 'obvious' rhythmic effects in prose, though does allow that certain writers of prose-poems such as Geoffrey Hill (e.g. 1971) show 'scrupulous control of the rhythmic form' (1982:317).

Syntax also causes expectations. We saw when discussing example (7.19) how expectations can be quite strict. In that case, they were governed by gapping. Sometimes they are raised by the start of the syntactic structure itself, rather than its repetition. For example, in

(7.27) He said he would go but I didn't believe –

the missing word is likely to be 'him', as the verb lacks an object, usually animate, and the reader makes an assumption that the pronoun in the space refers back to the subject. However, it could also be 'it'. And it is also possible to insert 'the weather forecast'; 'in miracles'; 'there were grounds for optimism' in the space. Expectations that syntax causes only have to do with the most likely continuation of the structure, and can be flouted, just as the metre is in (7.25). When the expectations to which syntax gives rise are contradictory, the resulting phenomenon is often called 'double syntax' (Furniss and Bath 2007:81), a term first used by Ricks (1963:96), for a phenomenon observed by Davie (1960). Usually, in double-syntax, the line-ending can on the one hand be interpreted as also ending the syntactic structure, because there is an expectation that the spatial reflects the structural, and at the same time another interpretation is possible in which the syntactic structure continues beyond the line ending. For example, in this poem by Ausländer(1977:110), the first few lines are ambiguous in this way:

(7.28) Dem Strom
    ruf ich zu
    mein Weidenwort
    gebeugt
    am Ufer

Two possible translations follow:

(7.29) I call out to the river
    my willow-word
    bowed on the bank
    (Boase-Beier and Vivis 1995:64)

(7.30) I call out
    to the river
    my willow-word
    bowed on the bank

Although the translations are very similar, the difference is in fact significant. In the original, there is ambiguity as to whether '*mein Weidenwort*' (my willow-word) is the object of 'call out' or the subject of a new clause: 'my willow-word (is) bowed on the bank'. The translation in (7.29) preserves this ambiguity by putting the first two lines together, so that the line 'my willow-word' can still conceivably be the object: 'I call out to the river my willow-word'. If the verb phrase 'I call out' is further separated from 'my willow-word' by the layout in (7.30), 'my willow-word' is much more likely to be read as the subject of a new clause. The German does not interpose the prepositional phrase 'to the river' between verb and (possible) object. (7.29) is thus closer to the German in layout but arguably less close in syntax, because the verb-second position of '*ruf ich zu*' ('I call out') in (7.28) is not possible in English. (7.29) has to place the VP first, but the layout compensates. The lines in (7.28) and (7.29) and to a lesser extent (7.30) exemplify double syntax.

Double syntax is an interesting case of what we met in Chapter 1 – see example (1.30) – as garden-pathing (Pinker 1994:212–217; Pilkington 2000:34), and relates to many other types of ambiguity, some of which will be looked at in the following two chapters. It is important to realize that ambiguity is rarely about two possible meanings of equal weight, because reading is linear. In the example in (7.28) above, the reader first reads the equivalent of 'I call out to the river my willow-word' and only when the next line is reached does one also read 'my willow-word bowed on the bank'. Because a reading is set up and then changed, the cognitive effect is much greater than that caused by something like a lexical ambiguity, where a word obviously has two meanings, though, as we shall see in Chapter 8, even in such cases the syntax usually suggests one meaning first.

It seems particularly important in cases such as (7.28) to consider the effect on the reader of the translation. One effect is that the structure will be re-read. In this case, the ambiguity acts as an instance of 'carrying forward' (Gendlin 2004:138) of the narrative, as a 'communicative clue' in Gutt's sense (2000:132) to a possible underlying ambiguity and a trigger for creative reading.

What the examples in this chapter have demonstrated is that the special shape of poems helps make foregrounding possible, and foregrounding draws the reader's attention, demands cognitive work and reprocessing, evokes feelings and slows down reading so all this can happen. So the notion of shape and position in a poem seems crucial. This is one reason that prose poems can seem so pointless: if the special shape of poems is not being exploited, then only its formal features such as alliteration or assonance distinguish it from non-poetic prose, features that depend upon proximity but not lineation. On the other hand, very good prose poems can be quite compelling, because they set up a tension between the rhythms and syntax of prose and those that usually interact with lineation. Translators of prose poems need to be very aware of how these elements of prose and poetry are combined.

But beyond making foregrounding possible, we have seen, in the examples in this chapter, that poetic shape interacts with syntax, sound and even metaphor, to create ever more subtle meanings and more profound effects. Furthermore, the shape of poems gives rise to expectations. This both enhances foregrounding and itself creates further cognitive effects, such as the rethinking we saw in (7.28).

All this can make it seem as though poetry must be impossible to translate. This brings us back to the earlier question of what translation is. If it means getting all the subtleties of effect that we saw, for example, in the Edward Thomas poem in (7.25) – and that was without even analysing it in detail – then it is impossible. But if it means to be aware of all the possible poetic effects and then make an informed choice about how to allow them in the translation, then translation is possible. Jakobson spoke of poetry as the focus on the form in its own right (2008:146–147) and up to now this has been reason enough to consider either that exact equivalence is not possible or that translation does not mean exact equivalence. But in fact the situation is far more complex. Because form in poetry is *never* the focus of attention in its own right, but only insofar as, because it is an element of style, it has a cognitive counterpart and so has poetic effects, merely capturing the form itself would not be a translation, even if it could be done. A poem like 'In Memoriam' will have many possible translations. But if the feeling caused by the break in metre does not happen when we read the translation, then it is not a good one.

7.4 Translation and the linearity of reading

It is important to remember that we read over time, and that reading is linear. If it were not, it would not be possible to build up expectations, and phenomena such as garden-pathing and the cumulative effects of repetition would be impossible. All reading is linear and all reading involves the construction and reconstruction and development of cognitive context in the reader's mind.

Because this is so, one of the aspects of shape the poet works with is the linear process of reading, and the way this affects the cognitive context of the reader. A poem in the shape of wings, such as George Herbert's 'Easter Wings', discussed above, will have an immediate visual impact that is not to do with the linear process of reading, but it is the latter that allows us to follow the decrease in man's estate to the central line 'Most poore' and its increase again beginning with the next line 'With thee / O let me rise' (2007:147). A translation which reproduced the shape but failed to allow the reader the experience of diminution and renewal in the semantics of the words would clearly not be a good translation. We saw also in example (7.9) how suspense in the poem arises because of the delayed subject. This is the sense of 'real-time unfolding' of which Attridge (2004:71) speaks. Cognitive processes such as blending (see Chapter 4) are also real-time processes, that happen 'online' (Slobin 2003).

In an article on the use of extended metaphor and allusion in Blake's 'A Poison Tree', Crisp (2008) argues that the reader is forced by the text to move from employing a conventional metaphor, which represents the 'wrath' felt by the speaker as a tree, to envisaging something which is a blend of the wrath the speaker feels and the tree of the title, and then to make a radical change to envisage a situation involving a real tree, so that from this point on the situation involving a real tree is read as an allegory. This is the poem he discusses:

(7.31) A Poison Tree
   1 I was angry with my friend:
   2 I told my wrath, my wrath did end.
   3 I was angry with my foe:
   4 I told it not, my wrath did grow.

   5 And I water'd it in fears.
   6 Night & morning with my tears;
   7 And I sunned it with smiles,
   8 And with soft deceitful wiles.

   9 And it grew both day and night,
10 Till it bore an apple bright;
11 And my foe beheld it shine,
12 And he knew that it was mine,

13 And into my garden stole
14 When the night had veil'd the pole:
15 In the morning glad I see
16 My foe outstretch'd beneath the tree
               (Blake 1967:49)

The reader's focus, according to Crisp, shifts during the actual reading of the poem from the real world in stanza 1 to a conceptual blend in stanza 2, to a possible but fictitious world which is introduced in the second line of stanza 3, when the blended wrath-tree becomes a real tree (but in an unreal world) by bearing an apple. If blending is something we do all the time, in order to process concepts such as 'red pencil' (Crisp's example, 2008:295), then the change to actually envisaging a new, fictional world is a significant one, because at this point in the reading of the poem we make a cognitive change from applying an everyday process to employing an imaginative one by entering a different but recognizable world. At this point thinking becomes literary in that it involves suspension of disbelief, a point made, though somewhat differently, in a much earlier study of metaphor by Levin, who argued that there comes a point in the understanding of metaphor at which we 'construe the world' (1977:33) or make the possible world described fit what the metaphor suggests. To take Crisp's observations further, one might note that Blake placed a great deal of importance on thought processes, on imagination, and on perception which allows the 'contrary states' (Blake 1967) to coexist in 'creative tension' (Kazin 1974:43). He was concerned to show that separate states of childlike innocence and adult experience must coexist. These states are, one could argue, exactly mirrored in the reader's thought processes in 'A Poison Tree', in that a blend in stanza 2 is replaced by a fictitious but unblended world. And the thought processes of the reader of this poem in fact mirror what we now know about the brain, to the extent that emotion is generated by the limbic system, which reacts to stimulation 'as though we were a two-year old' whereas 'insightful awareness' takes place in the right hemisphere of the cerebral cortex (Taylor 2009:8; 19–20), and involves further thinking about these childlike first reactions. It is interesting to note that Blake often used blends; this is what Furniss and Bath (2007:167) imply, without using that term, when they say that Blake's rose in 'The Sick Rose' is both a rose and not a rose. Moving beyond a blend to a coexistence of 'contraries' would seem to be the aim, in Blake's view, of human life and thought.

So it could be said that the thought process the reader goes through is manipulated quite carefully by Blake to echo what it means to pass from innocence to experience and attain a state where both coexist, to see the world as a child while still knowing what we have experienced. This suggests that a translator might wish to attempt to move the target text reader similarly from one thought process to another. In Hofmann's German translation (1975:100–101), this works particularly well because tree (*Baum*) and wrath (*Zorn*) are both masculine in German, so the reference to 'it' in line 9 is ambiguous (a blend-triggering effect of the genderless pronoun much exploited by religious and philosophical poets in English), and the blend of tree and wrath preserved at that crucial point.

Both these examples suggest that a reading process represents a thought process. It is a relationship of representation reminiscent of metaphor and iconicity: one thing (the reading process) stands for another (the thought process) and the latter, the target in metaphorical terms, can be grasped and experienced by processing the source. It is likely that philosophical and religious poetry in particular often aims in this way to give the reader a cognitive experience which is triggered by the physical object, the poem itself. This only works because of the particular linear process of reading. In this sense a religious poem might be said to function almost like a religious symbol such as a cross, which represents the crucifix in Christianity, and the intersection of the life-path with the death-path in some African religions (cf. Biedermann 1996:81) as well as in ancient Mexican and Egyptian thought (Biedermann 1996:82–3) and of course in the Jewish faith. A translation which ignored the linear nature of the reading process would thus lose the iconicity or the symbolic value of the poem. The use of lexical items that belong to the same semantic field rely on the linear process just as much as do the anaphoric references of pronouns. Consider the following example:

(7.32)   . . . And the darkness
         That is a god's blood swelled
         In him, and he let it
         . . . .

                    (Thomas 1993:324)

In these lines, from 'The Gap', we read 'he let it' either as 'he allowed it' or 'he let the blood', but the second meaning is only considered by the reader because the phrase immediately follows 'blood swelled'. In the translation (Perryman 2003:31) there is only the first meaning, to allow. Yet it seems important that a German reader should also experience doubt and ambiguity, leading to constant rereading, because such rereading, in this poem, is iconic of both the process of language acquisition by the human race in the Babel story and also of the gap between a word and its referent.

7.5 The eye of the poem

The Blake example, (7.31), shows that the poem is carefully shaped in order to guide the reading process so that it echoes a thought process which is not specific to the reading of this particular poem. The point that Crisp suggests for the radical change in cognition, from using a conceptual blend to entering an allegorical world, is in line 10 of the poem, though Crisp does suggest that the place might be different for different readers, or different readings by the same reader. Its position in Crisp's analysis suggests that it relates to something that has been referred to as 'the eye of the poem' (Freeman 2005:40; Boase-Beier 2006:93; Boase-Beier 2009).

The eye of the poem is a place in the poem which, according to Freeman (2005:40) is the 'central point on which the poem turns'. The term 'eye of the poem' refers to a point which is not usually spatially central, but semantically and stylistically of central significance. It is characterized by what Riffaterre called 'convergence', described as 'a heaping up of stylistic features working together' (1959:172). In his discussion of the Blake poem in example (7.31) above, Crisp points out that the 'it' in line 10, that up to this point was the speaker's wrath, metaphysically seen as a tree, changes to become a real tree in a fictitious world, because it bears fruit. As we have seen, Hofmann's German translation (1975) makes the same change possible because of the common gender of tree and wrath. In a discussion (Boase-Beier 2009) of poems by Michael Hamburger and Wilfred Owen (Hamburger 2000:64; Owen 1990:135), I locate the eye of the poem at, respectively, lines 10–14 of a 16-line poem and line 12 of a 14-line poem. I describe the eye of the poem as 'the locus for the poet's vision [which] ... serves at the same time to make the reader consider that vision carefully by searching for and reinterpreting her own contexts, thus mirroring, while reading the poem, the poet's (or narrator's) concerns' (2009:12).

In those examples what I identify as the eye of the poem occurs just beyond two-thirds of the way through the poem. There are obvious reasons for this: the thought needs to develop, often through two or more stages, before a point comes at which the reader is led by the text to rethink. Here is an extract from the Hamburger (2000:64) poem (also quoted in example 2.7), with lines numbered for clarity:

(7.33) Winter Solstice
    1 Dream of the trees found in a dubious garden

. . .

   8 Damp, dark and cold the dawn awakening,

   9 All my dead in it, dubious as the trees,

  10 No moonshine mixed into the grey of morning,

  11 Silence before the foraging birds descend,

  12 And no more mine in this light than in dream

  13 The garden was that once I must have tended,

  14 Than those will be whom in the street I pass

. . .

The 16-line poem describes a dreamlike early morning view of the garden. In the article mentioned I identify lines 10–14 as the point at which there is a change of perception, signalled by a number of things, including:

(i) the converging of semantic chains of words to do with gardens (there is such a word in almost every line of the poem), to do with dreams, and to do with light
(ii) the repeated sounds of 'no moonshine' in line 10 and 'no more mine' in line 12
(iii) the assonance of 'shine – silence – mine – light'
(iv) and, most importantly, the ambiguity of 'moonshine' in line 10, and of 'those' in line 14

The final point is in a way the most important, because ambiguity signals to the reader that there are at least two strands of thought to follow, and is thus a 'communicative clue' (Gutt 2000:132). 'Moonshine' both picks up on the half-light imagery, and also means 'visionary talk or ideas', according to the *Concise Oxford Dictionary* of 1976 (p.707). Unaccountably, this meaning is missing from later editions, but it is likely to have been a meaning familiar to Hamburger, and its negative thus suggests that at this moment in the poem reality begins to intrude upon the dreamlike view. Because the word 'moonshine' is also phonetically foregrounded, as noted above, it is especially striking and the ambiguity especially obvious. This lexical ambiguity is followed by the syntactic ambiguity in line 14, where 'those will be' seems to mean at first 'those gardens will be' in contrast to 'the garden was' in the previous line. But the 'whom' that follows makes the reader rethink 'those' as people rather than gardens. So people and gardens come together, in a specification of the conceptual metaphor PEOPLE ARE PLANTS (Turner 1991:221), and the reader rereads the poem, seeing the garden as an extended metaphor for relationships.

In fact, to pursue Crisp's ideas (2008), it could be argued that the poem is first read as a real description of a garden, though its possible allegorical nature is hinted at by the adjective 'dubious' in the first line. Line 10 suggests a real garden, and not a vision, because of the phrase 'no moonshine'. But then the phrase 'no more mine' 2 lines later that echoes 'no moonshine' so closely signals we are indeed entering the narrator's thoughts, and we become drawn into the eye of the poem. The phrase ' than those will be' in line 14 suggests first that we are talking about (possibly) metaphorical gardens, but then 'whom' shifts focus from the metaphor to its target, relationships, so we see the whole poem as an extended metaphor. At this point the oddness of this changing view, if it causes us to reread the poem, will cause us to view the extended metaphor as an allegory, because in fact real gardens and minute details of gardening – 'dug in too loosely', 'raised from a first-year seedling' – are referred to, and can be assigned counterparts in the history of the narrator's relationships.

In the article mentioned above, I discuss two different ways of deciding that this passage – lines 10–14 – constitutes the eye of the poem. One is that it is a convergence in Riffaterre's (1959) sense of a meeting-point of stylistic devices which draw attention and cause rereading. The other is that a comparison of the original poem with the translation shows a significant divergence at this point. The translation by Franz Wurm, *'Wintersonnenwende'* (in Dove 2004:104) has *'Mondlicht'*, which is unambiguous 'moonlight', and not ambiguous 'moonshine'. For the foregrounded 'the garden was once ... those will be whom ...', the German has no obvious link between garden and people because the relative pronoun *'denen'* does not, like its English counterpart, have to refer to people and in fact, because the repositioning of the lines removes the parallelism of the English, the reference to people is all but lost:

(7.34) Wie es im   Traum der Garten war, den ich einst
         as   it in-the dream the garden was that I once

         Besorgt haben muss, und wie es jene sein werden
         tended   have   must   and   as   it those will be

         An denen ich draußen vorübergehe
         on   which   I   outside   pass

The parallelism 'The garden was that once ... Than those will be' is not visible in this German translation. The link with Parks' observation, that 'divergences between original and translation tend to ... point to the peculiar nature of ... [the author's] style and the overall vision it implies' (1998:vii) is clear. What seems to be happening is that where we have a convergence in the source text, we have a divergence between source text and translation. A consideration of the translations of other poems such as those discussed later in this and the next chapter confirms this.

There are three possible consequences of the observation that divergences between target and source texts echo convergences in the source text itself:

(i) We can examine already translated texts and their translations to find clues to the important points in the original
(ii) When translating, we can look for convergences in an original text in order to find the vision behind the text
(iii) We can conclude that, if the target text works in terms of its structure it is likely to echo the source text more closely.

The first point is of most interest to the critic, and especially to the comparatist of language or literature and is the position put forward by Parks (1998 and 2007). Studying poems and their translations in this way can lead to some quite surprising insights. Consider, for example, the following lines, the first nine lines of a poem by R.S. Thomas (2004:139):

(7.35) *Agnus Dei*
   1 No longer the lamb
   2 but the idea of it.
   3 Can an idea bleed?
   4 On what altar
   5 does one sacrifice an idea?
   6 It gave its life
   7 for the world? No
   8 it is we give our life
   9 for the idea . . .

If we look at the German translation of this poem, we note that it is fairly close until line 6. At this point the German translation has:

(7.36) 6 Es gab sein Leben
     it gave its life

   7 für die Welt? Nein
     for the world no

   8 wir sind es, die ihr Leben geben
     we are it who their life give

9 für die Idee
   for the idea . . .
            (Perryman 2003:35)

There is a rather surprising difference here. '*Es*' in line 6 of the German cannot refer back to 'the idea', because '*die Idee*' is feminine and '*es*' is the neuter pronoun, and so must be 'the lamb' which is in line 1. And yet, there is the proximity of 'idea' both in line 5 (which seems the obvious antecedent) and in line 9, suggesting this is what '*es*' refers to. Furthermore, the contrast of 'It gave its life for the world – No, it is we give our life for the idea' also suggests 'it' is the idea. On the other hand, when reading the original poem, the reader is aware that it is the lamb that in Christian tradition gives its life. Thus semantically, and in terms of the Christian background to the poem, 'it' in line 6 seems to be the lamb, whereas syntactically 'it' seems to be the idea. This clash between semantics and the most likely syntactic possibility becomes especially obvious when one reads the German and sees that there is no clash there at all.

Thus the comparison of German translation with English original suggests important differences in the interpretations the English and German reader will have. The English reader will be very aware of the conflict between the lamb as a (metaphorical) human being and as an idea – or between the word made flesh and the word itself – whereas the German reader will not. It is interesting to note that studies of R.S. Thomas in English show him as a deeply contradictory man, ironical, very aware he was seen as 'an outsider' but also 'full of fun' (Rogers 2006:64;310). German criticism, of which there is of course far less, makes much of his concern for the absent God, his 'reduced language' (Exner 1998), but there is no sense of the contradictions, irony and humour of his person and his poetry. Reading Thomas' poetry in English is to become involved in an intellectual game; there is less room for such involvement in the German. More than this, though, the result of such a comparison will be to highlight the importance for the original poem of the ambiguity the translator misses. It leads the reader not to confusion but to increased speculation about the relationship between the idea and the lamb, and the extent to which they are or are not different, and so to the extent to which 'the lamb' is a symbol for an idea, or a metaphor for a sacrificed human. The 'it' at the beginning of line 6 thus triggers a wide-ranging examination of the reader's cognitive context, at the same time as it leads to a rereading of the poem from the beginning.

Point (ii) above is of most interest to the translator, especially of poetry, because it is linked to the notion that poems have shape, and the shape, and the reading it guides, are crucial to the thought processes the reader, or translator, goes through, including rereading, examining of contexts, putting oneself in the position of the narrator, seeing the world through the poet's eyes. Recall Edward Thomas' 'In Memoriam', discussed as example (7.25) above. As we saw there, 'never again' in the final line is probably the most foregrounded phrase, and the phrase that the reader hears most clearly, suggesting the futility of war and the hope that it will not happen: that the 'never again' of the gathering of flowers will not itself happen again. But the point in the poem at which most patterns converge, in the way Riffaterre (1959) meant, is the enjambed 'should / have' that links the end of the previous line with this final line. The word 'should', in itself a rather unlikely rhyme for 'wood' in line 1, receives emphasis by virtue of this end-rhyme, and also the phrase 'should have' provides a contrast to 'will do' in the final line, the phrase that I suggested a performance of the poem would lose. With its suggestions of absence – the men should have gathered the flowers but cannot – it also equally strongly indicates the mind of an observer (or the narrator, or the poet) who has this thought. And thus it picks up the suggestion earlier in the poem that the men are only in the mind: the phrase 'call into mind' suggests the call into battle that has happened before and caused their absence. 'Should have' thus suggests a vision of men who are gone similar to the vision held in the mind of those who have left the flowers. A translator of this poem will need to preserve many things: the difficult fit of sense with rhythm in the final line, suggested in (7.26), the enjambed 'should have', and the various patterns of which it forms part.

Point (iii) above is particularly important because it further underlines the importance of writing a target text poem that works in itself, as the best way of ensuring a good translation of the original. It is unlikely that every poem has an identifiable eye, but certainly for many poems this does seem to be the case. Identifying such a point – which in the Edward Thomas, R.S. Thomas and Michael Hamburger poems was two-thirds to three-quarters of the way through – and making sure that the translated poem also has an eye, the point at which stylistic devices converge and the reader's way of thinking changes, will go some way towards assuring the proper shape of the target poem.

Ambiguity, Mind Games and Searches 8

Chapter Outline

8.1 The reader's search for meaning

The vicar of Tarporley had taken as his theme for the Easter service the open ending of Mark's Gospel: the disciples had seen Jesus' body was gone from the tomb and they left and told no-one: 'for they were afraid' (Chapter 16, verse 8). Later endings were added by other writers but the original ending, said the vicar (and cf. also Green and McKnight 1992:524), could be considered more powerful because it was up to the listener to work out what happened next.

This sense of 'what happened next' is inherent in the concept of narrative and is seen by cognitive stylisticians such as Turner as fundamental to the way we think, because it is part of the 'predicting, planning and explaining' (1996:5) that characterizes our cognitive processes. For Turner, all thinking is essentially literary, and the capacity to tell stories is one of the most basic ways this can be shown to be true. Telling stories is linked to our conceptualizing of events as actions, or as spatial stories, such as a river flowing down to the sea or a building collapsing (Turner 1996:47). For example, in Armitage's poem 'Greenhouse', a greenhouse has 'gone to seed' (Armitage 1989:13), and here a spatial story of a plant such as the lettuce developing too far and becoming useless (in terms of its food value) is projected onto a greenhouse. Often the concepts of a spatial story and an action overlap and interact in the way we conceptualize events. In another poem by Armitage 'Night-Shift', we are told that 'water in the pipe finds its level' and, in the next line 'Here are other signs of someone having left', where the word 'other' signals that the water is in fact finding its level because someone has just used it (Armitage 1989:14). Actions are intentional; we conceptualize stories as having an actor with the power to act and hence with the power to decide what comes next, and we conceptualize the event of the telling of the story itself as an action with an instigator. This is especially so where there is an implied narrator, such as the 'I' of Armitage's two poems: someone (who is often intuitively associated with the author, as the Proxy Principle suggested; see Chapter 6) who is recounting to us the various stories in the text. In the poem 'Greenhouse', we read the final line, in which a ghost walks 'one step behind' the addressee of the poem as a prefiguration of what is to come, perhaps the imminent death of the addressee.

The sense of what happens next is also inherent in philosophical views that explain how 'the present *occurs into* the previous implying and brings it forward as the new implying' (Gendlin 2004:138). This is what Gendlin calls 'carrying forward'. For him, the phenomenon of 'carrying forward' is connected with the view that real meaning is found in what is peripheral, that is, what is implied, a view mentioned throughout this book in relation to style, inferences, weak implicatures, and especially figures such as ambiguity. This sense of implication, that what we say is the basis for what might follow, is also behind Benjamin's view of the 'afterlife' of a literary text or other work of art (2004:76), and of views that follow it, such as Berger's view that a photograph of a painting, for example, allows the original painting to become subject to a multiplication of uses and meanings in different contexts and with different viewers (Berger 1972:19). If a text is to work in a way that is appropriate to literature, then it needs to invoke this sense that something comes after it. As suggested in Chapter 3, what comes after it might be interpretation, criticism, another text, a musical adaptation, a translation. In other words, it encourages and demands the reader's engagement. In this chapter I will be concerned with examining how this crucial openness to the reader's engagement can be preserved when a text is translated, and how translation affects it.

When a reader envisages what will happen next in terms of the story of a text, then there are always several possibilities. This is true whether we are talking about the ending of Mark's Gospel of a film, or of a children's story. The film '*The Italian Job*', which ends with the main character saying 'I've got a great idea', has recently been the subject of a competition by the Royal Society of Chemistry to find the best solution to the predicament the characters find themselves in. When an Enid Blyton character ends a story with 'here's to our next adventure!' (2003:276) the reader is left to imagine what that might be, and to buy the next book if there is one, or to invent stories if the series is ended.

But texts engage their reader in such acts of completion in other ways than in terms of 'what happens next'. The most important of these ways is through the use of ambiguity. In Chapter 7 we saw ambiguity, along with other figures of style, in its interaction with the linear process of reading; it was central to the pivotal point we called the 'eye of the poem'. Poetry contains ambiguities of all types: these may be gaps, or lexical ambiguities, or double syntax. We saw in the previous chapter how an ambiguity about what 'it' refers to created this sort of pivotal point in R.S. Thomas' poem 'Agnus Dei' (Thomas 2004:139). What is important in a cognitive view of the way texts work is that the reader is not only able to see a variety of meanings but to think each of them through. In 'Agnus Dei', the reader reading 'It gave its life / for the world' not only processes the ambiguity of whether the idea or the lamb can be said to have given its life, but also reconstructs each of the possible scenarios without the other. That is, 'it' can be read as an idea, and the whole poem is then about the uses of ideas to narrow 'the gap between word and deed', as the poem later puts it. Or 'it' can be understood, as in the German translation, as 'the lamb', which is then seen not to have given its life for the world, because human beings are too intent on concentrating on the idea of an idea, something which cannot bleed, or have life, and which leads to the sense of there being 'no God'. It is not just that we see a contradictory view, but that we are able to envisage two different scenarios, as well as the third one, which is a blend of the other two: the metaphorical human lamb and the actual idea combined in one being.

What happens when we read such a poem with an ambiguous 'it', or a story with an open ending, is what might be called 'creative reading', a term used also by Carey (2005: Chapter 7) and Attridge (2004:79–83). This view, mentioned in Chapter 3, largely derives from the Reader-Response Theories of critics such as Iser (1974) and also from the ideas of uncertainty and lack of fixed meaning in post-structuralism (e.g. Barthes 1977; Derrida 1981).

Religious poems are particularly characterized by the creativity they demand of the reader, as we saw in the examples from R.S. Thomas. Other religious texts, too – the final part of Mark's gospel, and the sermon based upon it – often aim specifically to make the reader think, to reach an understanding of faith as interpretative and creative, employing many of the cognitive processes such as blending and the use of mental spaces that we see in the literary mind and in everyday thinking (Sørensen 2002, Barrett 2002). Religious poems are thus a particularly good illustration of how ambiguity works to engage the reader in literary texts. In '*Agnus Dei*', the main ambiguity is ambiguity of reference, just as it is in Blake's poem 'The Poison Tree', discussed above in example (7.31).

The translator's task, when faced with such ambiguity, has not always been seen as clear. Sometimes ambiguity in texts is regarded as a fault, and then the translator will attempt to disambiguate. This is the position suggested by Tytler, when he says 'to imitate the obscurity or ambiguity of the original is a fault' (in Robinson 2002:210). Tsur (2002:280) points out that some readers are 'intolerant of ambiguity or uncertainty' whereas other readers expect it, and there will thus be a variety of possible or likely responses to a text which exploits ambiguity, as most literary texts (and many non-literary ones, such as advertisements) do. In religious poetry, and indeed in all poetry, and in most literary texts, ambiguity is not a fault but is the very stylistic feature that allows the desired creative reading. So the question for the literary translator is how to preserve it: as Hamburger says of his Celan translations, the ambiguities are 'not to be resolved at all, but accepted and respected' (2007:407). Consider the following, where each English example is followed by its translations. In the first case, ambiguity has been preserved, but not in the other two:

(8.1) . . . but he is no more here
       than before

(8.2) er aber   ist genausowenig da wie   davor
       he though is   just-as-little here as earlier/in-front

(8.3) Garden Organic

(8.4) Öko-Garten
       organic garden

(8.5) no moonshine

(8.6) kein Mondlicht
       no moonlight

Example (8.2) is not the translation of (8.1) (from a poem by R.S. Thomas: 1993:361) by Perryman (2003:39); the latter renders 'before' as '*zuvor*', thus limiting the possibility of either a temporal or a spatial meaning to just the temporal. Yet the possible spatial meaning is central to this poem, which is about an absence felt by the person who both precedes and follows, and thus is always in 'the vestibule', waiting. Temporal and spatial senses of 'before' are blended in the use of this word in (8.1), which also suggests religious blended imagery such as 'before the altar' or 'one who goes before'. The suggested German translation in (8.2) thus uses a German word '*davor*' which also has both spatial and temporal meanings.

The phrase 'Garden Organic', in (8.3), the name of the organization which promotes organic gardening, is both a descriptive NP (noun phrase) with the adjective following the noun (as in the NP *Café Rouge*, which keeps the French word order) and an imperative VP (verb phrase, as in Drive carefully! Eat healthily!), though of course we would usually expect an adverb: Garden organically! To translate it as in (8.4) is to ignore the imperative meaning. (8.6) is from the translation by Franz Wurm (Dove 2004:104), which we met in (7.34), of the preceding phrase in (8.5) which suggests visionary talk or imagination, besides actual moonlight. As we saw in the discussion there, the reduction of Hamburger's 'moonshine' (2000:64) to '*Mondlicht*' in (8.6) loses an important implicature in the poem.

It is difficult to capture lexical ambiguity or ambiguity of reference in the target text, because, as the three examples above illustrate, such ambiguities depend on the linguistic contingencies of the source language. While (8.1) and (8.5) could be translated in a way that captured the ambiguity, it is not possible to find a phrase in German that, like the English one in (8.3), could be either an NP or a VP.

Another way to examine the translation of such cases is therefore to consider the two or more possible cognitive scenarios they give rise to and what the nature of their relationship is. In the examples we have just been considering, both (8.1) and (8.5) suggest blended meanings, as well as separate ones. It is important that the translation should both capture the various possible meanings and enable the complex thinking that blending entails. It is important to know that the poem quoted in (8.5) gives rise to ambiguity rather than vagueness: it is not that there is a general uncertainty of interpretation but rather 'the certainty of different scenarios, each one of which has equal validity with the others' (Zeki 1999:263). When Zeki describes ambiguity thus, he is talking about the sort of ambiguity in pictures such as Vermeer's 'The Music Lesson'. But the same applies to most literary texts. We see 'moonshine' in the Michael Hamburger poem as either moonlight or vision or a blend of both: the sort of visionary thinking that moonlight might give rise to. These meanings, though the blended one is complex, are all quite clear and there do not seem to be other possible meanings besides these three. In all these examples, whether ambiguity is lexical as in (8.1) and (8.5), or syntactic as in (8.3), as well as in the cases of 'double syntax' in Chapter 7, there is no vagueness. Thus a translation which rendered such examples as vague would make the cognitive process of blending impossible for the reader, because blending involves combining two clear meanings or mental spaces.

The examples up to now in this chapter have illustrated lexical and syntactic ambiguity. But we saw in the previous chapter that even metrical patterning could be said to rest on ambiguity, because there is always, in a good poem, a conflict between the rhythm that meaning dictates (or would dictate, if one were to read poetry as if it were speech) and the rhythm that the metre dictates. Leech (2008:Chapter 6) in fact notes four levels of metrical form – performance, rhythm, metre and musical scansion – any of which can contradict the others.

As we saw in the case of the Edward Thomas poem in (7.25) it is exactly this sort of contradiction – in this case between normal speaking rhythm and metre – that causes the reader to stumble over 'will do never again' and to emphasize 'never', by reading 'will never do again'. The cognitive effect comes from the ambiguity: whereas metre demands a repetition of the stress pattern of the previous three lines, with weak stress on 'never', normal reading rhythm highlights 'never'. It is the conflict between regular and irregular that matters. The reader follows through both scenarios: a repetitive (metrical) one and a broken (rhythmic) one, and it is in the contrast between them that the poignancy of the final words arises.

Metaphor, too, can interact with ambiguity, and in fact very often does. Furniss and Bath (2007:151) discuss the simile in Burns' 1796 song 'my luve's like a red, red rose' (Burns 1991:75) and point out that it leaves it up to the reader to work out whether 'my luve' is his feeling or the woman he loves, and in what ways she is 'like' a red rose. In general, it is also the case that implicit metaphors (Furniss and Bath 2007:152) require more work than explicit metaphors, because they give 'one side of the equation' (Furniss and Bath 2007:152). To pursue Furniss and Bath's useful example a little further, we could say that, if Burns' line had read 'My red red rose will never fade', not only would the reader need to work out whether the rose was the love itself or the loved one, and in what way either of these could be a red rose, but she would also have to entertain other possibilities for what the red rose metaphorically referred to. Perhaps the woman's beauty, or the speaker's memory of her, or the memory of their relationship. Furniss and Bath (2007:153) point out that implicit metaphor is especially important in literature because it is a way of engaging the reader in making meanings, and these will relate to the context of the poem. However, they will also depend upon the reader's context, and the more implicit the metaphor, the more this is the case. Implicit metaphor gives the reader great freedom, and so does not lead to some of the conflict of possible scenarios we saw in earlier examples. It is the sort of conflict caused by ambiguous expressions like 'my luve', or 'moonshine' that will involve the reader in most mental work, because the two paths the mind will tend to follow are clear but difficult to reconcile, and it is this difficulty of reconciliation which gives rise to the possibility of a blend: the love and the woman blended or visionary talk blended with half-light. Indeterminate metaphor is easy to translate, because the openness of interpretation will translate with it almost automatically. It is the guided conflict of ambiguous words or expressions that causes linguistic problems and risks loss of cognitive effect.

Furniss and Bath (2007:157) say that religious and philosophical poetry especially uses concrete metaphor to speak of intangible or abstract things. But the example from R.S. Thomas' 'Agnus Dei', discussed in Chapter 7 (see 7.35), suggests something a little different. Seeing the lamb as a concrete metaphor for the idea of sacrifice and salvation is only part of Thomas' point. As we have seen, the reader must go much further from this, and think about whether the concrete is merely a representation of the abstract or a thing to be revered in its own right. Thomas, who was a vicar, caused consternation when he stated that the crucifixion was a metaphor. Some people interpreted this as meaning that it did not happen, but Thomas explained that he had not meant it was 'a metaphor', but 'metaphor' (Rogers 2006:302–303). What he presumably meant was that it was both real and stood for something else, 'a kind of new life' (ibid.), but that if it did *not* stand for something else (that is, if it was *not* metaphor) then it had lost its meaning. He is suggesting, in fact, that it is a blend of historical event and metaphor. The poetic effects of this poem will be such considerations in the mind of the reader of 'Agnus Dei' and other such poems; the core of both religion and poetry, according to Thomas, is 'imagination' (Rogers 2006:302).

Furthermore, the lamb, like the cross, is a conventional Christian symbol, and one of the ways Christian poetry such as Thomas' works is to call upon the reader to question the nature of symbols themselves. A blend of lamb and idea is a very real possibility, as is a blend of history and idea. These are big issues, and they happen in the mind of the reader. A translation that does not trigger them there has failed.

The sense of 'what happens next' and the cognitive development of ambiguity on the part of the reader are both interactions of the text with the reader's cognitive context. The translator must take into account that contexts, because they are cognitive, are individual. They are also unstable and changing. As described by Stockwell (2002:155–158), context is built up, adapted, added to and subtracted from during the processes of reading and comprehension.

Sometimes writers on translation seem to suggest that a context is something fairly stable, and that the original writer's context is more important than the translator's, and more decisive in determining how a translation is done. For example, in a 2005 article, Gutt suggests that sometimes the 'originally intended context' can be supplied by the translator in order that the reader can get to the originally intended interpretation (2005:38–41). But these notions of intended context and intended interpretation are based on a view of Relevance Theory that assumes that the reader who is no longer getting cognitive effects in terms of changes to his or her context will stop interpreting. Stopping interpreting can be seen as successful because the meaning that makes sense in the reader's context matches (to some degree) the intended one. This seems also to be the view of reading suggested by Pilkington when he says that the 'the real reader has to manoeuvre himself into the position of the implied reader by supplying contextual assumptions that are needed for an interpretation' (2000:63). Similarly, van Peer (2000:39) says that literary interpretation is driven by the promise of reaching 'higher certainty' about meaning. For translation, this view would suggest that the translator reading the source text arrives at a satisfactory meaning, at which point she stops reading and translates the poem in such a way that the same or a similar meaning can be arrived at by the target text readers, along with the various effects caused by stylistic devices such as rhyme, metre or metaphor.

What I have been arguing for, however, is an approach to literary texts that sees reading not as satisfying optimal relevance but maximal relevance (cf. MacKenzie 2002:7). The cognitive context of the reader keeps changing in order to maximize relevance. For example, if I read the poem 'The Absence', by R.S. Thomas (1993:361), from which (8.1) was taken, I will come to the final lines:

(8.7) . . . . What resource have I
other than the emptiness without him of my whole
being, a vacuum he may not abhor?

The final phrase is ambiguous; one possible way of translating it is to say that 'to abhor a vacuum' means either to fill it or to shun it, and that the translator must decide for one of these. This is in fact what the following translation, by Kevin Perryman, (2003:39) does:

(8.8) Welches andere Mittel bleibt   mir
   which   other means remains to-me

   als die Leere – ohne ihn –   meines ganzen
   but the emptiness without him of-my   whole

   Wesens, ein Vakuum, das   er vielleicht nicht
   being   a vacuum which he maybe   not

   verabscheut?
   shuns

The interpretation that is arrived at when the German reader reads this translated poem is that God might not refuse to enter the emptiness in one's being. It is thus understood against a particular cognitive background: a present God, or at least a hoped-for presence. This is the sense of 'abhor' in the English Christmas carol 'O Come All Ye Faithful', where we are told reassuringly that 'he abhors not a virgin's womb' (Dearmer *et al* 1968:78). Whether or not the German reader of (8.8) knows the English carol, or links it to the original English presented opposite the German translation in Perryman's book (2003:38), the German poem suggests a reassurance, though tempered with the word '*vielleicht*' ('maybe'). However, this is not what happens to the reader of the original poem in English. Here context is built and altered during reading. There are at least four possible interpretations of the phrase 'a vacuum he may not abhor':

   (i) a vacuum he might enter
   (ii) a vacuum he must enter
   (iii) a vacuum he might not enter
   (iv) a vacuum he cannot enter

The English reader therefore needs to keep contexts compatible with all four readings in mind, whereas the German poem only allows the creation of contexts that are compatible with (i). The difference between (i) and (ii) rests on different meanings of 'may not' in the English poem ('might not' or 'is not able to'). This ambiguity is not present in the German. But in fact the even greater ambiguity is that (iii) and (iv) are also possible readings of the English original. There are two reasons to suppose they might apply. One is that it can be assumed (and assumed that R.S. Thomas assumed) that the phrase 'nature abhors a vacuum', meaning that air rushes in to fill a vacuum, is part of the existing background context of the reader of the English poem. The other is that Thomas liked to say God was absent, and should be met with awe, rather than with humanized love (cf. Rogers 2006:301). Whether or not the latter knowledge of the poet's views is part of the reader's cognitive context, the former knowledge about nature abhorring a vacuum almost certainly will be, and thus the reader will see (iii) and (iv) as possible interpretations by building contexts that allow each one, and keeping all four possibilities open.

It is in the nature of literature, and especially poetry, to suggest different changes to the context of each individual reader, depending on their background knowledge. But readers do not seek and find a context that is compatible with this poem in order to arrive at a possible meaning, or any of the four interpretations above would be equally possible. The purpose of reading poetry is the search itself, not the finding of a possible context, presumably because the changing and creating of contexts is pleasurable. As Fabb suggests, it is in the cognitive processes, in the relationship of one mental representation to another, that what we feel as the aesthetic and emotional response to a text is experienced (1995: 155); this is the notion of affect, discussed in Chapter 6. If the search has to end too quickly, much of the pleasure is lost. This, perhaps, is one of the reasons that some poetry readers say they do not like to read translations. If poetry is not carefully and poetically translated it might give us some sense of the original, but too few possibilities to search for contexts. What is pleasurable about reading 'The Absence' is its very complexity. And, as we saw earlier with 'Agnus Dei', the reader goes even further than just to keep open contexts that fit several meanings. Once it is clear that there is a conflict between two sets of meanings – (i) and (ii) as opposed to (iii) and (iv) –, it becomes possible to imagine a blended scenario in which all four possibilities exist at once. The very beginning of the poem speaks of 'this great absence / that is like a presence', an idea that is in fact inherent in the concept of the *via negativa*, or negative theology: the view that God can only be understood in terms of what he is not (Rocca 2004). For some readers, context-building will stop with a complex set of contexts compatible with all four readings. For others, further elements to add to the context will be actively sought, and a blend obtained. Then, for example, further reading on the theological concept of the *via negativa* might follow.

In such texts there are always triggers that activate a more concentrated search for contexts. In '*Agnus Dei*', it was the word 'it', in 'The Absence', it was the phrase 'may not abhor' and in Hamburger's poem it was 'no moonshine'. All these expressions are the result of convergences. We saw this in the case of the Michael Hamburger poem in Chapter 7. But in '*Agnus Dei*', the semantic clashes in the earlier questions 'can an idea bleed?' and 'On what altar / does one sacrifice an idea' have already suggested that the contrast of idea and lamb is crucial. In 'The Absence', the notions of absence and presence are given in the first line. In all the poems, too, other stylistic devices build up around the ambiguity in question.

A translated poem cannot aim to match the possible contexts the original gave rise to, for these are not finite in number, but depend on the readers themselves, their cultural and religious backgrounds, their experience of reading poetry, and so on. And it should not attempt to match them. If, as Fabb (1995) suggests, the response to a poetic text is in the spaces between representations, then a translation that treats the source text as a code, and matches one representation with another, or even a finite set of contexts with another, will fail to trigger the 'density' (ibid.) of its readers' response. A translation is always the translator's interpretation and different translators will see different aspects as important. However, ambiguity has a central function in allowing the building and examination of contexts, and in preventing too early an end to the process of searching for meaning.

8.2 Voices, attitudes and implicatures

I suggested in the previous section, and indeed in earlier chapters, that whenever there is ambiguity in a text, whether lexical, syntactic or metrical, the result is a greater involvement of the reader. But I have also been suggesting throughout this book that the effects of translation do not merely echo those of the original text, and that the task of the translator is not to use stylistic analysis to enumerate and try to reproduce those effects.

This is in fact exactly what Gutt says when he states that producing a translation cannot involve a counting-up of implicatures and explicatures and an attempt to render something like the same overall number (2000:98–101), because translation is not just the conveying of message but involves an interpretation on the part of the translator that takes the target-text reader's context into account (2000:116) according to what the translator interprets as relevant to the target-reader (in a Relevance-Theory sense, that is, as not making the reader work for no returns).

What seems to be missing from Gutt's detailed account is, however, any sense that equivalence (of message, of implicatures and explicatures, of the amount of relevance to the reader's cognitive context) may be in itself an inadequate basis for understanding translation. Though equivalence in Gutt's sense (as Pym 2010:37 points out) is a sophisticated notion that operates on 'the level of beliefs, of fictions, or of possible thought processes', it still seems inadequate. Substituting equivalence of the degree of relevance to the reader's cognitive context for equivalence of message may get us nearer to what translation does than checking implicatures and explicatures, but it still appears to ignore the notion I suggested in Chapter 4 as crucial to translation: that translation is a text-type in its own right and gives rise to a different type of reading and a different degree of relevance. To put it in Relevance-Theory terms: if a reader reads a novel or poem originally written in a different language, more work will be needed to achieve similar effects to the source text effects, but this extra work will in fact give rise to extra effects associated with the fact that she or he is reading a translation. Remember example (4.12), from Hamburger's translation of Celan (2007:49), repeated here as (8.9):

> (8.9) Oaken door, who lifted you off your hinges?
> My gentle mother cannot return.

We noted when discussing this example in Chapter 4 that the English reader would need all the knowledge of the German language and its idioms and history that the original reader needed. This in itself demands more effort on the part of the English reader. We noted also that the reader of the translation from which (8.9) is taken has to process the way Hamburger's voice has overlaid and added to Celan's. Hamburger chose not to repeat the verb 'to come', used earlier in the poem, in the second line of (8.9), opting instead for 'return'. This has the effect of suggesting an open door and a mother permanently in exile, whereas the German suggests also that the mother might be within, and cannot come to the door. The sense of sadness and absence is perhaps greater in the English; the language is less colloquial, the mother more distant.

The translated text differs from the source text in that it demands more work of its reader and, in a good translation, has the chance to effect greater cognitive changes, and also because, containing the voice of the translator as well as that of the original author, it is able to convey a greater array of attitudes than the source text. But what happens, then, when ambiguity in the source text is a particularly central characteristic and the voice it suggests is a silent one? I have discussed in (6.32) the use of a gap in the von Törne poem *'Beim Lesen der Zeitung'*, where a missing auxiliary forces the reader to choose whether to supply a subjunctive, thus interpreting the speaker as merely reporting what the newspaper said, or an indicative, thus endorsing it (see also Boase-Beier 2006:122–127). The English translation of von Törne's complete poem, from which (6.32) was taken, is as follows:

(8.10) Butchers ignorant of slaughter
        – so at least the papers say.
        (And I watched my sister with her dolls,
        sewing yellow patches on in play.)

This translation tries to preserve the uncertainty by making the first line sound like a headline, with the verb missing, so that it is unclear whether the paper said they are ignorant, or were said to be, and whether the newspaper endorses the view that they were ignorant, or merely reports that they were said to be. But as with all good poems, the attempt to translate von Törne's original constantly throws up new questions. We can add now that in fact there is a further layer, engendered by the fact that this is a translation. The yellow patches will seem the child's approximation of the yellow stars that Jews were forced to wear under the Nazi occupation. The child's view which turns stars to patches recalls Celan's use (in the poem from which (8.9) is taken) of the expression 'round star', where the star is both the Nazi symbol, and a star as it appears to the human eye. But in England, people were not forced to wear yellow stars, so the effort required to make this link is considerably greater, and will depend on background knowledge about the situation in other European countries at that time.

The English reader might initially assume that 'butchers' must either be a designation chosen by the German newspaper in question or it represents the interpretation by the narrator (and newspaper reader) of what the German newspaper said. Were either of these the case, the extra work the English reader has to do would not be much greater than it would be had the poem been written in English. But in fact it was not written in English, and 'butchers' is not the word used by the German newspaper in the poem, but the word used by the translator, which echoes in sound the later 'patches'. Thus, in the English poem, the butchers and the child are brought into close focus, and the action of the butcher (cutting) contrasted with the child's play (sewing). This gives rise to a possible blend of butchers and tailors, or even of butchers and doctors (- a blend also discussed by Lakoff 2008:33 -) and a blend of this blend with the Nazi perpetrators. None of this discussion is meant to suggest that (8.10), which is my translation of the von Törne poem, is a better poem than the original. But it does suggest that translation adds layers of interpretation that the reader must process, with the concomitant cognitive effects.

Poetry about the Holocaust is often characterized by silences and gaps. As Schlant (1999) notes, events were too terrible to speak of, people were silenced, people chose silence. Poetry that represents these events does so by avoiding conscious artifice, by being fragmented, or hermetic, by having gaps, or unfinished sentences, and contradictions, of which Celan's 'black milk' (Hamburger 2007:71) is one of the most famous. Ambiguity is used to express both the unfathomable and unspeakable nature of the historical events and also to iconically reflect the ambiguous state of mind of perpetrators and bystanders, who both knew what was going on and at the same time did not know (see Boase-Beier 2004a) or chose not to know; in fact this 'split-self' (Emmott 2002) phenomenon might be just a particular instance of a very basic (cognitive) process that allows for ambiguity. There may even be ambiguity about whether a poem is 'about' the Holocaust or not. In '*Aufruf*' (Call to Action), by von Törne (1981:13), the final three lines read

> (8.11) (Wenn sie kommen
>   when/if they come
>
>   ich weiß
>   I know
>
>   von nichts.)
>   (of) nothing

This poem, which suggests life under a totalitarian regime, could be 'about' any such situation. Its final lines give rise to many questions, but, just to focus on one of them, we note that the sentence in these final three lines has no inversion after the wenn-phrase. This sentence would normally read: '*Wenn sie kommen, weiß ich von nichts*' that is, the subject and verb in the main clause 'I know nothing' would change places. The fact that there is no inversion suggests this main clause is not just the voice of the narrator, as in the rest of the poem, but is an echo of words actually spoken.

The line could be translated:

(8.12) (When they come
        I know
        nothing.)

which echoes the original closely, but although it could be seen as syntactically equivalent to the inversion in the sense that it keeps exactly this word-order in English, the English has no suggestion of speech. First, this is so because it is the word-order of both direct speech that stands alone and indirect or reported speech that depends upon a subordinate 'when'-clause. But more importantly, no-one would actually say 'I know nothing'. An alternative translation would be:

(8.13) (When they come:
        I don't know
        anything.)

The addition of the colon before the main clause turns it into a possible actual speech, as does the change to 'I don't know anything'. These details make the voice more clearly that of a possible speaker and thus, even though German word order is lost, it is easier to see the voice in (8.13) as that of the 'ordinary German', during and after the Holocaust, of whom was often said that he or she used the phrase 'I didn't know' or 'I didn't know anything' (see e.g. Cohen 2002:84).

The translation of such poems as this seems especially important. The author of '*Aufruf*', Volker von Törne, living in the GDR under the Communists, was clearly haunted by what he saw as his father's complicity in Nazi crimes, and his poems suggest that, unless poets speak out about them, people will continue in ignorance.

So translating this poetry is a way of preserving the voice of those who were silenced, or of those who are afraid the facts will be forgotten, or that history will repeat such silences, and it is a way of making those people speak who chose not to speak at the time. The point here is that the translation cannot possibly be a way of creating the same or similar contextual effects as the reader of the source text might have experienced. The subject matter, the name of the poet, all make it clear that the reader of the target text must read the poem against a different context, and must alter his or her context as reading progresses. These examples suggest that translation should not be judged alone by its ability to show us the source text (to be documentary) nor only by its ability to act as a proxy, but at least in part by its ability to be more demanding than the original. I take this ability to be one of the effects of what Venuti calls foreignizing (Venuti 2008: 152–163), especially relevant in the translation of poetry.

Thinking and Doing Translation

9

Chapter Outline

9.1 Description, theory and practice of translation

In Chapter 5, I noted that theories are not static pictures of the world, but cognitive constructs and, like the cognitive constructs which form the contexts that readers bring to the reading of a text, they are altered and augmented as they come up against the world and as they interact with other theories, and other views, and with practices.

But the question of the interaction of theory and practice, especially in Translation Studies, is never just about building theories. We also need to ask how this interaction helps develop practices. There is a naïve view that a theory is meant to be applied: this is the view suggested by Wagner, and argued against by Chesterman at the beginning of their joint book (Chesterman and Wagner 2002:1–4). Chesterman says 'Most modern translation theorists find this view very odd' (2002:2), but I suggested in Chapter 5 that, though the idea that a theory is meant to be applied is simply a misunderstanding of the nature of theory, which is a partial description of aspects of a particular area or phenomenon, this does not mean that theory has no effect on practice. On the contrary, theory can and does have profound effects on practice, and this is the final point – point (xii) – of my list at the end of Chapter 5. It is these effects that I will be examining in this final chapter.

When considering in concrete terms the effects of theory upon practice there are two types of approach we can take. The first, more general, approach is to ask what effects theory can have, given that it is a description and not a set of instructions. The second is to use the case of a particular theory and to illustrate with a particular text or set of texts what effects it has. I shall return to this second approach, picking up the points made at the end of Chapter 5, in the next section, but first I want to consider the general senses in which theory can affect practice. There are four main ways in which this happens:

(i) theory broadens the mind
(ii) theory embodies a particular way of seeing
(iii) theory tells us what the issues are
(iv) theory is preparation for action

As far as (i) is concerned, translation theory is useful as a representation of a body of knowledge. Consider, for example, one of the best-known translation theories, that of the translator's invisibility (e.g. Venuti 2008). When one just reads Venuti's theory, initially published in 1995, one becomes aware of a vast number of things, from the fact that it is possible to think of translation in terms of invisibility or visibility, to the fact that Venuti has translated Milanese poet Milo de Angelis (2008:239). Or consider Gutt's Relevance-Theory approach, first published in 1991 (Gutt 2000). A reader of this theory will learn about the difference between the technical term 'relevance' and its ordinary-language meaning, will learn that some scholars see no need for a separate theory of translation, and will learn many facts about translations of the Bible, among other things. Such facts, approaches, views and developments can and should become part of what one knows about translation. This is important whether one is a translator or a translation scholar. Wilful ignorance of what others have to say is sometimes excused on grounds that it risks 'negatively impacting the final result' (Landers 2001:50). Yet this seems a strange idea, rather like saying we will no longer be able to bake a good cake if we understand the chemical effect of baking powder, or that knowing who invented baking powder will somehow be detrimental to its use. This is clearly nonsense, and it would be better if translators who dislike theory were honest and said merely that they found it difficult and uncongenial. One can rarely argue that too much knowledge is a bad thing; where translation is concerned, this is just as true as in any other case.

The possible effects of such increased knowledge are many and various. For example, recognizing the insidious effects of a cult of fluency (Venuti 2008:1–6) or 'locating what has been dominated or excluded in the past' (Venuti 2008:33) can lead to greater awareness of the reasons for a publisher's comments on translations. I was told by a publisher some years ago that the poetry of Volker von Törne was 'too German' to be appealing in English translation to an English audience. Understanding why the history of translation might have led to such a view can have various consequences. One would be to seek other works, less typical of their culture of origin, to translate. Another would be to domesticate the translation, in order not to tax the reader too much. Yet another, and my own preferred response, would be to set about re-educating publishers, academics, translators and readers at every appropriate opportunity. To take a completely different type of theory and its associated approach, we might note that a concrete effect of understanding a Relevance-Theory approach to translation could be to build a large amount of ambiguity, tension, foregrounding and openness into a translated poem so that the reader does not feel too easily satisfied.

In the two instances just given, it is not important to accept the theory in its entirety. A theory is always a partial explanation and presents a partial picture. Theory is a way of seeing: this is point (ii) above. Thus one might question foreignizing translation as an answer to invisibility (see Davis 2001:87–90; Pym 2010:112). Or one might argue that Relevance Theory tells us little about literary texts or literary translation (Malmjkaer 1992). Because a theory is a way of seeing, knowing about theories means accepting that there are different views. Because understanding different ways of seeing is fundamental to translation it could be argued that the very act of attempting to see translation through a variety of approaches is practice for the act of translation. Venuti argues for foreignizing translation for a variety of reasons: his background in English Renaissance literature and Marxist criticism (see Venuti 1989), his own experiences of translating de Angelis, his experience of limited views of translation, and so on. Gutt argues from his experience as Bible translator and interest in the work of other Bible translators. Understanding the background and ideology of these and other theorists of translation is crucial to putting oneself in their position and recognizing that translation means different things to different people and fulfils different functions.

In both these cases we can see the importance of point (iii) above, that theory tells us what the issues are. We might not realize that it is possible to do a foreignizing translation if we have never heard of such a thing. Worse, we might think that domesticating translation is simply translation, and that there is no alternative, as indeed Venuti suggests was a common view until recently (Venuti 1998:11). Until we have read Gutt's view that translation is a type of communication and must therefore obey the laws of communication, we might be unable to explain why certain translations fail or why the words of the text have been seen as so important to the translation of sacred texts (cf. Gutt 2000:22).

Point (iv) above was that theory is preparation for action. What I mean by this is that it is impossible to carry out any action, unless it is a reflex, without a theory of how it is done. The theory will probably be a partial model of the action, and may or may not explain all its details, but some sort of mental model is always necessary (cf. Boase-Beier 2010a). In the case of translation, it is reasonable to suppose that a particular sort of engagement with the text, a particular sort of reading, and a particular linguistic mindset are involved (see Slobin 2003:164; Boase-Beier 2006:23–25). Many translators have testified to the fact that they read with a view to possibilities of expression in the target language (e.g. Bell 1991:186; Scott 2008:17). It is unlikely that such reading could be unaffected by the theories of translation we know about, and the theories to which we subscribe. I have discussed elsewhere (Boase-Beier 2010a) the dangers of particular theories. The danger is not so much that the theory may be wrong, but that it may, in the first case, be taken as a complete representation, and secondly that it may be naively applied. In the first case, translators who believe, for example, that translations are 'windows, not veils' (Boland 2004:11), could be led to see translation as not involving the intervention of the translator in any important way. The view is not unreasonable, just incomplete. And because it is not possible to translate without interventions, since translation is an interpretative act (see e.g. Gutt 2000:105), its impossibility can lead to the sort of view I have just mentioned, namely that translation is *per se* impossible. This view is not only absurd, but potentially damaging to the work of translators. In the second case, naïve application leads to the sort of 'self-annihilation' that Venuti laments in translators (2008:7). The consequences of both taking the window metaphor as a complete representation of translation, and of trying to apply it in practice, can be either a complete domestication of the translated text or, alternatively, a lack of consideration of the need to engage the reader of the target text, and a sort of closeness to the source text which ignores its style in the belief that the translator has no important role to play (see e.g. Trask in Honig 1985:11–21, whom Venuti quotes (2008:7) as an example of a view that the translator is invisible.

It is essential to recognize that a theory is a mental construct and engages the mind of its reader in the ways suggested as (i) to (iv) above. We cannot, therefore, simply take a theory of translation and apply it to the act of translation so that we translate in a particular way. There is no Relevance Theory way of translating because, according to the theory, all translation, as an act of communication, will be subject to the principles of Relevance Theory. There is no 'polysystem' translation and no 'stylistic' translation. Every translation, according to polysystem theory, will have its place in the system, and every translation, according to stylistic theory, can be read and analysed, and its reading analysed, using the tools of stylistics. In order to derive methods of translating or reading, the theory itself must undergo conversion (or translation) just as critical theories can be translated into methods of critical reading (Iser 2006:10) or even of writing (Iser 2006:126). But this translation of theory into practice is an essential step and is by no means straightforward. Some theorists suggest, as part of their theory, what such a translation might look like. When Venuti labels one of his chapters 'Call to action' (Venuti 2008: Chapter 7), he is presenting methods by which the description he has set out in his book, of the conditions that cause and typify 'the marginal position of translation in contemporary Anglo-American culture' (2008:viii), can become easier to 'resist and change' (2008:13). When, towards the end of *Stylistic Approaches to Translation*, I offer a chapter on 'A Stylistic Approach in Practice' (Boase-Beier 2006: Chapter 5), I am offering the reader concrete ways of translating the observations of earlier chapters into strategies. Theories describe situations, processes or events; the strategies that follow build upon such descriptions as they interact with historical, cultural, literary and other situations. Based on this understanding, each translator needs to decide upon and develop a strategy.

9.2 The poetics of translation

The particular theory that has been argued for throughout this book is a development of the points that were established at the end of Chapter 5, and subsequently, as the cognitive nature of the theory was developed. Central to this theory is the importance of the style of both the text to be translated and the resulting target text, because the style reflects its author's choices and unconscious influences, and is also the basis for the cognitive effects on the reader. Because style is a cognitive entity it is best examined using insights from cognitive stylistics. These include a notion of meaning that resides to a large extent in the nuances, gaps, ambiguities and connotations that allow a reader to make inferences, and also other important insights such as the structuring effect of conceptual metaphor. In particular, as Chapter 6 suggests, the effect of the EVENTS ARE ACTIONS metaphor will be that the translator as reader will always reconstruct the mind of an author who is responsible for the text being translated. But another insight from cognitive stylistics (again via its origins in cognitive linguistics and conceptual metaphor theory) is the emphasis placed on thought, reading, understanding and poetic effect as physical and emotional processes, not merely mental ones in a narrow sense. If poetics or stylistics is the theory that applying linguistics to read the text will help explain how we arrive at particular readings (cf. Leech 2008:6 and Stockwell 2002:8), then a poetics of translation involves placing emphasis on explaining why we read the way we do. A translator needs to be able to analyse how she or he reads and how the source text achieves its effects on the reader. Furthermore, the translator needs to be aware of how texts work and what makes them literary, so that the resulting translation works both as a literary text, in that literary reading is possible, and as a translation, in that the resulting text is seen as to some degree a proxy for the source text. In the terms discussed in Section 1.2 of Chapter 1, it is both instrumental (in that it works as a literary text) and documentary (and hence a proxy for the source text). In particular, it is worth just summarizing what is new about the approach taken here, because in this way the reader can compare it more easily with other approaches. The main differences from earlier theories, and the effects of this approach in practice, are set out in the remainder of this chapter.

First, though there is little or no consensus about what constitutes a translation, as Chapter 1 showed, and though some non-literary translations (such as instructions) are in fact rewriting, it is possible to say what literary translation is. *All* literary translation, whether the (successful) translation of literary texts or the literary translation (that takes style and effect on board) of any other text, is translation in its true sense in that it is both documentary and instrumental. Seeing translation as both documentary and instrumental can have profound effects on how we carry it out.

Understanding the translation of poetry helps us understand the translation of literary texts in general. Consider the example:

> (9.1) 'No need to apologize'
>   says God to his conscience.
>
>   . . . . . .
>
>   'The answer is at the back
>   of the mirror', says Alice, 'where truth lies'
>   (Thomas 2004:303)

A translator (and most probably any reader) will see a link between 'apologize' and 'lies', because the words rhyme. The words rhyme not simply because they fulfil the phonological criteria of rhyme (that is, the stressed vowel and following consonants are identical) but because in addition they fulfill positional criteria. Though they are separated by six lines of verse, and there is no strong metre to throw the emphasis on the two words, they are at the end of, respectively, the first and the last lines of the poem, and are thus foregrounded. So they rhyme, and the rhyme will be taken by the translator to be significant. Its significance is not that it points the way to a particular meaning (for example, that there *is* a need to apologize) as will have become clear from discussion in Chapter 10, but that it signals to the reader that there are links, over and above those of sound and position, between 'apologize' and 'lies'. The rhyme thus acts as a trigger for rereading and re-evaluation by enhancing the ambiguity of 'where truth lies'. Engaging with the poem becomes a search for the questions it poses as much as a search for answers.

It is not so much the case that we can perform either a documentary or an instrumental translation, or one which combines both types. In fact, every translation of this poem, simply because it is the translation of a poem, is likely to combine both. But the notion of instrumentality is itself important. No one will question that every translation, in order to be considered one, is to some degree documentary. But the notion of instrumentality involves making the reader work. Awareness of instrumentality could be the difference between translating (9.1) as (9.2) or (9.3) below:

(9.2) 'Kein Grund zum Entschuldigen',
    sagt Gott zu seinem Gewissen.

    . . . .

    'Die Antwort ist hinter
    dem Spiegel', sagt Alice 'wo Wahrheit liegt'.

(9.3) 'Keine Entschuldigung nötig
    sagt Gott seinem Gewissen.

    . . . .

    Sagt Alice: 'Hinten liegt die Antwort
    im Spiegel, wo Wahrheit falsch ist'

In (9.2), one meaning of the original is kept. But the discussion of (9.1) suggested the rhyme of 'apologize – lies' triggers literary reading: we regard the enjambement causing double syntax of 'answer at the back' (just one as in an exercise book) and 'answer at the back of the mirror' (in an unreal world) as significant, and further examine the ambiguity of 'truth lies'. (9.3) is an instrumental translation done by Philip Wilson for this book that attempts to allow the reader creative engagement with all these issues of truth, reality and the nature of questioning. All translations, including (9.2), are by definition documentary but it is the instrumental nature of the resulting text that renders literary translation different. To make an instrumental translation is to write a target text that encourages the creative reading which distinguishes literary texts. In order to do this, the translator has to take the style of the source text into account.

Secondly, I have argued in this book that literary translation differs from non-literary translation in that the process of instrumental translation involves creating a text which has profound cognitive effects on its readers. It makes them rethink what they previously knew, search for new meanings, and create new contexts. Consider the following extract (the first and final stanzas) of a poem by Rose Ausländer (1977:24):

> (9.4) Wir kamen heim
> we came home
>
> ohne Rosen
> without roses
>
> sie blieben im Ausland
> they stayed in-the abroad
>
> . . . .
> Wir sind Dornen geworden
> we are thorns become
>
> in fremden Augen
> in foreign eyes

If we focus for a moment on the final stanza, we note that a reader of this poem in German will be aware of at least the following points:

(i) 'Dornen', thorns, relates both to the poet's first name, Rose, and to the first two lines of the poem, which literally mean 'we came home / without roses'. 'Thorns' thus suggests that the 'we' of the poem are seen in a negative light.

(ii) The idiom 'jemandem ein Dorn im Auge sein' means to be a severe irritant to someone, literally, to be a thorn in their eye.

(iii) The word 'fremd', foreign, suggests the poet's second name: Ausländer means 'foreigner'. It also suggests the use of the word 'Ausland', a foreign country, abroad, in the first stanza.

Each reader of the German poem will start from a different background context and will alter and add to the context as part of the search for meaning when reading the poem. The three points just given form part of the basic contextual framework probably shared by most German readers, but others will, for example, add their particular knowledge of the poet – perhaps the fact that she lived in America for a long time or that she was Jewish – or their own interpretation of the sense in which the speaker, and other unspecified persons, are 'thorns in foreign eyes'. Against this background, the reader's interpretation of the original poem might involve understanding the 'we', which is the first word of the poem, as referring to Ausländer and other exiled Jews, or only to herself in that she felt fragmented into the English-language poet that she became for many years and the German-speaking poet she started out as. Or we understand it as referring to all who live in exile, and so on. An interpretation might involve seeing the '*Dorn im Auge*' image as referring to all exiled Jews, all exiles in general, all Jews in general or to poets. My contention in this book has been that a translation of the poem cannot work if it does not take into account that a similar process of context-building and -changing occurs in the reader of the translated poem, whereby allusions help establish the contextual framework and ambiguities help to explore ways it might develop. Allusions to Ausländer's second name might be difficult to keep, but they are not impossible. The first stanza could be translated

(9.5) We came home
      with no roses
      they stayed out in that land

There is also the question of how to translate the 'thorn in the eye' image. It is quite possible to understand it in English, and so we might opt for a translation which is foreignizing both in the sense that it keeps close to the original text (following Berman's suggestion (2004:286) and in Venuti's sense, in that it uses unusual language that helps us see things differently (e.g. Venuti 2008). Osers (1977:51) does just this, translating this stanza:

(9.6) We've become thorns
      in the eyes of others

The usual translation would be 'a thorn in the flesh', but this less painful image does not allow for a reference to other ways of seeing. What is important is that the English reader is able to construct a number of contexts into which images of roses and thorns, of foreign lands and home, and of others' ways of seeing, all have their place.

It is also worth noting that the English reader of this poem in the translation from which (9.6) is taken has to work harder than the German reader. He or she might need to find out more about the situation of Jews who went abroad during the Nazi occupations of Eastern Europe, to rethink what it means to be a 'foreigner', might ponder on the difference between the English idiom 'a thorn in the flesh' and the expression used by Osers, or might find out more about Osers' background and his reasons for keeping close to the German idiom. The more involved and creative reading of translated literary texts actually increases their literary effects. Knowledge of the enhanced literariness of literary translations leads to the sort of end- or footnotes translators use to incorporate into the reader's context allusions not necessarily obvious to the target reader. An example is in the translations by Howard and Plebanek (2001) of the Polish poet Różewicz. Endnotes allow the English reader to incorporate knowledge of Polish painters, of German slogans and dishes, and even of the original poet's (professed) views and thoughts, into the context built during reading. Such additional notes are often controversial; some critics (e.g. Newmark 2009:35) have argued that they make things easier for the reader of the translation, by providing information. To some extent this is true, because, as we have seen, it is mostly the implicatures, suggestions and stylistic nuances of the text that allow for creative context-building. However, the informational content of a literary text – and this applies to its end- and footnotes, too – always interacts with its stylistic features and so can lead to enhanced engagement with the text and increased effects.

A third way in which the theory here presented differs from earlier ones is that in this book the translated text is seen as a conceptual blend that combines elements of the real source text and an imaginary text that has been originally written in the target language. This view can explain how an English native speaker with no German can say 'Yes, I have read Rilke', if someone asks whether she knows the German poet's work, but the same person might also say 'I have read Paterson's Rilke but not Hamburger's' (see Paterson 2006, Hamburger 2003). In the first case, the book is conceived of as a blend with relatively few characteristics of an English book by an English poet-translator, though enough to make the verb 'read' possible. In the second case, the characteristics of an English text, including the stylistic elements of each English poet's style, have a stronger presence in the blend. If a translation is seen as a blend, the enhanced effects mentioned in the previous section are easy to explain: the translation does not displace or replace the original text, but the effects created by translation are added to it, and result from the increased engagement with the text that its blended nature gives rise to. The voices in the original text are multiplied as the translator's voice is added, and the possibilities for interpretation may be enhanced by the translator's interpretation. Even the language of the text may be hybrid, as examples in Chapter 4 illustrate. An understanding of a translation as a blend may lead the translator to use elements of foreignization (as Venuti 2008 suggests), to keep the idioms of the source text, as Berman (2004) suggests, to allow the creation of new words and new situations.

Fourthly, I stated in Chapter 6 that a translated text is subject to the Proxy Principle. It will stand in for the original text. This is of itself neither a good nor a bad thing, it is simply a fact, and depends upon the larger principle by which one thing can serve as proxy for another, whether in metonymy, in family relationships, or in a public meeting. Venuti has shown some of the potential pitfalls of this principle (e.g. 2008:7) and that the status of a translation as a proxy and so of secondary value is so broadly questioned, at least in academia, is largely as a result of his work. But this does not mean the Proxy Principle is in itself problematical. There is nothing wrong with imagining that John Thaw (playing Inspector Morse in the British television series) had a heart attack in Oxford, or that the events described in Jodi Picoult's *Nineteen Minutes* (2008) actually occurred, or that Hamburger's work is Rilke's poetry. Acting would be pointless, novels would offer no escape, and translations would be unsuccessful, if there were. Instead, we need to be aware both that the principle exists, and that it can potentially have dangerous effects. Some of these effects, such as occur when readers copy what happens in crime novels, or children attempt to fly having read Batman comics, or become terrified of the dark after reading ghost stories, can be profound. Others, like the invisibility of the translator, might not threaten lives, but can have a huge impact on livelihoods, academic careers and research funding, besides self-esteem. In terms of effects on the way we translate, the Proxy Principle might lead both to attempted compliance and to avoidance. Michael Hamburger, for example, whose academic background made him more aware than many translators of the translation's potential as proxy, states that he sees his translation work as not 'trying to impose himself on the text' but 'trying to render the text' (Honig 1985:177), so that, for example, people get to know foreign poets they would not otherwise have heard of. For Hamburger there are different types of translation: those we read to see the original and those we read because we like the translator's work (Honig 1985:179). What he is saying, then, is that some translations act as proxies for the original poet's writing and some do not. An example of the latter is Lowell's 1961 book *Imitations* which can be read 'as a sequence, one voice running through many personalities' (Lowell 1990:xi). This has enabled Lowell to translate freely, and it is unlikely that Lowell's translations would ever be seen as the originals. On the other hand, those publishers who avoid putting the name of the translator prominently on the covers of their books probably do so in order that people will think they are reading the original. A view of translation as a proxy might suggest the 'window' metaphor mentioned above, and might lead, paradoxically, to domesticating language so that the text does not draw attention to itself as a translation. The ability of a translation to be viewed as a proxy for the original is closely connected with the translator's sense of allegiance to the original, discussed in Chapter 3.

It might seem that there is a link between the degree to which a translation is regarded as a proxy and the translator's creativity, in that a translator who clearly wants to show the reader 'what the original [was] actually like' (Hamburger in Honig 1985:179) is less creative. Translators themselves do sometimes seem to support this view: Hamburger said he translated when he could not do his own work. He regarded translation as like 'playing music' rather than composing it. Lowell, too, said the translations were 'written from time to time when I was unable to anything of my own' (1961:xii). But, as Holman and I argued in the Introduction to *The Practices of Literary Translation* (Boase-Beier and Holman 1999:2–17), constraint can of itself lead to greater creativity, so that literary translation enhances both creative writing and creative reading.

Finally, I have been maintaining throughout this book that analysing literary translations leads to an understanding of the processes involved in both literary and non-literary translation. My basis for saying this was partly an extension of the view of cognitive linguists and stylisticians that literary thinking is central to how we think in general (Turner 1996:11), and partly also that many non-literary texts such as advertisements use literary style, and have cognitive effects on the reader, even if these are likely to be less profound than those caused by literary texts. That they are less profound is a result of the fact that literary reading differs from non-literary in that it requires more creative engagement. And I have tried to show that understanding the translation of poetry will help understand literary translation in general, because the same rules apply, though in a more concentrated way, because shape and position play a greater role. This suggests that a study of the translation of poetry is useful for all translators, literary and non-literary. The study of poetry and its translation is often seen as an important part of training in literary criticism (Barlow 2009:52–65), and this is as true for the student of literary translation as it is for the student of literature, and as true for the translator as for any creative writer. In example (9.1), it was the position of 'apologize' and 'lies' at line-ends that determined they be seen as rhymes, whereas they are not in (9.2), a position more easily foregrounded in poetry. The issues of freedom and constraint, discussed in Chapter 7, are important in all texts, and especially in literary texts, and are even more significant when these constraints of shape, that affect metre and sound repetition, are added. As I have suggested, these are all elements that are likely to lead to particularly creative translations, partly because all such constraints are stylistic devices that have cognitive effects on the reader, and translation aims to recreate such effects for the reader of the target text. Ambiguity in particular is a powerful tool to engage the reader, as discussed in Chapter 8. Poems possibly rely on ambiguity more than other literary texts, and clearly much more than non-literary texts. But we also saw that a writer uses ambiguity whenever the reader is to be engaged: in newspaper headlines, advertisements, or political speeches. The engagement of the reader, as we saw particularly in Chapter 7 – and recall example (9.4) above – involves the reader processing her or his cognitive contexts in order to search for meaning, and obtaining all sorts of effects – changing views, adding new information, gaining new insights, experiencing emotion – in the process.

Cognitive effects occur in any reading. We recall the emotive use of 'the creeps' in a book of popular psychology, discussed in Chapter 1 in example (1.18). If we read other factual works, perhaps about the history of Europe or the current plight of the citizens of the Democratic Republic of Congo, they will enable us to enhance our knowledge and perhaps review our position. The difference is that cognitive effects are the whole purpose of poetry. Understanding the translation of poetry, therefore, is essential to an understanding of any literary translation and of literature in general.

But studying translation is not just a way of understanding how translation has worked in any particular case, or how it might work in particular circumstances, or how literary texts work, or how the mind works. Because knowledge informs action, it also has potential consequences for the translator, as many of the examples discussed here aim to show. Thinking about translation in all the ways given here is thus likely to lead to particular ways of doing translation. The sort of translation that the thinking in this book would expect to give rise to would be both documentary and instrumental, it would encourage creative reading and have potentially profound cognitive effects on the reader, obtained as contexts are built and searched. Such translation would be hybrid in language and situation, foreignizing and possibly strange, yet convincing enough to be acceptable to its readers as embodying the essence of the original.

Bibliography

Abbott, C. (ed.) (1955), *The Letters of Gerard Manley Hopkins to Robert Bridges*. London: Oxford University Press.

Adams, R. (1973), *Proteus, His Lies, His Truth: Discussions of Literary Translation*. New York: Norton.

Agnorni, M. (2002), *Translating Italy for the Eighteenth Century*. Manchester: St Jerome Publishing.

Anderson, E.A. (1998), *A Grammar of Iconism*. London: Associated University Presses.

Apollinaire, G. (2003), *Calligrammes*. Paris: Gallimard.

Armitage, S. (1989), *Zoom!* Highgreen: Bloodaxe Books.

Arndt, W. (tr) (1989), *The Best of Rilke*. London: University Press of New England.

Arnold, M. (1994), *Selected Poems*. London: Penguin.

Arup, J. (1981), *Ibsen: Four Major Plays*. Oxford: Oxford University Press.

Attridge, D. (1982), *The Rhythms of English Poetry*. London: Longman.

Attridge, D. (1995), *Poetic Rhythm: An Introduction*. Cambridge: Cambridge University Press.

Attridge, D. (2004), *The Singularity of Literature*. London: Routledge.

Ausländer, R. (1977), *Gesammelte Gedichte*. Cologne: Literarischer Verlag Braun.

Austin, J.L. (1962), *How to do Things with Words*. Oxford: Oxford University Press.

Badiou, A. (2001), *Ethics*, tr. P. Hallward. London: Verso.

Baker, M. (2000), 'Towards a methodology for investigating the style of a literary translator'. *Target* 12(2): 241–266.

Barlow, A. (2009), *World and Time: Teaching Literature in Context*. Cambridge: Cambridge University Press.

Barnstone, W. (1993), *The Poetics of Translation: History, Theory, Practice*. New Haven and London: Yale University Press.

Barrett, J. (2002), 'Dumb gods, petitionary prayer and the cognitive science of religion', in I. Pyysiäinen and V. Anttonen (eds), *Current Approaches in the Cognitive Science of Religion*. London: Continuum, pp. 93–109.

Barthes, R. (1977), 'The death of the author', in S. Heath (tr and ed.), *Image – Music – Text*. London: Fontana, pp.142–148.

Bartoloni, P. (2009), 'Renunciation: Heidegger, Agamben, Blanchot, Vattimo', *Comparative Critical Studies* 6(1): 67–92.

Bassnett, S. (1998), 'When is a translation not a translation', in S. Bassnett and A. Lefevere (eds), *Constructing Cultures: Essays on Literary Translation*. Clevedon: Multilingual Matters, pp. 25–40.

Bassnett, S. (2002), *Translation Studies*. London: Routledge.

Bassnett, S. and H. Trivedi (eds) (1999), *Post-Colonial Translation*. London: Routledge.

Beckett, S. (1999), *Worstward Ho*. London: John Calder.

Bell, A. (tr) (1992), *Christian Morgenstern: Lullabies, Lyrics, Gallows Songs*. London: North-South Books.

Bell, R. (1991), *Translation and Translating: Theory and Practice*. London: Longman.

Benjamin, W. (2004), 'The task of the translator', tr. H. Zohn, in L. Venuti (ed.), *The Translation Studies Reader* (second edn). London: Routledge, pp. 75–85.

Bennett, A. and N. Royle (2004), *Introduction to Literature, Criticism and Theory* (third edn). London: Longman.

Berger, J. (1972), *Ways of Seeing*. London: Penguin.

Berman, A. (2004), 'Translation and the trials of the foreign', tr. L. Venuti, in L. Venuti (ed.), *The Translation Studies Reader* (second edn). London: Routledge, pp. 276–289.

Bex, T., M. Burke and P. Stockwell (2000), *Contextualized Stylistics: In Honour of Peter Verdonk*. Amsterdam: Rodopi.

Bhabha, H. (1994), *The Location of Culture*. London: Routledge.

Biedermann, H. (1992), *The Wordsworth Dictionary of Symbolism*, tr. J. Hulbert. Ware: Wordsworth.

Blackburn, N. (2005), *Truth: A Guide for the Perplexed*. London: Penguin.

Blake, W. (1967), *Songs of Innocence and Experience*. Oxford: The Trianon Press.

Blakemore, D. (1987), *Semantic Constraints on Relevance*. Oxford: Blackwell.

Blakemore, D. (2002), *Linguistic Meaning and Relevance: The Semantics and Pragmatics of Discourse Markers*. Cambridge: Cambridge University Press.

Blyton, E. (2003), *The Ring O'Bells Mystery*. London: Award Publications.

Blyton, E. (2007), *The Mountain of Adventure*. London: Macmillan.

Boase-Beier, J. (2004), 'Knowing and not knowing': Style, intention and the translation of a Holocaust poem'. *Comparative Critical Studies* 2(1): 93–104.

Boase-Beier, J. (2006), *Stylistic Approaches to Translation*. Manchester: St Jerome Publishing.

Boase-Beier, J. (2009), 'Translating the eye of the poem'. *CTIS Occasional Papers*, 4: 1–15.

Boase-Beier, J. (2010a), 'Who needs theory?', in A. Fawcett, K. Guadarrama García and R. Hyde Parker (eds), *Translation: Theory and Practice in Dialogue*. London: Continuum, pp. 25–38.

Boase-Beier, J. (2010b), 'Translation and timelessness'. *Journal of Literary Semantics*, 38(2): 101–114.

Boase-Beier, J. (2010c), 'Introduction' to R. Dove (tr), Ludwig Steinherr: Before the Invention of Paradise. Todmorden: Arc Publications, pp. 28–32.

Boase-Beier, J. and M. Holman (eds) (1999), *The Practices of Literary Translation: Constraints and Creativity*. Manchester: St. Jerome Publishing.

Boase-Beier, J. and A. Vivis (trs) (1995), *Rose Ausländer: Mother Tongue*. Todmorden: Arc Publications.

Boase-Beier, J. and A. Vivis (trs) (2011), *Rose Ausländer: Mother Tongue* (second edn). Todmorden: Arc Publications.

Boland, E. (tr) (2004), *After Every War: Twentieth-Century Women Poets*. Princeton: Princeton University Press.

Bolinger, D. (1968), *Aspects of Language*. New York: Harcourt, Brace and World.

Booth, W. (1983), *The Rhetoric of Fiction* (second edn). Chicago: University of Chicago Press.

Boroditsky, L. (2004), 'Linguistic relativity' in L. Nagel (ed.), *Encyclopedia of Cognitive Science*. London: Macmillan, pp. 917–922.

Bühler, K.C. (1965), *Sprachtheorie: die Darstellungsfunktion der Sprache*. Stuttgart: Fischer.

Burke, S. (2007), *The Death and Return of the Author* (second edn). Edinburgh: Edinburgh University Press.

Burns, R. (1991), *Selected Poetry*. London: Penguin.

Burnshaw, S. (ed.) (1960), *The Poem Itself*. Harmondsworth: Penguin.

Carey, J. (2007), *What Good Are the Arts?* London: Faber and Faber.

Carper, T. and D. Attridge (2003), *Meter and Meaning: An Introduction to Rhythm in Poetry*. London: Routledge.

Carston, R. (2002), *Thoughts and Utterances: The Pragmatics of Explicit Communication*. Oxford: Blackwell.

Carter, R. (2004), *Language and Creativity: The Art of Common Talk*. London: Routledge.

Catford, J.C. (1965), *A Linguistic Theory of Translation*. Oxford: Oxford University Press.

Chesterman, A. (1997), *Memes of Translation*. Amsterdam and Philadelphia: John Benjamins.

Chesterman, A. and E. Wagner (2002), *Can Theory Help Translators?*, Manchester: St. Jerome Publishing.

Chomsky, N. (1957), *Syntactic Structures*. The Hague: Mouton.

Chomsky, N. (1965), *Aspects of the Theory of Syntax*. Cambridge, Massachusetts: MIT Press.

Chomsky, N. (1972), *Language and Mind*. New York: Harcourt, Brace and World.

Chomsky, N. (2000), *New Horizons in the Study of Language and Mind*. Cambridge: Cambridge University Press.

Clancy, P. (2006), 'Nine years in Provence'. *In Other Words* 27: 6–12.

Cohen, S. (2002), *States of Denial: Knowing about Atrocities and Suffering*. Cambridge: Polity Press.

Concise Oxford Dictionary of Current English (1976). Oxford: Clarendon Press.

Concise Oxford English Dictionary (2008). Oxford: Oxford University Press.

Constantine, D. (tr) (2005), *Johann Wolfgang von Goethe: Faust Part I*. London: Penguin.

Cook, G. (1994), *Discourse and Literature*. Oxford: Oxford University Press.

Crisp, P. (2008), 'Between extended metaphor and allegory: is blending enough?', *Language and Literature* 17(4): 291–308.

Croft, W. and D. Cruse (2004), *Cognitive Linguistics*. Cambridge: Cambridge University Press.

Crystal, D. (2003), *The Cambridge Encyclopedia of the English Language*. Cambridge: Cambridge University Press.

Damasio, A. (1994), *Descartes' Error: Emotion, Reason, and the Human Brain*. New York: Avon.

Damasio, A. (1999), *The Feeling of What Happens*. London: Vintage.

Davie, D. (1960) 'Syntax and music in *Paradise Lost*', in F. Kermode (ed.), *The Living Milton*, pp. 70–84.

Davis, K. (2001), *Deconstruction and Translation*. Manchester: St Jerome Publishing.

Dearmer, P., R. Vaughan Williams and M. Shaw (eds) (1968), *Songs of Praise*. London: Oxford University Press.

Diaz-Diocaretz, M. (1985), *Translating Poetic Discourse: Questions on Feminist Strategies in Adrienne Rich*. Amsterdam: John Benjamins.

Die Heilige Schrift (n.d.), tr. M. Luther, Stuttgart: Württembergische Bibelanstalt.

van Dijk, T.A. (1972), *Some Aspects of Text Grammars*. The Hague: Mouton.

van Dijk, T.A. (1977), *Text and Context*. London: Longman.

Dove, R. (ed.) (2004), *Michael Hamburger: Unterhaltung mit der Muse des Alters.* Munich: Carl Hanser Verlag.

Dryden, J. (1992), 'On translation', in R. Schulte and J. Biguenet (eds), *Theories of Translation: An Anthology of Essays from Dryden to Derrida.* Chicago: University of Chicago Press, pp. 17–31.

Eco, U. (1976), *A Theory of Semiotics.* Bloomington: Indiana University Press.

Eco, U. (1981), *The Role of the Reader.* London: Hutchinson.

Ellsworth, J. (tr) (2007), *Enid Blyton: Der Berg der Abenteuer.* München: dtv.

Elsworth, B. (tr) (2000), *Michael Strunge: A Virgin from a Chilly Decade.* Todmorden: Arc Publications.

Emmott, C. (2002) '"Split selves" in fiction and in medical "life stories": cognitive linguistic theory and narrative practice', in E. Semino and J. Culpeper (eds), *Cognitive Stylistics: Language and Cognition in Text Analysis.* Amsterdam: Benjamins, pp. 153–181.

Evans, I. (1970), *The Wordsworth Dictionary of Phrase and Fable.* Ware: Wordsworth.

Even-Zohar, I. (1978), 'The position of translated literature within the literary polysystem', in J. Holmes, J. Lambert and R. van den Broeck (eds), *Literature and Translation: New Perspectives in Literary Studies.* Leuven: acco, pp.117–127.

Exner, R. (1998), 'Nachwort', in K. Perryman (ed. and tr), *R.S. Thomas: Laubbaum Sprache.* Denklingen: Babel, pp. 75–80.

Fabb, N. (1995), 'The density of response: a problem for literary criticism and cognitive science' in J. Payne and N. Fabb (eds), *Linguistic Approaches to Literature: Papers in Literary Stylistics.* Birmingham: University of Birmingham English Language Research, pp. 143–156.

Fabb, N. (1997), *Linguistics and Literature.* Oxford: Blackwell.

Fabb, N. (2002), *Language and Literary Structure.* Cambridge: Cambridge University Press.

Fairley, I. (tr) (2001), Paul Celan: *Fathomsuns and Benighted.* Manchester: Carcanet.

Fauconnier, G. (1994), *Mental Spaces: Aspects of Meaning Construction in Natural Language.* London: MIT Press.

Fauconnier, G. and M. Turner (2002), *The Way We Think.* New York: Basic Books.

Faulkner, W. (1993), *The Sound and the Fury.* London: Picador.

Felstiner, J. (1995), *Paul Celan: Poet, Survivor, Jew.* New Haven: Yale University Press.

Ferreira, F., K. Christianson and A. Hollingworth (2000), 'Misinterpretations of garden-path sentences: implications for models of sentence processing and reanalysis'. *Journal of Psycholinguistics Research,* 30(1): 3–20.

Fish, S. (1980), *Is There a Text in This Class?* Cambridge, Massachusetts: MIT Press.

Fowler, R. (ed.) (1975), *Style and Structure in Literature.* Oxford: Blackwell.

Fowler, R. (1977), *Linguistics and the Novel.* London: Methuen.

Fowler, R. (1996), *Linguistic Criticism.* Oxford: Oxford University Press.

Freeman, D. (2008), ' Notes towards a new philology', in S. Zyngier, M. Bortolussi, A. Chesnokova and J. Auracher (eds), *Directions in Empirical Literary Studies.* Amsterdam: Benjamins, pp.35 – 47.

Freeman, M. (2005), 'The poem as complex blend: conceptual mappings of metaphor in Sylvia Plath's "The Applicant"', *Language and Literature* 14(1): 25–44.

Frye, N. (1957), *The Anatomy of Criticism.* Princeton: Princeton University Press.

Furniss, T. and M. Bath (2007), *Reading Poetry: An Introduction* (second edn). London: Longman.

Garvin, P. (ed.) (1964), *A Prague School Reader on Esthetics, Literary Structure, and Style*. Washington: Georgetown University Press.

Gavins, J. (2007), *Text World Theory: An Introduction*. Edinburgh: Edinburgh University Press.

Gendlin, E. (2004), 'The new phenomenology of carrying forward', *Continental Philosophy Review* 37: 127–151.

Gibbs, R. (1994), *The Poetics of Mind: Figurative Thought, Language and Understanding*. Cambridge: Cambridge University Press.

Gifford, T. (2008), *Ted Hughes*. London and New York: Routledge.

Glasheen, A.-M.(tr) (2009), *Anise Koltz: At the Edge of Night*. Todmorden: Arc Publications.

Goodrick, A. (tr) (1962), *Johann Jakob Christian von Grimmelshausen: The Adventurous Simplicissimus*. Lincoln: University of Nebraska Press.

Green, J. and S. McKnight (eds) (1992), *Dictionary of Jesus and the Gospels*. Leicester: InterVarsity Press.

Greenbaum, S. (1996), *The Oxford English Grammar*. Oxford: Oxford University Press.

Gumperz, J. and S. Levinson (eds) (1996), *Rethinking Linguistic Relativity*. Cambridge: Cambridge University Press.

Gutt, E.-A. (2000), *Translation and Relevance* (second edn). Manchester: St. Jerome Publishing.

Gutt, E.-A. (2005), 'On the significance of the cognitive core of translation'. *The Translator* 11(1), 25–49.

Halliday, M. (1978), *Language as Social Semiotic*. London: Edward Arnold.

Hamburger, M. (tr) (1966), *Friedrich Hölderlin: Poems and Fragments*. London: Routledge and Kegan Paul.

Hamburger, M. (1991) *String of Beginnings*. London: Skoob.

Hamburger, M. (1995), *Collected Poems 1941–1994*. London: Anvil.

Hamburger, M. (2000), *Intersections*. London: Anvil.

Hamburger, M. (tr) (2003), *Rainer Maria Rilke: Turning-Point: Miscellaneous Poems 1912–1926*. London: Anvil.

Hamburger, M. (tr) (2004), *Peter Huchel: The Garden of Theophrastus*. London: Anvil.

Hamburger, M. (tr) (2007), *Poems of Paul Celan*. London: Anvil.

Hardy, T. (1974), *Jude the Obscure*. London: Macmillan.

Hardy, T. (1977), *Poems of Thomas Hardy*, ed. T. Creighton. London: Macmillan.

Hartley Williams, J. and M. Sweeney (2003), *Teach Yourself Writing Poetry*. London: Teach Yourself Books.

Harvey, M. (2005), *The Sum of My Parts*. Halesworth: The Poetry Trust.

Hatfield, G. (2003), *Descartes and the 'Meditations'*. London: Routledge.

Havránek, B. (1964), 'The functional differentiation of the standard language', in P. Garvin (ed.), *A Prague School Reader on Esthetics, Literary Structure, and Style*. Washington: Georgetown University Press, pp. 3–16.

Heaney, S. (1995), *The Redress of Poetry*. London: Faber and Faber.

Heidegger, M. (1957), *Der Satz vom Grund*. Pfullingen: Neske.

Herbert, G. (2007), *The English Poems of George Herbert*, ed. H. Wilcox. Cambridge: Cambridge University Press.

Hermans, T. (1996), 'The translator's voice in translated narrative'. *Target* 8(1): 23–48.

Hermans, T. (2002), 'Paradoxes and aporias in translation and translation studies', in A. Riccardi (ed.), *Translation Studies: Perspectives on an Emerging Discipline*. Cambridge: Cambridge University Press, pp. 10–23.

Hermans, T. (2007), *The Conference of the Tongues*. Manchester: St. Jerome.

Hermans, T. (2009), 'Translation, ethics, politics', in J. Munday (ed.), *The RoutledgeCompanion to Translation Studies*. London: Routledge, pp. 93–105.

Hill, G. (1971), *Mercian Hymns*. London: André Deutsch.

Hiraga, M. (2005), *Metaphor and Iconicity: A Cognitive Approach to Analyzing Texts*. Basingstoke: Macmillan.

Hofmann, W. (1975), *William Blake: Lieder der Unschuld und Erfahrung*. Frankfurt am Main: Insel.

Holmes, J. (1998), *Translated! Papers on Literary Translation and Translation Studies*. Amsterdam: Rodopi.

Holy Bible (1939), Authorized King James Version. London: Collins.

Honig, E. (ed.) (1985), *The Poet's Other Voice: Conversations on Literary Translation*. Amherst: University of Massachusetts Press.

Hopkins, G.M. (1963), *Poems and Prose*, ed. W.H. Gardner. London: Penguin.

Howard, T. and B. Plebanek (trs) (2001), *Tadeusz Różewicz: Recycling*. Todmorden: Arc Publications.

Hughes, T. (tr) (1997), *Tales from Ovid*. London: Faber and Faber.

Hulse, M. (tr) (1993), *W.G. Sebald: Vertigo*. London: Vintage.

Ibsen, H. (1962), 'Hedda Gabler' in *Natidsdramaer*. Oslo: Gyldendal Norsk Vorlag, pp. 383–484.

Ingarden, R. (1973), *The Cognition of the Literary Work of Art*. Evanston: Northwestern University Press.

Iser, W. (1971), 'Indeterminacy and the reader's response in prose fiction', in J. Hillis Miller (ed.) *Aspects of Narrative*. New York: Columbia University Press, pp. 1–45.

Iser, W. (1974), *The Implied Reader: Patterns of Communication in Prose Fiction from Bunyan to Beckett*. Baltimore: Johns Hopkins University Press.

Iser, W. (1979), *The Act of Reading: A Theory of Aesthetic Response*. London: Routledge and Kegan Paul.

Iser, W. (2006), *How to do Theory*. Oxford: Blackwell.

Jakobson, R. (2004), 'On linguistic aspects of translation', in L. Venuti (ed.), *The Translation Studies Reader* (second edn). London: Routledge, pp. 138–143.

Jakobson, R. (2008), 'Linguistics and poetics', in D. Lodge and N. Wood (eds), *Modern Criticism and Theory: A Reader* (third edn). London: Pearson, pp. 141–164.

Johnson, M. (1987), *The Body in the Mind*. Chicago: University of Chicago Press.

Johnson, M. (2007) *The Meaning of the Body: Aesthetics of Human Understanding*. Chicago: University of Chicago Press.

Jones, F.R. (2009), 'Embassy networks: translating post-war Bosnian poetry into English', in J. Milton and P. Bandia (eds), *Agents of Translation*. Amsterdam: Benjamins, pp. 301–325.

Joyce, J. (2000), *A Portrait of the Artist as a Young Man*. Oxford: Oxford University Press.

Kazin, A. (1974), 'Introduction' to A. Kazin (ed.), *The Portable Blake*. Harmondsworth: Penguin, pp. 1–55.

Kerr, J. (1968), *A Tiger Comes to Tea*. London: Collins.

Kinnell, G. and H. Liebmann (trs) (1999), *The Essential Rilke*. New York: Ecco Press.

Kiparsky, P. (1973), 'The role of linguistics in a theory of poetry', *Daedalus* 102: 231–244.

Kirkup, J. (2002), *Shields Sketches*. Sutton Bridge: Hub Editions.

Kleist, H. (1973), *Der zerbrochne Krug*. Stuttgart: Reclam.

Knight, M. (tr) (1963), *Christian Morgenstern: Galgenlieder*. Berkeley: University of California Press.

Koch, E. (2006), 'Cartesian corporeality and (aesth)etics', *PMLA* 121(2): 405–420.

Kövecses, Z. (2002), *Metaphor and Emotion*. Cambridge: Cambridge University Press.

Kristeva, J. (1986), 'Freud and love' in *The Kristeva Reader*, Oxford: Blackwell, pp. 240–271

Kuiken, D. (2008), 'A theory of expressive reading', in S. Zyngier, M. Bortolussi, A. Chesnokova and J. Auracher (eds), *Directions in Empirical Literary Studies*. Amsterdam: Benjamins, pp.49–68.

Lakoff, G. (2008), 'The neural theory of metaphor', in R. Gibbs (ed.), *The Cambridge Handbook of Metaphor and Thought*. Cambridge: Cambridge University Press, pp.17–38.

Lakoff, G. and M. Johnson (1980), *Metaphors We Live By*. Chicago: University of Chicago Press.

Lakoff, G. and M. Johnson (1999), *Philosophy in the Flesh*. New York: Basic Books.

Lakoff, G. and M. Turner (1989), *More Than Cool Reason: A Field Guide to Poetic Metaphor*. Chicago: University of Chicago Press.

Landers, C. (2001), *Literary Translation: A Practical Guide*. Clevedon: Multilingual Matters.

Lawson, S. (2002), *Poems of Jacques Prévert*. London: Hearing Eye.

Lee, D. (2001), *Cognitive Linguistics: An Introduction*. Oxford: Oxford University Press.

Leech, G. (2008), *Language in Literature: Style and Foregrounding*. London: Longman.

Lefevere, A. (ed.) (1992), *Translation / History / Culture: A Sourcebook*. London: Routledge.

Leimberg, I. (tr) (2002), *George Herbert: The Temple*. Munich: Waxmann Münster.

Lewes, G.H. (1855), *The Life and Works of Goethe*. London: Everyman.

Lewis, C.S. (1947), *Miracles*. London: Bles.

Lowell, R. (1990), *Imitations*. New York: Farrar, Straus and Giroux.

MacKenzie, I. (2002), *Paradigms of Reading*. London: Palgrave.

MacNeice, L. (2007), *Collected Poems*. London: Faber.

Madsen, D. (2003), *A Box of Dreams*. Sawtry: Dedalus.

Malmkjær, K. (1992) '[Review of] E.A. Gutt: "Translation and Relevance: Cognition and Context"'. *Mind and Language* 7(3): 298–309.

Malmkjær, K. (2005), *Linguistics and the Language of Translation*. Edinburgh: Edinburgh University Press.

Mankell, H. (2002), *One Step Behind*, tr. E. Segerberg. London: Vintage.

Martindale, C. (2007), 'Deformation forms the course of literary history'. *Language and Literature* 16(2): 141–153.

McCrone, J. (1990), *The Ape that Spoke*. London: Macmillan.

McCrum, R. (1999), 'Ghost writer'. *The Observer*, December 12, 1999.

McCully, C. (1998), 'The beautiful lie: towards a biology of literature', *PN Review* 121: 22–24.

Mehrez, S. (1992), 'Translation and the postcolonial experience: the francophone North African text', in L. Venuti (ed.) *Rethinking Translation: Discourse, Subjectivity, Ideology*. London: Routledge, pp. 128–138.

Mey, J.L. (2001), *Pragmatics* (second edn). Oxford: Blackwell.

Miall, D. (2007), 'Foregrounding and the sublime: Shelley in Chamonix'. *Language and Literature* 16(2): 155–168.

Miall, D. and D. Kuiken (1994a), 'The form of reading: empirical studies of literariness'. *Poetics* 25: 327–341.

Miall, D. and D. Kuiken (1994b), 'Foreground, defamiliarization, and affect: response to literary stories'. *Poetics* 22: 389–407.

Milroy, J. and L. Milroy (1991), *Authority in Language* (second edn). London and New York: Routledge.

Mithen, S. (1996), *The Prehistory of the Mind*. London: Phoenix.

Montgomery, M., A. Durant, N. Fabb, T. Furniss and S. Mills (2000), *Ways of Reading: Advanced Reading Skills for Students of English*. London: Routledge.

Morgenstern, C. (1965), *Gesammelte Werke*. München: Piper.

Morrison, B. (tr) (1996), *The Cracked Pot*. London: Samuel French.

Mukařovský, J. (1964), 'Standard language and poetic language', in P. Garvin (ed.), *A Prague School Reader on Esthetics, Literary Structure, and Style*. Washington: Georgetown University Press, pp. 17–30.

Munday, J. (2008), *Style and Ideology in Translation: Latin American Writing in English*. London: Routledge.

Munday, J. (ed.) (2009), *The Routledge Companion to Translation Studies*. London: Routledge.

Newmark, P. (1988), *A Textbook of Translation*. London: Phoenix.

Newmark, P. (1993), *Paragraphs on Translation*. Clevedon: Multilingual Matters.

Newmark, P. (2009), 'The linguistic and communicative stages in translation theory', in J. Munday (ed.), *The Routledge Companion to Translation Studies*, London: Routledge, pp. 20–35.

Nida, E. (1964), *Toward a Science of Translating*. Leiden: Brill.

Nietzsche, F. (1998), *Beyond Good and Evil*. Oxford: Oxford University Press.

Nord, C. (1997), *Translating as a Purposeful Activity: Functionalist Approaches Explained*. Manchester: St. Jerome Publishing.

Oakley, B. (2007), *Evil Genes*. New York: Prometheus Books.

O'Hear, A. (1985), *What Philosophy Is*. Atlantic Highlands: Humanities Press International.

Osers, E. (tr) (2007), *Rose Ausländer: Selected Poems*. London: London Magazine Editions.

Osers, E. (2001), *The Snows of Yesteryear*. London: Elliott and Thompson.

Owen, W. (1990), *The Poems of Wilfred Owen*, ed. J. Stallworthy. London: Chatto and Windus.

Parks, T. (1998), *Translating Style*. London: Cassell.

Parks, T. (2007) *Translating Style* (second edn). Manchester: St Jerome Publishing.

Paterson, D. (tr) (2006), *Rilke: Orpheus*. London: Faber and Faber.

van Peer, W. (1986), *Stylistics and Psychology: Investigations of Foregrounding*. London: Croom Helm.

van Peer, W. (2000), 'Hidden meanings', in T. Bex, M. Burke and P. Stockwell (eds), *Contextualized Stylistics*. Amsterdam: Rodopi, pp. 39–47.

van Peer, W. (2007), 'Introduction to foregrounding: a state of the art', *Language and Literature* 16(2): 99–104.

Peirce, C.S. (1960), *Collected Papers of Charles Sanders Peirce*, Vol I and II, ed. C. Hartshorne and P. Weiss. Cambridge, Massachusetts: Harvard University Press.

Perryman, K. (tr and ed.) (1998), *R.S. Thomas: Laubbaum Sprache*. Denklingen: Babel.

Perryman, K. (tr and ed.) (2003), R.S. Thomas: *Die Vogelscheuche Nächstenliebe*. Denklingen: Babel.

Picoche, J. (1994), *Dictionnaire Étymologique du Français*. Paris: Les Usuels.

Picoult, J. (2008), *Nineteen Minutes*. London: Hodder and Stoughton.

Pilkington, A. (2000), *Poetic Effects: A Relevance Theory Perspective*. Amsterdam and Philadelphia: Benjamins.

Pinker, S. (1994), *The Language Instinct: The New Science of Language and Mind*. London: Penguin.

Pinker, S. (1999), *Words and Rules*. London: Weidenfeld and Nicolson.

Pinker, S. (2007), *The Stuff of Thought*. London: Penguin.

Pope, R. (1995), *Textual Intervention*. London: Routledge.

Pope, R. (2005), *Creativity: Theory, History, Practice*. London: Routledge.

Pym, A. (2010), *Exploring Translation Theories*. London and New York: Routledge.

Qvale, P. (2003), *From St. Jerome to Hypertext*. *Manchester*: St Jerome Publishing.

Rahner, H. (1983), *Greek Myths and Christian Mystery*. London: Burns and Oates.

Ratey, J. (2001), *A User's Guide to the Brain*. London: Little, Brown and Company.

Reah, D. (2003), *Bleak Water*. London: Harper Collins.

Reidel, J. (tr) (2006), *Thomas Bernhard: In Hora Mortis; Under the Iron of the Moon*. Princeton: Princeton University Press.

Reiβ, K. (1971), *Möglichkeiten und Grenzen der Übersetzungskritik*. Munich: Hueber.

Reiβ, K. and H.J. Vermeer (1984), *Grundlegung einer allgemeinen Translationstheorie*. Tübingen: Niemeyer.

Richards, I.A. (1970), *Poetries and Sciences*. New York: Norton.

Richardson, L.L. (1983), *Committed Aestheticism: The Poetic Theory and Practice of Günter Eich*. New York: Peter Lang.

Ricks, C. (1963), *Milton's Grand Style*. Oxford: Oxford University Press.

Ricœur, P. (2006), *On Translation*. London: Routledge.

Riffaterre, M. (1959), 'Criteria for style analysis'. *Word* 15: 154–174.

Riffaterre, M. (1992), 'Transposing presuppositions on the semiotics of literary translation', in R. Schulte and J. Biguenet (eds), *Theories of Translation*. Chicago: University of Chicago Press, pp. 204–217.

Rimbaud, A. (2001) *Collected Poems*, tr. Martin Sorrell. Oxford: Oxford University Press.

Roberts, I. (1997), *Comparative Syntax*. London: Arnold.

Robinson, D. (ed.) (2002), *Western Translation Theory from Herodotes to Nietzsche*. Manchester: St Jerome Publishing.

Rocca, G. (2004), *Speaking the Incomprehensible God: Thomas Aquinas on the Interplay of Positive and Negative Theology*. Washington: Catholic University of America Press.

Rogers, B. (2006), *The Man Who Went into the West*. London: Aurum Press.

Ross, H. (1982), 'Hologramming in a Robert Frost poem: the still point', in The Linguistic Society of Korea (eds), *Linguistics in the Morning Calm*. Seoul: Hanshin Publishing, pp. 685–691.

Russell, B. (1957), *Why I am not a Christian*. London: Allen and Unwin.

Salinger, J.D. (1987), *The Catcher in the Rye*. Harmondsworth: Penguin.

Sansom, P. (1994), *Writing Poems*. Highgreen: Bloodaxe.

Sapir, E. (1949), *Selected Writings in Language, Culture and Personality*, ed. D. Mandelbaum. Berkeley: University of California Press.

Saussure, F. de (1966), *Course in General Linguistics*. New York and London: McGraw-Hill.

Sayers Peden, M. (1989), 'Building a translation, the reconstruction business: poem 145 of Sor Juana Inés de la Cruz', in J. Biguenet and R. Schulte (eds), *The Craft of Translation*. Chicago: University of Chicago Press, pp. 13–27.

Schlant, E. (1999), *The Language of Silence: West German Literature and the Holocaust*. London: Routledge.

Schlegel, W. and L. Thieck (trs) (1916), *William Shakespeare: Hamlet*. Jena: Eugen Diederichs.

Schleiermacher, F. (1992), 'On the different methods of translating', in R. Schulte and J.Biguenet (eds), *Theories of Translation*. Chicago and London: University of Chicago Press, pp 36–54.

Schulte, R. and J. Biguenet (eds) (1992), *Theories of Translation*. Chicago and London: University of Chicago Press.

Scott, C. (2008), *Translating Baudelaire*. Exeter: University of Exeter Press.

Scott, C. (2008), 'Our engagement with literary translation'. *In Other Words* 32: 16–29.

Scott Moncrieff, C. (tr) (1929), *Stendhal: The Red and the Black*. University of Virginia: The Modern Library.

Sebald, W.G. (1990), *Schwindel. Gefühle*. Frankfurt am Main: Eichborn Verlag.

Semino, E. (1997), *Language and World-Creation in Poems and Other Texts*. London: Longman.

Semino, E. (2002), 'A cognitive stylistic approach to mind style in narrative fiction', in E. Semino and J. Culpeper (eds), *Cognitive Stylistics: Language and Cognition in Text Analysis*. Amsterdam: Benjamins, pp. 95–122.

Sendak, M. (1963), *Where the Wild Things Are*. Harmondsworth: Penguin.

Shakespeare, W. (1956), *The Works of Shakespeare*, ed. W. Clark and W. Wright. London: Macmillan.

Shklovsky, V. (1965), 'Art as technique', in L. Lemon and M. Reis (eds), *Russian Formalist Criticism: Four Essays*. London: University of Nebraska Press, pp. 3–24.

Short, M. (1996), *Exploring the Language of Poems, Plays and Prose*. London: Longman.

Simmonds, K. (1988), Sunday at the Skin Launderette. Bridgend: Seren.

Simpson, P. (1993), *Language, Ideology and Point of View*. London: Routledge.

Slobin, D.I. (1987), 'Thinking for speaking'. *Proceedings of the 13th Annual Meeting of the Berkeley Linguistics Society* 30: 435–444.

Slobin, D. (2003), 'Language and thought online: cognitive consequences of linguistic relativity', in D. Gentner and S. Gocklin-Meadow (eds), *Language in the Mind: Advances in the Study of Language and Thought*. Cambridge, Massachusetts: MIT Press, pp. 157–192.

Snell-Hornby, M. (1988), *Translation Studies: An Integrated Approach*. Amsterdam: John Benjamins.

Snell-Hornby, M. (2006), *The Turns of Translation Studies*. Amsterdam: Benjamins.

Sontag, S. (2000), 'On W.G. Sebald', *Times Literary Supplement*, February 25, 2000.

Sørensen, J. (2002), '"The morphology and function of magic" revisited', in I. Pyysiäinen and V. Anttonen (eds), *Current Approaches in the Cognitive Science of Religion*. London: Continuum, pp. 177–202.

Sorrell, M. (tr) (2001), *Claude de Burine: Words Have Frozen Over*. Todmorden: Arc Publications.

Sperber, D. (1996), *Explaining Culture: A Naturalistic Approach*. Oxford: Blackwell.

Sperber, D. and D. Wilson (1995), *Relevance: Communication and Cognition*. Oxford: Blackwell.

Spigge, E. (tr.) (1995), 'August Strindberg: The Father' in E. Spigge (tr and ed.), *Six Plays of Strindberg*. New York and London: Anchor, pp. 1–57.

Spolsky, E. (1993), *Gaps in Nature: Literary Interpretation and the Modular Mind*. Albany: SUNY Press.

Spolsky, E. (2002), 'Darwin and Derrida: cognitive literary theory as a species of post-structuralism'. *Poetics Today* 23(1): 43–62.

Steiner, G. (1966), *The Penguin Book of Modern Verse Translation*. Harmondsworth: Penguin.

Stockwell, P. (2002), *Cognitive Poetics: An Introduction*. London: Routledge.

Stockwell, P. (2009), *Texture: A Cognitive Aesthetics of Reading*. Edinburgh: Edinburgh University Press.

Strachan, J. and R. Terry (2000), *Poetry*. Edinburgh: Edinburgh University Press.

Strindberg, A. (1984), 'Fadren' in *Samlade Verk* Vol 27. Stockholm: Almqvist and Wiksell Förlag, pp. 7–98.

Strubel, A. (2008), *Kältere Schichten der Luft*. Frankfurt am Main: Fischer.

Tabakowska, E. (1993), *Cognitive Linguistics and Poetics of Translation*. Tübingen: Narr.

Tan, Z. (2006), 'Metaphors of translation', *Perspectives: Studies in Translatology*, 14(1): 40–54.

Taylor, J.B. (2008), *My Stroke of Insight*. London: Hodder and Stoughton.

Tennyson, A. (1894), *The Works of Alfred Lord Tennyson, Poet Laureate*. London: Macmillan.

Tennyson, H. (1897), *Alfred Lord Tennyson: A Memoir*, Vol I. London: Macmillan.

Thomas, E. (1997), *Edward Thomas* (ed.) W. Cooke. London: Dent.

Thomas, R.S. (1993), *Collected Poems 1945–1990*. London: Orion.

Thomas, R.S. (2004), *Collected Later Poems 1988–2000*. Highgreen: Bloodaxe Books.

Thurner, D. (1993), *Portmanteau Dictionary: Blend Words in the English Language, Including Trademarks and Brand Names*. London: McFarland.

von Törne, V. (1981), *Im Lande Vogelfrei: Gesammelte Gedichte*. Berlin: Wagenbach.

Tourniaire, C. (1999), 'Bilingual translation as a re-creation of the censored text: Rhea Galanaki in English and French', in J. Boase-Beier and M. Holman (eds), pp. 71–80.

Toury, G. (1980), *In Search of a Theory of Translation*. Tel Aviv: Tel Aviv University.

Toury, G. (1995), *Descriptive Translation Studies and Beyond*. Amsterdam and Philadelphia: John Benjamins.

Trotter, D. (1992), 'Analysing literary prose: the relevance of relevance theory'. *Lingua* 87: 11–27.

Tsur, R. (1992), *What Makes Sound Patterns Expressive*. Durham: Duke University Press.

Tsur, R. (2002), 'Some cognitive foundations of "Cultural Programs"'. *Poetics Today* 23(1): 63–80.

Turner, M. (1991), *Reading Minds: The Study of English in the Age of Cognitive Science*. Princeton: Princeton University Press.

Turner, M. (1996), *The Literary Mind: The Origins of Thought and Language*. Oxford: Oxford University Press.

Turner, M. and G. Fauconnier (1999), 'A mechanism of creativity'. *Poetics Today*, 20(3): 397–418.

Tymoczko, M. (2007), *Enlarging Translation, Empowering Translators*. Manchester: St. Jerome Publishing.

Tytler, A.F. (2002) 'The proper task of a translator', in D. Robinson (ed.), pp. 209–212.

Vardy, P. (1999), *The Puzzle of Evil*. London: Fount Books

Vendler, H. (1995), *Soul Says: On Recent Poetry*. Cambridge, Massachusetts: Harvard University Press.

Venuti, L. (1998), *The Scandals of Translation*. London: Routledge.

Venuti, L. (2008), *The Translator's Invisibility: A History of Translation* (second edn). London: Routledge.

Verdonk, P. (ed.) (1993), *Twentieth-Century Poetry: From Text to Context*. London: Routledge.

Verlaine, P. (2001), *Romances sans paroles*. Paris: Gallimard.

Verschueren, J. (1999), *Understanding Pragmatics*. London: Arnold.

Vincent, J. (2002), *Queer Lyrics: Difficulty and Closure in American Poetry*. New York: Palgrave Macmillan.

Vogler, C. (2007), *The Writer's Journey*. Studio City, California: Michael Wiese.

de Waard, J. and E. Nida (1986), *From One Language to Another*. New York: Thomas Nelson Publishers.

Wales, K. (2001), *A Dictionary of Stylistics*. London: Longman.

Wechsler, R. (1998), *Performing Without a Stage: The Art of Literary Translation*. North Haven: Catbird Press.

Weissbort, D. (ed.) (1989), *Translating Poetry: The Double Labyrinth*. London: Macmillan.

Werth, P. (1999), *Text Worlds: Representing Conceptual Space in Discourse*. London: Longman.

Westerweel, B. (1984), *Patterns and Patterning: A Study of Four Poems by George Herbert*. Amsterdam: Rodopi.

Whorf, B.L. (1956), 'An American Indian model of the universe', in J. Carroll (ed.) *Language, Thought and Reality: Selected Writings of Benjamin Lee Whorf*. Cambridge, Massachusetts: MIT Press, pp. 57–64.

Wimms, J. (1915), *An Introduction to Psychology for the Use of Teachers*. London: Charles and Son.

Wimsatt, W.K. (ed.) (1954a), *The Verbal Icon*. Lexington: University of Kentucky Press:

Wimsatt, W.K. (1954b), 'The intentional fallacy' in W. Wimsatt (ed.), pp. 3–18.

Woolf, L.S. and V. Woolf (1917), *Mark on the Wall*. London: Hogarth.

Zeki (1999), 'The neurology of ambiguity', in H. Turner (ed.) *The Artful Mind*. Oxford: Oxford University Press, pp. 243–270.

Zhu, Chunshen (2004), 'Repetition and signification; a study of textual accountability and perlocutionary effect in literary translation'. *Target* 16(2): 227–252.

Zola, E. (1995), *L'Assommoir*, tr. M. Mauldon. Oxford: Oxford University Press.

Index